CHAPTERS ON PHARMACEUTICAL LAW

S. Callens (ed.)

CHAPTERS ON PHARMACEUTICAL LAW

Editor:

S. CALLENS

Authors:

S. CALLENS
F. DE VISSCHER
L. HOMBROECKX
B. JANSE
A. MENCIK
T. SCHOORS
J. ter HEERDT
A. VIJVERMAN

Intersentia
Antwerpen – Groningen – Oxford

Chapters on Pharmaceutical Law
S. Callens (ed.)

©   2000 Intersentia
     Antwerpen – Groningen – Oxford
     http://www.intersentia.be

ISBN: 90-5095-086-8
D/2000/7849/7
NUGI 691

FOREWORD

The editing of this book on pharmaceutical law was not possible without the help of many persons. Some of them I would like to thank in particular.

Firstly, I am indebted to the contributors to this publication for the time to write a practical and detailed chapter on pharmaceutical law despite their busy job or practice.

Moreover, I am deeply indebted to thank An Vijverman and Joyce ter Heerdt, lawyers at the law firm CALLENS who did research for several chapters. I thank Anne De Decker who did an excellent job in typing, editing, correcting all the chapters. Without her work, the book would never be ready for printing.

Finally, I must record a great debt to David Pactwa, who reviewed as a native speaker in a very short time the book and who made it possible to communicate our legal thoughts in a more understandable way.

Stefaan CALLENS

TABLE OF CONTENTS

ABOUT THE AUTHORS

S. CALLENS, member of the Brussels Bar; attorney-at-law at law firm Callens; professor of Health Law at the Faculty of Medicine at the K.U. Leuven.

F. DE VISSCHER, member of the Brussels Bar, attorney-at-law at Braun Bigwood, partner; lecturer in intellectual property at Strasbourg University (CEIPI).

L. HOMBROECKX, Secretary at the Commission of Medicines of the General Pharmaceutical Inspection of the Ministry of Social Affairs, Public Health and Environment ; professor at the Faculty of Pharmacy at the K.U. Leuven.

B. JANSE, member of the Brussels Bar, attorney-at-law at Loeff Claeys Verbeke.

A. MENCIK, member of the Brussels Bar, attorney-at-law at Squire, Sanders & Dempsey L.L.P.

T. SCHOORS, member of the Brussels Bar, attorney-at-law at Loeff Claeys Verbeke

J. TER HEERDT, Doctor of Laws; Post doctoral investigator at the U.I. Antwerpen; member of the Brussels Bar; attorney-at-law at law firm Callens; secretary of the Belgian Journal of Health Law.

A. VIJVERMAN, member of the Brussels Bar; attorney-at-law at law firm Callens.

INTRODUCTION

Pharmaceutical law is a division of health law. Health law deals with law and health and describes the legal issues on different health players, such as patients, health care professionals, hospitals, insurers, public authorities, advisory boards and pharmaceutical companies. Pharmaceutical law encompasses the legal issues on pharmaceutical products, such as medicinal products from the developing of the active substance to the selling of the product by the pharmacist to the public.

Pharmaceutical law, like health law, requires analysis of different fields of law, such as administrative law, civil law, intellectual property, European law, torts, penal law and commercial law. This book deals with these diverse issues while always keeping in mind the legal issues related to medicinal products.

It is a strategic choice on our part to limit the chapters on pharmaceutical law to medicinal products for human beings. We recognise that other products with other rules are increasingly important such as medical devices and specific biotechnology products. Nevertheless, it seems more important to devote, in a classical way, a book to the medicinal products as such, including the high tech products, and to give an overview of the most relevant European legal issues on these products. Contrary to some books on pharmaceutical law, this book does not deal merely with intellectual property rights. Rather, it gives an overview of the legal issues on medicinal products from the development of the products to the selling of them. At the same time, the contributing authors give specific guidance in interpreting rules and jurisprudence. It is the purpose of this book to be a vade mecum for lawyers and non-lawyers working in Europe in one way or another with medicinal products. Although many of the contributors work in Belgium, the focus of the book is primarily to give an overview of pharmaceutical law as it is applied in the European Community. Those issues that pose primarily practical or technical problems, like pharmacovigilance are not extensively analysed in this book.

The first chapter describes the subject of the book, i.e. the medicinal product for human use. The first chapter encompasses the European jurisprudence that has been developed in the last decades. The second chapter describes the research and development of medicinal products. Specific attention is given to the clinical trials which are an important phase in the development of the product. This chapter deals also with the agreements drafted between companies and investigators. The third chapter analyses the marketing authorisation that is required before a medicinal product can be put on the market. The different national and European procedures are described as well as the procedure to be followed in case of variations to an authorisation. Chapter three deals also with the possibility of filing an abridged authorisation procedure. The fourth chapter gives an overview of the distribution agreements between a manufacturer and a distributor and it discusses in particular the impact of Article 81 and Article 82 of the EC Treaty as well as of the Good Distribution Practices on the distribution agreements. It is impossible to manufacture medicinal products without having valid intellectual property rights. Chapter five deals with the general intellectual property aspects, such as patent law, trademark law and copyright law. The recent case law of the European Court of Justice on the parallel import of medicinal products is discussed in chapter six. The putting on the market of a medicinal product requires compliance with the specific rules on leaflets and labelling. These rules are analysed in chapter seven. The impact of internet and ecommerce on the pharmaceutical sector is rapidly growing. Chapter eight examines the legal issues at stake when introducing ecommerce solution at the retail level. Before a medicinal product will be put on the market, it is required to obtain a price for the product. Whether the product will also be successfully be marketed depends also of the fact whether the product will or will not be reimbursed. The procedures to be followed to get a price and to put it on the list of reimbursable products are discussed in chapter nine. Manufacturers of medicinal products, as well as distributors and pharmacists process personal data, and this data is often very sensitive. The impact of the European Data Protection Directive on several types of processing is described in chapter 10. The last chapter deals with the different legal issues of selling medicinal products through a pharmacy.

The law as stated is, as far as possible, accurate to January 2000.

Stefaan Callens
16 August 2000

1. DEFINITION OF MEDICINAL PRODUCTS

1.1. Introduction

1. Medicinal products[1] are strictly regulated. Their research and development must follow a specific legal procedure (see Chapter 2 and Chapter 3).

2. Specific licences are required to manufacture, import and distribute medicines. Public advertising campaigns are limited to well-defined medicinal products under strict conditions (see Chapter 8). Only qualified persons may prescribe medicinal products to patients and medicinal products are sold only by qualified health care professionals (see Chapter 11). Cosmetics and other products such as foodstuffs however are less heavily regulated.

3. The boundary between the definition of a medicinal product and other products has been discussed in jurisprudence. These discussions were usually related to cases concerning concoctions of herbs, slimming aids, products against itching, fatigue, smoke addiction or substances to aid digestion or circulation, eye lotion, baby milk, disinfectant, soap, hair growing product(s), vitamins, tooth paste, hawthorn, echinacea drops etc.

4. An analysis of the case law shows that some producers of slimming aids, teas, etc. often intentionally remove their products from the strict regulation of medicinal products by presenting these products as "foodstuffs[2]". At the same time, other producers are trying to place their goods within the distribution system of medicinal products, even though they do not consider their goods medicinal products. By selling their products through the pharmacist, they try to make the consumer believe that their products have a therapeutic effect or are at least more efficient than similar products not sold in the pharmacy[3]. This strategy seemed to be successful for parapharmaceutical products, i.e. products that concern personal hygiene (e.g. antiseptics) cosmetics and specific foodstuffs (e.g. sport foods), that are all distributed through the pharmaceutical circuit[4].

5. The demarcation of the concept is difficult and complicated because so many products are situated somewhere on the borderline between cosmetics or foodstuffs and medicinal products[5]. New manufacturing procedures make it hard

---

[1] This article is based on CALLENS, S., "Definitie van het geneesmiddel" in *Het geneesmiddel juridisch bekeken*, Gent, Mys & Breesch, 1995, p. 1.

[2] GOYENS, M., "Le statut ambigu de la distrubution parafarmaceutique en Belgique", *D.C.C.R.*, 1996, p. 339.

[3] GOYENS, M., "Le statut ambigu de la distrubution parafarmaceutique en Belgique", *D.C.C.R.*, 1996, p. 335.

[4] PETIT, Y., "La notion de médicament en droit communautaire", *E.C.R.*, 1992, p. 571; PELLISTRANDI, B., "Distribution et circulation des médicaments et des produits pharmaceutiques", *L'observateur de Bruxelles*, 1996, No 19, p. 25; see more in detail GOYENS, M., "Le statut ambigu de la distrubution parafarmaceutique en Belgique", *D.C.C.R.*, 1996, p. 333-349.

[5] DE MEIJER, A.H.R. and HOMBROECKX, L., "Definitie 'geneesmiddel' geïnterpreteerd in de Belgische rechtspraak", *Vl. T. Gez.*, 1993, p. 23.

to clearly delineate between medicinal products and medicinal aids or even biocides.

6.   The question of defining a medicinal product has arisen in both civil and criminal cases. In criminal cases, public health is particularly stressed. A person suspected of selling and/or promoting products contrary to the regulations on medicinal products, regularly uses the defence that the products are foodstuffs. In most civil cases the parties have economic motives as opposed to the protection of public health. Often the major players are on the one hand big chainstores who sell "foodstuffs" and on the other hand organisations (order, unions) who defend pharmacists' interests and claim that the products sold by chainstores are medicinal products[6].

7.   In this chapter I will describe the interpretation that the Court of Justice of the European has given to the definition of "*medicinal product*". I will also distinguish briefly medicinal products from other products such as cosmetic products. This chapter considers also how the Member States have interpreted the definition of a medicinal product[7].

1.2. The Definition of a Medicinal Product in Community Law

8.   Now, we are looking into the definition of a medicinal product as given in Article 1 of Directive 65/65/EEC of 26 January 1965 on the approximation of provisions laid down by law, regulation or administrative action relating to medicinal products (hereinafter "Directive 65/65/EEC"[8]). This Article defines medicinal product[9] as follows:

> "Any substance or combination of substances presented for treating or preventing disease in human beings or animals.
>
> Any substance or combination of substances which may be administered to human beings or animals with a view to making a medicinal diagnosis or to restoring, correcting or modifying physiological functions in human beings or animals is likewise considered a medicinal product."

9.   The concept "substance" occurs in both parts of the definition. The Directive defines it as:

> any matter irrespective of origin which may be:

---

[6]   In this case it is not Hygeria, the goddess of health but Mercurus, the god of trade, who plays the major role (Conclusion of advocate-general (TESAURO, E.C.J., 21 March 1991, Monteil en Sammani, case C-60/90, *E.C.R.*, 1991, I-1556).

[7]   The consequences of characterising something as a medicinal product, e.g. problems concerning the pharmacists' monopoly, distribution methods, advertising regulations, etc., as well as the difference between a medicinal product and a medical device are not considered in this contribution.

[8]   *O.J.* EG, L 369, 9 February 1965, p. 65.

[9]   Directive 65/65/EEC gives also a definition for the word "proprietary medicinal product". This term stands for any ready-prepared medicinal product placed on the market under a special name and in a special pack (Article 1).

- human, e.g. human blood and human blood products;
- animal, e.g. micro-organisms, whole animals, parts of organs; animal secretions, toxins, extracts, blood products, etc.;
- vegetable, e.g. micro-organisms, plants, parts of plants, vegetable secretion, extracts, etc.;
- chemical, e.g. elements, naturally occurring chemical materials and chemical products obtained by chemical change or synthesis[10]

10. The concept "substance" contains many elements and this broadens the definition of "medicinal product".

11. Article 1 of the Directive 65/65/EEC tells us that a medicinal product can be identified by its presentation, its announcement (the presentation criterion), its contents, or by its function (the function criterion). The definition provides, in other words, the two aforementioned criteria to define a product as a medicinal product. As soon as a product meets one of these criteria, it is a medicinal product[11]. It is not necessary for both criteria to apply simultaneously for a product to qualify as a medicinal product.

12. Even if it is not necessary that a product meets the two criteria, it is clear that most classical medicinal products meet the two criteria. A classical medicinal product modifies, corrects or restores a physiological function; otherwise it would not pass the registration procedure (see Chapter 3)[12]. Further these products are always presented in the package insert or on the package as having therapeutic or prophylactic properties.

13. If a product does not fall under the first or the second part of the Community definition, it may not be regarded as a medicinal product within the meaning of Directive 65/65/EEC[13].

1.3. Medicinal Product according to the Presentation Criterion

14. As explained above, Article 1 of Directive 65/65/EEC contains two criteria to define a product as a medicinal product, i.e. the presentation criterion and the function criterion. A product that is presented for treating or preventing disease will be considered as a medicinal product because of the presentation criterion. This criterion of presentation is intended to prevent products from being marketed, under the guise of medicinal product, where their manufacturer or seller attributes or purports to attribute to them properties for treating or preventing disease when they are devoid of such properties. It therefore aims to combat quackery[14].

15. In the *van Bennekom* case, the Court of Justice stated that, by basing itself on the criterion of the product's presentation, Directive 65/65/EEC is

---

[10] Article 1, 3 of Directive 65/65/EEC.
[11] E.C.J., 21 March 1991, Delattre, case C-369/88, *E.C.R.*, 1991, I-1532, r. 15.
[12] BOGAERT, P., *EC Pharmaceutical Law*, London, Chancery Law Publishing, 1992, 2-3.
[13] E.C.J., 30 November 1983, van Bennekom, case 227/82, *E.C.R.*, 1983, 3902, r. 23.
[14] Conclusion of advocate-general ROZES, E.C.J., 30 November 1983, van Bennekom, case 227/82, *E.C.R.*, 1983, 3909.

designed to cover both medicinal products with a genuine therapeutic or medical effect and also those which are not sufficiently effective or do not have the effect that consumers are entitled to expect in view of their presentation[15].

16. In later cases the Court pointed out that the consumer should not only be protected from harmful or toxic medicinal products as such, but also from a variety of products used instead of the proper remedies[16].

17. According to the Court, the concept of "presentation" of a product must be broadly construed[17].

18. The Court has obviously been inspired by the purpose of Directive 65/65/EEC in interpreting the presentation criterion so broadly[18]. Directive 65/65/EEC aims indeed both to safeguard public health [19] and to remove the obstacles due to disparate national provisions. The Directive 65/65/EEC aims to develop the trade of medicinal products into a common market[20]. According to the Court, a broad interpretation is necessary, because the Directive 65/65/EEC aims to protect the consumer[21].

19. Applying a broad interpretation is criticised by Valette who regrets that products that are neither effective nor harmful, are considered as medicinal products[22]. Valette is of the opinion that referring to the protection of public health is wrong when a consumer uses a product that is not of vital interest and that is not efficient but is also harmless. The Court erroneously equated the protection of public health with the interest of consumer protection.

20. Based on the broad interpretation of the presentation criterion, a product that is presented to a person as having therapeutic qualities, such as a placebo that is used in a clinical study, will be considered a medicinal product[23].

21. We explained above that the Court of Justice gives a broad interpretation of the presentation criterion. The question then is: what is meant by a presentation. The *van Bennekom* case of the Court indicates that a product is presented for treating or preventing disease when

---

[15] E.C.J., 30 November 1983, van Bennekom, case 227/82, *E.C.R.*, 1983, 3901, r. 17.

[16] E.C.J., 16 April 1991, Upjohn, case C-112/89, *E.C.R.*, 1991, I-1741, r. 16.

[17] E.C.J., 30 November 1983, van Bennekom, case 227/82, *E.C.R.*, 1983, 3901, r. 17; 21 March 1991, Delattre, case C-369/88, *E.C.R.*, 1991, I-1536, r. 39; E.C.J., 16 March 1991, Upjohn, case C-112/89, *E.C.R.*, 1991, I-1741, r. 16; E.C.J., 20 May 1992, Commission agains. Federal Republic of Germany, case C-290/90, *E.C.R.*, 1992, I-3333, r. 3.

[18] See also BOGAERT, P., *EC Pharmaceutical Law*, London, Chancery Law Publishing, 1992, 2-20.

[19] See recital 1 of Directive 65/65/EEC.

[20] See recitals 2, 3 and 4 of Directive 65/65/EEC.

[21] E.C.J., 30 November 1983, van Bennekom, case 227/82, *E.C.R.*, 1983, 3401, r. 17; E.C.J., 16 April 1991, Upjohn, case C-112/89, *E.C.R.*, 1991, I-1741, r. 16; PETIT, Y., "La notion de médicament en droit communautaire", *Rev. dr. sanit. et soc.*, 1992, p. 575.

[22] VALETTE, M.-F., "Le juge communautaire et l'harmonisation des législations nationales relatives aux médicaments à usage humain", *RTD Eur.*, 1996, p. 33.

[23] LEENEN, H.J.J., *Handboek Gezondheidsrecht*, 1995, p. 138.

(a)   it is expressly indicated or recommended as such, possibly by means of labels, leaflets or oral representation[24]; and

(b)   any reasonably well-informed consumer gains the impression, that the product in question should, having regard to its presentation, have an effect as described by the first part of the Community definition[25].

22.   The Court specified in a case on Echinacea drops of 15 May 1997 that the external look of the product, like tablets, pills, capsules, can be a serious indication of the intention of the seller or the manufacturer to market the product as a medicinal product. The Echinacea drops were composed of a tincture of fresh plants containing 95% Echinacea purpura e herga and 5% Echinacea purpura e radice and also 65 volume-percent alcohol. The description of the accuracy or preventive characteristics of the products as well as the form of the packaging of the product, the administration and selling were elements for the Court to consider the products as medicinal products[26]. In this case the Court did not decide on the applicability of Article 1 Directive 65/65/EEC. The case concerned the applicability of heading 3004 (medicinal products) of annex I of Regulation (EEC) No 255/93 concerning the tariff and statistic nomenclature and the common customs tariff[27]. In cases concerning the interpretation of Article 1 Directive 65/65/EEC the Court usually pointed out that the external form cannot provide conclusive evidence[28]. If it did, many foodstuffs sold in grains or in powder would fall within the scope of the Directive 65/65/EEC.

23.   The indication of the form of a product as an element for interpreting Article 1 Directive 65/65/EEC is refined in later cases. Form must be taken to mean not only the form of the product itself (tablets, pills or capsules), but also the form of the packaging of the product, which may tend to make it resemble a medicinal product[29]. The external form given to a product may serve as strong evidence of the seller's or manufacturer's intention, but it cannot be the sole or conclusive evidence[30].

24.   In other cases the Court applied the presentation criterion to products for which reference was made to research by pharmaceutical laboratories or for which methods or substances developed by medical practitioners were described or for which testimonials from medical practitioners commending the qualities of the product on the packing or the leaflet of the product were given. These types of presentation provided persuasive evidence that a national court may consider. However, presentation is not in itself conclusive, as was said in the *Delattre* case[31]. In other cases the Court of Justice has decided that products presented as counteracting certain sensations or states such as hunger, heaviness

---

[24]   E.C.J., 30 November 1983, van Bennekom, case 227.82, *E.C.R.*, 1983, 3901, r. 17.
[25]   E.C.J., 30 November 1983, van Bennekom, case 227.82, *E.C.R.*, 1983, 3901, r. 18; E.C.J., 21 March 1991, Monteil en Sammani, case C-60/90, *E.C.R.*, 1991, I-1566, r. 23.
[26]   E.C.J., 15 May 1997, Bioforce, case C-405/95.
[27]   *O.J.*, L 241, 1993, p. 1.
[28]   E.C.J., 21 March 1991, Delattre, case C-369/88, *E.C.R.*, 1991, I-1536, r. 38.
[29]   E.C.J., 21 March 1991, Delattre, case C-369/88, *E.C.R.*, 1991, I-1536, r. 40.
[30]   E.C.J., 21 March 1991, Delattre, case C-369/88, *E.C.R.*, 1991, I-1536, r. 38.
[31]   E.C.J., 21 March 1991, Delattre, case C-369/88, *E.C.R.*, 1991, I-1536, r. 41; 28 October 1992, Ter Voort, case C-219/91, *E.C.R.*, 1992, I-5510, r. 26.

in the legs, tiredness or itching may be a medicinal product within the meaning of Directive 65/65/EEC. Such states or may be the symptoms of a disease or illness and, combined with other clinical signs, may reveal a pathological condition. However, a reference to such states or sensations in the presentation of a product is not decisive[32]. Other facts will be taken into account before one may consider a product as a medicinal product.

25. In the *Ter Voort* case the Court decided that a third party may provide the product's presentation. In that case a brochure described and recommended a product as having therapeutic or prophylactic effects. The brochure was sent to the purchaser at his request by a person who acted on behalf of the manufacturer or the seller of the product or who was connected with them.

26. It is generally accepted in European case law that a product fits the presentation criterion[33] if the conduct of the manufacturer or the seller discloses his intention to make the product he markets appear to be a medicinal product in the eyes of a reasonable well-informed consumer. In contrast, the dissemination of information about the product, in particular about its therapeutic or prophylatic properties, by a third party acting on his own initiative and completely independently, both at law and in fact, of the manufacturer or the seller, does not in itself constitute a presentation within the meaning of the directive. The manufacturer or the seller shows no intention to market the product as a medicinal product[34].

27. Some producers of goods put a statement on the package of the product according to which the product is not a medicinal product even if the product is presented in the form of tablets, gel or cream. Such a statement does not prevent the product from being regarded as a medicinal product. This statement is persuasive evidence that the national court may consider, but is not in itself conclusive[35].

1.4. Medicinal Product according to the Function Criterion

28. With the second part of the definition on medicinal products of Article 1 of Directive 65/65/EEC (i.e. the criterion of function), the Community definition protects the consumers against all medicinal products that are in themselves harmful or toxic[36]. If a product is to be considered as a medicinal product according to this criterion, this product may be administered with a view to making a medical diagnosis or to restoring, correcting or modifying physiological functions. Some products are indeed not presented as medicinal products but are potentially dangerous and may restore physiological functions. Based on this function criterion, they may be regarded as medicinal products. In the *van Bennekom* case, the Court emphasised that a substance with properties for treating or preventing disease in human beings or animals within the meaning of the first part of the Community definition, but which is not presented as such, falls in principle within the scope of the second part of the Community

---

[32] E.C.J., 21 March 1991, Delattre, case C-369/88, *E.C.R.*, 1991, I-1535, r. 34.
[33] E.C.J., 28 October 1992, Ter Voort, case C-219/91, *E.C.R.*, 1992, I-5509, r. 29.
[34] E.C.J., 28 October 1992, Ter Voort, case C-219/91, *E.C.R.*, 1992, I-5512, r. 32.
[35] E.C.J., 21 March 1991, Delattre, case C-369/88, *E.C.R.*, 1991, I-1537, r. 41.
[36] E.C.J., 16 April 1991, Upjohn, case C-112/89, *E.C.R.*, 1991, I-1741, r. 16.

definition of a medicinal product[37]. In view of the aims of the Directive 65/65/EEC, the Court held that this criterion should be construed broadly[38].

29. This is emphasised in the *Tissier* case. The Court examined whether the function criterion only covers substances that can be administered as they are to human beings or animals, or whether it also applies to substances that are administered after processing, for example after having been mixed with other substances. Considering the purpose of Directive 65/65/EEC, the Court interpreted the criterion to include substances that are not administered as they are to human beings or animals, but rather are manufactured separately and are intended to be used mixed with other substances, either as simple combinations of substances after chemical transformation, or as carrier substances[39]. In the *Upjohn* case the Court repeated its broad interpretation of Article 1 Directive 65/65/EEC. Any substance capable of having an effect on the actual functioning of the body is a medicinal product[40].

30. According to the Court[41], it is irrelevant for the function criterion whether that substance is made available to the public or sold only to radiologists working in hospitals or in private practice.

31. The function criterion is applied as a result of intrinsic qualities of products[42]. In other words, the function criterion is an objective criterion in considering a product as a medicinal product. The intention of the seller or manufacturer is not at all relevant[43]. The Court will only pay attention to the pharmaceutical properties of the product, which presumes scientific knowledge. However, since this knowledge is not absolute and still evolving, the criterion of the function of a product never gives a fixed definition for "medicinal product"[44].

32. This means that the national courts must always classify each product case-by-case, i.e. in regard to its pharmacological properties as they may be ascertained in the current state of scientific knowledge[45].

33. If a product is antiseptic or antibacterial, this is not in itself conclusive[46] to classify it as a medicinal product by virtue of its function. The range of

---

[37]   E.C.J., 30 November 1983, van Bennekom, case 227/82, *E.C.R.*, 1983, 3902, r. 22; E.C.J., 16 April 1991, Upjohn, case C-112/89, *E.C.R.*, 1991, I-1742, r. 18.

[38]   E.C.J., 20 March 1986, Tissier, case 35/85, *E.C.R.*, 1986, 1216, r. 26; E.C.J., 16 April 1991, Upjohn, case C-112/89, *E.C.R.*, 1991, I-1742, r. 19.

[39]   E.C.J., 20 March 1986, Tissier, case 35/85, *E.C.R.*, 1986, 1216, r. 26.

[40]   E.C.J., 16 April 1991, Upjohn, case C-112/89, *E.C.R.*, 1991, I-1742, r. 21.

[41]   E.C.J., 20 March 1986, Tissier, case 35/85, *E.C.R.*, 1986, 1216, r. 26.

[42]   PETIT, Y., "La notion de médicament en droit communautaire", *Rev. dr. sanit. et soc.*, 1992, p. 573.

[43]   Conclusion of advocate-general ROZÈS, E.C.J., 30 November 1983, van Bennekom, case 227/82, *E.C.R.*, 1983, 3911.

[44]   See also VALETTE, M.-F., "Le juge communautaire et l'harmonisation des législations nationales relatives aux médicaments à usage humain", *RTD Eur.*, 1996, p. 31.

[45]   And to the way in which it is used, to the extent to which it is sold and the consumers' familiarity with it (E.C.J., 16 April 1991, Upjohn, case C-112/89, *E.C.R.*, I-1742, r. 23; Conclusion of advocate-general VAN GERVEN, E.C.J., 20 May 1992, Commission against Federal Republic of Germany, case C-290/90, *E.C.R.*, 1992, I-3346, r. 21).

[46]   E.C.J., 21 March 1991, Monteil en Sammani, case C-60/90, *E.C.R.*, 1991, I-1566, r. 25.

antiseptic and antibacterial products is enormous, but we are only concerned with products used to prevent diseases or treat patients. To determine whether a product is a medicinal product by virtue of its function, one should take into account the adjuvants also entering into the composition of the product, how it is used, the extent of its distribution, its familiarity to consumers and the risks which its use may entail[47].

34. The Court takes into account the results of international scientific research and the work of specialised community committees[48] as well as of the European Committee to qualify a product.

35. According to the Court an eye lotion that is used when a harmful substance has come into contact with the eye, can be a medicinal product if it is mentioned in the European Pharmacopoea[49]. The Court used similar reasoning in a case concerning hawthorn drops. These are used both therapeutically and prophylactically and in medically prescribed dosages, for neuro-vegetative imbalances, sleeplessness and cardio-vascular disorders The Court considered these products medicinal products because they have clearly defined therapeutic and, above all, prophylactic characteristics, whose effect is concentrated on precise functions of the human organism, namely the neuro-vegetative, circulatory and cardiac functions[50].

36. It should be stressed that only those substances that affect the actual functioning of the body are regarded as medicinal products. Although cosmetics have an effect on the human body, they do not significantly affect the metabolism and thus do not strictly change the way it functions. Therefore they are not medicinal products, presuming that they are not presented as medicinal products[51] (see above).

37. The function criterion, as mentioned in Article 1 of the Directive 65/65/EEV does not mention therapeutic or prophylactic properties. Rather, it refers to making a medicinal diagnosis or restoring, correcting or modifying physiological functions. This is no coincidence. Indeed, there are products that modify physiological functions without having therapeutic or prophylactic properties, e.g., a contraceptive[52]. Therefore, a product which alters

---

[47] E.C.J., 21 March 1991, Monteil en Sammani, case C-60/90, *E.C.R.*, 1991, I-1568, r. 29.

[48] See for an application hereof: E.C.J., 21 March 1991, Delattre, case C-369/88, *E.C.R.*, 1991, I-1533, r. 20.

[49] E.C.J., 20 May 1992, Commission against Federal Republic of Germany, case C-290/90, *E.C.R.*, 1992, I-3347, r. 19.

[50] E.C.J., 14 January 1993, Bioforce, case C-177/91, *E.C.R.*, 1993, I-62, r. 10 and r. 12. In this case however, the interpretation of Article 1 of Directive 65/65/EEC was not a point of discussion, but heading 3004 (pharmaceutical products) of the Common Customs Tariff as published in the Annex of Regulation (EEC) No 2886/89 of the Commission of 2 August 1989 to adapt Annex I of Regulation (EEC) No 2658/87 (*O.J.*, L 282, 1989, p 1) was.

[51] E.C.J., 16 April 1991, Upjohn, case C-112/89, *E.C.R.*, 1991, I-1742, r. 22; E.C.J., 25 Januari 1994, Angelopharm, case C-212/91, *E.C.R.*, 1994, I-205, r. 15; Conclusion of advocate-general VAN GERVEN, E.C.J., 20 May 1992, Commission against Federal Republic of Germany, case C-290/90, *E.C.R.*, 1992, I-3344, r. 21.

[52] Conclusion of advocate-general ROZES, E.C.J., 30 November 1983, van Bennekom, case 227/82, *E.C.R.*, 1983, 3914; see also conclusion of advocate-general LENZ, E.C.J., 16 April 1991, Upjohn, case C-112/89, *E.C.R.*, 1991, I-1719.

physiological functions in the absence of disease, also falls within the scope of that definition[53]. So a product can still fall within the definition of a medicinal product, e.g. a hair growing product against boldness, even if it is not related to any disease. If the function criterion does not apply, the product may still fall within the scope of the presentation criterion. By isolating the concepts "medicinal product" and "disease", many products with certain ancillary functions in a medicinal context (e.g. narcotics), may fall under the wide formulation of the function criterion[54] of medicinal products, although they are not used directly to treat or prevent disease.

1.5. Medicinal Products derived from Cosmetics and Foodstuff

38. According to the third recital of Directive 65/65/EEC, foodstuffs and hygienic products do not fall within the scope of the Directive. Cosmetic products and feeding stuffs are subject to different European regulations that aim to safeguard public health. Council Directive 76/768/EEC of 27 July 1976 on the approximation of the laws of the Member States relating to cosmetics defines cosmetics as follows:

> "Any substance or preparation intended for placing in contact with the various external parts of the human body (epidermis, hair system, nails, lips and external genital organs) or with the teeth and the mucous membranes of the oral cavity with a view exclusively or principally to cleaning them, perfuming them or protected them in order to keep them in good condition, change their appearance or correct body odours"[55].

39. At first view this definition appears broad[56]. According to the fifth recital of this Directive, the Directive does not apply to products that are exclusively intended to protect against diseases.

40. The protection of public health is also stressed in regulations on foodstuffs. According to Article 2, 2 b) of Directive 79/112/EEC from the Council of 18 December 1978[57]. No medical qualities can be ascribed to foodstuffs. Council Directive 80/777/EEC of 15 July 1980[58] on the exploitation and marketing of natural mineral waters is an exception to the previous rule. Indications like "stimulates digestion", "may facilitate the hepaot-biliary functions" are authorised without being regarded as medicinal products[59].

41. As mentioned above the Court of Justice interprets broadly the concept of medicinal product. The question arises as to what kind of criteria the Court uses to distinguish between medicinal products and other products. Are the Directives concerning cosmetics and foodstuff interpreted as broadly as the medicinal products Directive?

---

[53]   E.C.J., 16 April 1991, Upjohn, case C-112/89, *E.C.R.*, I-1742, r. 19.
[54]   Conclusion of advocate-general LENZ, E.C.J., 16 April 1991, Upjohn, case C-112/89, *E.C.R.*, 1991, I-1719.
[55]   *O.J.*, L 262/169, 27 September 1976.
[56]   BOGAERT, P., *EC Pharmaceutical Law*, London, Chancery Law Publishing, 1992, 2-15.
[57]   *O.J.*, L 33, 8 February 1979.
[58]   *O.J.*, L 229, 30 August 1980.
[59]   Article 9, 2, c) Directive 80/777/EEC.

42. Analysing the Court's previous judgements does not clarify the delimitation criteria[60]. No-one has ever thoroughly compared the directives on medicinal products and foodstuffs. The Court has only stated that in dubious cases, the definition of a cosmetic product might be considered in conjunction with that of a medicinal product before the product is classified as a medicinal product[61]. But the Court has always stated that a product which displays the character of a medicinal product or a proprietary medicinal product, does not fall within the scope of Directive 796/768[62]. According to the Court that is the only conclusion consistent with the aim of protecting public health, pursued by the cosmetic products directive. However the medicinal products Directive are more strict than the Directive governing cosmetic products in view of the particular risks to public health that medicinal products may cause but that cosmetic products do not generally display[63].

43. When a product falls within the definition of a medicinal product, the Court will apply the strict regime to the product, even if the product is also a cosmetic product[64]. The Court will systematically apply the strictest regime to all products that fall within both definitions[65].

44. Nevertheless in the *van Bennekom* case, the Court gave the impression that certain criteria such as the criterion of consumption are useful in delimiting the products. This case concerned the following questions: assuming that vitamins in legal concentrations may be regarded as foodstuffs and not as medicinal products, although marketed in the form of pills, tablets or capsules, should a higher concentration of the same vitamin in the same form be regarded as a medicinal product within the meaning of the Directive? The Court reasoned that in as much as vitamins are usually defined as substances which, in minute quantities, form an essential part of the daily diet and are indispensable for the proper functioning of the body, as a general rule, they may not be regarded as medicinal products when consumed in small quantities[66].

45. Similarly, vitamin or multivitamin preparations are sometimes used in large doses for therapeutic purposes to combat diseases other than those caused by a vitamin deficiency. In those cases, the vitamin preparation definitively constitutes a medicinal product[67]. Ultimately the Court's response remains

---

[60] For critics see VALETTE, M.-F., "Le juge communautaire et l'harmonisation des législations nationales relatives aux médicaments à usage humain", *RTD Eur.*, 1996, p. 38 e.s.; WAELBROECK, D. and COUYNE, D., "Vers une libre circulation des médicaments grâce à l'harmonisation des procédures d'autorisation de mise sur le marché", *J.T. Dr. Eur.*, 1997, p. 102.

[61] E.C.J., 21 March 1991, Delattre, case C-369/88, *E.C.R.*, 1991, I-1533, r. 20.

[62] E.C.J., 21 March 1991, Delattre, case C-369/88, *E.C.R.*, 1991, I-1533, r. 20; E.C.J., 16 April 1991, Upjohn, case C-112/89, *E.C.R.*, 1991, I-1744, r. 30.

[63] E.C.J., 21 March 1991, Delattre, case C-369/88, *E.C.R.*, 1991, I-1533, r. 22; E.C.J., 16 April 1991, Upjohn, case C-112/89, *E.C.R.*, 1991, I-1744, r. 31.

[64] See e.g. E.C.J., 16 April 1991, Upjohn, case C-112/89, *E.C.R.*, 1991, I-1744, r. 33.

[65] FAURAN, B., "La Cour de Justice des Communautés et la définition du médicament", *Gaz. Palais*, 1992, 17 September 1992, p. 657; BOGAERT, P., EC Pharmaceutical Law, London, Chancery Law Publishing, 1992, p. 2.32.

[66] E.C.J., 30 November 1983, van Bennekom, case 227/82, *E.C.R.*, 1983, 3902, r. 26.

[67] E.C.J., 30 November 1983, van Bennekom, case 227/82, *E.C.R.*, 1983, 3902, r. 27.

vague. It does not provide the national court with a concrete and definite answer. Whether a vitamin is classified as a medicinal product within the meaning of the second part of the definition is determined case by case. The Court considers the pharmacological properties of each vitamin to the extent that they have been established in the present state of scientific knowledge[68].

46. In more recent cases the Court has repeated that to determine whether a product is a medicinal product one should take into account:

- its pharmacological properties[69] as they may be ascertained in the current state of scientific knowledge;
- how it is used;
- the extent to which it is sold and;
- consumers' familiarity with it[70] (see above).

47. The Court has not followed advocate Tesauro's delimitation proposals in his conclusions to the *van Bennekom, Monteil and Sammani* cases. This advocate general suggested distinguishing between medicinal products, and cosmetic products and other foodstuffs according to the European regulations for the products themselves. Council Directive 89/398 of 3 May 1989 on the approximation of the laws of Member States in relation to foodstuffs for particular nutritional uses[71] states that although it restores, corrects or modifies physiological functions, a product does not cease to be classified as a product if its purpose continues to be essentially nutritional. This is so, even if it is used, albeit as a food product, either for its beneficial effect on a natural physiological condition (such as a few pounds excess weight) or as an effective adjunct to the treatment (using medicinal products) of an illness properly so called (such as diabetes)[72].

48. According to advocate-general Tesauro, a product will be medicinal where it is used exclusively or at least mainly to treat an illness or where it has a sufficiently far-reaching impact on the physiological functions to exceed the effects that food products have on such functions, whether they are everyday foods or are intended for special nutritional purposes[73]. In the *Monteil and Sammani* case advocate general Tesauro defended a similar vision. The question was whether products such as eosin with a strength of 2% and modified alcohol with a strength of 70% should be regarded as medicinal products.

49. He considered that an average well-informed consumer, even if treated as having no intellectual capacity at all, could not attribute to alcohol and still less to eosin, properties making them suitable for the treatment of a disease.

---

[68]   E.C.J., 30 November 1983, van Bennekom, case 227/82, *E.C.R.*, 1983, 3902, r. 29.
[69]   E.C.J., 21 March 1991, Delattre, case C-369/88, *E.C.R.*, 1991, I-1537, r. 43.
[70]   E.C.J., 16 April 1991, Upjohn, case C-112/89, *E.C.R.*, 1991, I-1742, r. 23.
[71]   *O.J.*, L 186/27.
[72]   Conclusion of advocate-general TESAURO, E.C.J., 21 March 1991, Delattre, case C-369/88, *E.C.R.*, 1991, I-1513.
[73]   Conclusion of advocate-general TESAURO, E.C.J., 21 March 1991, Delattre, case C-369/88, *E.C.R.*, 1991, I-1514.

50. While it is true that alcohol and eosin are undeniably products with disinfectant properties, (...) it is similarly true that they are also used as hygienic products for other purposes. In other words, their possible general application, which to some extent has broadened their functionality, means that they cannot be presented as medicinal products by implication[74].

51. The vision of advocate-general Tesauro was shared by his colleague Lenz in the case of *Commission v Hellenic Republic*. This case concerned the compatibility of a decision of the Hellenic Minister of Public Health prohibiting the sale of processed milk for infants outside pharmacies, with Article 30-36 EC Treaty.

52. Advocate-general Lenz argued that the Member States have a relatively wide discretion to categorise particular products as medicinal products. However, in this case the Greek government was precluded from classifying infant formula as a medicinal product in the light of Community legislation. The advocate general referred to Commission Directive 91/32 of 14 May 1991 on infant formula and follow-on formula[75], based on Directive 89/398/EEC (see above). In view of the binding definitions of these directives a Member State is left with no leeway to subject the foodstuff in question for healthy infants to the special rules for medicinal products. Moreover, since the focus is expressly on healthy infants, the characteristics required to comply with the definition of medicinal products set out in Directive 65/65/EEC are not present[76]. Product characteristics going beyond the effects that any healthy nutrition has in warding off human illness cannot be attributed to the product by mere presentation. Restoring, correcting or modifying physiological functions first assumes that these functions deviate from the norm and this cannot be assumed in the case of healthy infants. The Court did not follow the advocate-general. It did not pursue the problem of clarifying the boundary between medicinal products and foodstuffs.

1.6. The Appreciation of the Member States under Pressure

53. Unusual as it seems, the decisions of the Court of Justice do not clarify whether products are in fact medicinal products in the sense of Directive 65/65/EEC. In most cases the Court only provides elements for interpreting the Community definition of a medicinal product. The national courts must consider, case by case, whether a product presented as being intended to facilitate certain functions must ultimately be classified as a foodstuff or as a medicinal product. They must consider the pharmacological properties of the product concerned, to the extent that they may have been established in the present state of scientific knowledge[77].

---

[74]   E.C.J., 21 March 1991, Monteil en Sammani, case C-60/90, *E.C.R.*, 1991, I-1558.
[75]   *O.J.*, 1991, L 175/35, E.C.J., 29 June 1995, Commission against Hellenic Republic, *E.C.R.*, 1995, I-621.
[76]   Conclusion of advocate-general LENZ, E.C.J., 29 June 1995, Commission against Hellenic Republic, *E.C.R.*, 1995, I-1636.
[77]   E.C.J., 21 March 1991, Delattre, case C-369/88, *E.C.R.*, 1991, I-1534, r. 26; E.C.J., 25 January 1994, Angelopharm, case C-212/91, *E.C.R.*, 1994, I-205, r. 15.

54. The Court has reiterated that until harmonisation of the measures necessary to ensure the protection of health is more complete, there will be differences in the classification of products between Member States[78]. In the *van Bennekom* case the Court stated that Directive 65/65/EEC is designed to eliminate, at least in part, obstacles to trade in proprietary medicinal products[79].

55. In the later *Delattre* case, as in the *Monteil and Sammani* case and in *Commission v Federal Republic Germany* the Court ruled that in the absence of harmonised rules on distributing medicinal products, the Member States may choose the level to which they wish to ensure the protection of public health[80]. It is paradoxical that the Court maintains that a product may be differently classified in different Member States, because the medicinal product sector[81] is not fully harmonised, despite numerous European directives and regulations on medicinal products (such as clinical research, the manufacturing and the distribution of medicines, the packaging of and advertising for medicines, etc.).

56. Since 1965 a number of changes in medicinal products have occurred (see Chapter 3). Directive 65/65/EEC was in fact the first step towards harmonising the national laws on manufacture and distribution of medicinal products. This Directive's scope has gradually expanded and covers both generic medicinal products[82] (see also Chapter 3) like immunological medicinal products for human purposes including vaccines, toxins, serums, or allergens[83], radio pharmaceuticals for human purpose[84], medicinal products prepared on the basis of blood elements[85], and homeopathic medicinal products[86]. Europe regulates the registration of a medicinal product, the research of medicinal products[87], their method of labelling[88], their advertisement and their distribution[89]. Finally – and of decisive importance – a "decentralised"[90] and "centralised" registration procedure has recently developed, separate from the classic national recognition procedure for medicinal products (see Chapter 3). All these initiatives illustrate that the medicinal products sector has become a highly harmonised sector[91]. There is indeed harmonisation when the

78 E.C.J., 21 March 1991, Monteil en Sammani, case C-60/90, *E.C.R.*, 1991, I-1568, No 28.
79 E.C.J., 30 November 1983, van Bennekom, case 227/82, *E.C.R.*, 1983, 3900, r. 13.
80 E.C.J., 21 March 1991, Delattre, case C-369/88, *E.C.R.*, 1991, I-1540, r. 53; E.C.J., 21 March 1991, Monteil en Sammani, case C-60/90, *E.C.R.*, 1991, I-1568, r. 28; E.C.J., 20 May 1992, Commission against Federal Republic Germany, case C-290/90, *E.C.R.*, 1992, I-3347, r. 15.
81 LHOEST, O., "Autorisations de mise sur le marché de médicaments: reconnaissance mutuelle ou procédures communautaires centralisées?", *Ann. Dr. Louv.*, 1993, p. 299.
82 See Directive 89/341/EEG, *O.J.*, L 142, 25 May 1989, p. 11.
83 See Article 1 of Directive 89/342 EEG of the Board of 3 May 1989, *O.J.*, L 142, 25 May 1989, p. 14.
84 See Article 1 of Directive 89/343/EEG of the Board of 3 May 1989, *O.J.*, L 142, 25 May 1989, p. 16.
85 See Article 1 of Directive 89/381/EEG of the Board of 14 June 1989, *O.J.*, L 181, 28 June 1989, p. 44.
86 See Article 2 of Directive 92/73/EEG of the Board of 22 September 1992, *O.J.*, L 297/8.
87 See Directive of the Board 75/318/EG, *O.J.*, 9 June 1975, L 147/1.
88 See Directive 92/27/EEG, *O.J.*, L 113/8.
89 See Directive 92/25/EEG of the Board of 31 March 1992, *O.J.*, L 113/1.
90 See Directive 93/39/EEG of 14 June 1993 modifying Directives 65/65/EEG, 75/318/EEG and 75/319/EEG concerning pharmaceutical products (*O.J.*, L 214, 24 August 1993).
91 DEBOYSER, P., "Les nouvelles procédures communautaires pour l'autorisation et la surveillance des médicaments", *Rev. Marché Un. Eur.*, 1995, No 4, p. 77.

classification of a product and the licence is granted at the community level[92]. Given the 1993 European harmonisation initiatives (the mutual recognition procedure and the procedure of central recognition), we should reconsider the classic decisions of the Court on the appreciation of the Member States. The recent regulations will undoubtedly restrain the appreciation of the Member States[93].

---

[92] LHOEST, O., "Autorisations de mise sur le marché de médicaments: reconnaissance mutuelle ou procédures communautaires centralisées?", *Ann. Dr. Louv.*, 1993, p. 301.

[93] WALBROECK, D. and COUYNE, D., "Vers une libre circulation des médicaments grâce à l'harmonisation des procédures d'autorisation de mise sur le marché", *J.T. Dr. Eur.*, 1997, p. 102; CASSIA, P. and SAULNIER, E., "L'autorisation de mise sur le marché des médicaments à usage humain dans l'union européenne", *Rev. Marché comm.*, 1996, p.

2. RESEARCH AND DEVELOPMENT OF MEDICINAL PRODUCTS: CLINICAL TRIALS

2.1. Necessity of Clinical Trials

57. Artificial procreation techniques, organ donation... the media is full of spectacular developments in the field of medicine. Developments or improvements in medical technology have also led to an explosion of new drugs[94]. More and more illnesses and handicaps can be prevented and/or treated with "breakthrough" medicinal products. The pharmaceutical industry has thus become a powerful and influential branch of the medicinal activity.

58. The progress of medicinal products implies necessarily the performance of clinical trials. Every year, pharmaceutical companies spend a serious amount of their budget on research and development. Research and development have become an important business branch. The process between the development of an idea and the final marketing of that medicinal product takes also several years, occasionally up to more than 10 years.

59. The concern for safe and effective drugs is the direct result of the thalidomide disaster. It appeared that the administration of thalidomide, known under the name of Softenon or Contergan, caused foetal abnormalities in pregnant women. They gave birth to deformed children. From this case forward, a medicinal product must prove its safety and efficacy. The inherent possibility that medicinal products can enhance the health and well being of humans implies that inevitably these products are tested on human beings, sick as well as healthy persons. Most documents, treating clinical trials, acknowledge this explicitly[95]. Medical progress is based on research that ultimately must rest in part on experimentation involving human subjects[96]. Being an important part of the pharmaceutical industry, pharmaceutical companies must follow not only national but also European regulations.

60. The possibility to obtain an authorisation to market is becoming more and more difficult. There is a duty to obtain prior registration, price control, supervision of the manufacturing and distribution, the regulation of the publicity, and so on. To avoid these leaden obligations, companies try to escape the application of the drug regulation by the marketing of so-called parapharmaceutical products[97].

---

[94] DEWATRIPONT, J. "De farmaceutische specialiteiten", *Medi-ius*, 1994, p. 9, No 1; VOSSENAAR, T. and PAUW, H.S.P., "De farmaceutische industrie en klinisch onderzoek" , in *Medische experimenten met mensen. Mogelijkheden en grenzen*, Wolters, W.H.G. (ed.), Utrecht, Bohn, Scheltema & Holkema, 1980, p. 126.

[95] Declaration of Helsinki (Preambule); Recommendation R(90)3 of the Committee of the Council of Europe; Belgian Code of Deontology (Article 89);

[96] *"Introduction"* of the Declaration of Helsinki.

[97] GOSSELINCKX, F., "Geneesmiddelenregistratie en geneesmiddelenbewaking als instrumenten van bescherming van de volksgezondheid" in *Het geneesmiddel juridisch bekeken*, Gent, Mys & Breesch, 1998, p. 74.

61. In this chapter, the legal and deontological aspects of clinical trials are discussed. In view of the applicable regulations, the marks for the admissibility of clinical trials can be set. Typical for research are the different and sometimes conflicting interests of the trial subject, the researcher, the physician, the pharmaceutical industry and insurance companies. As such, every interest is legitimate, but they can easily interfere with each other. It is one of the primary tasks of the legislator to get them into harmonious tracks, in order to protect the integrity of the subject. Therefore, the regulations will be set out and evaluated.

2.2. Clinical Trials

2.2.1. Definition of Clinical Trials

62. The competent authorities may only grant a marketing authorisation if the medicinal product meets certain criteria. For instance, the application has to contain the results of the clinical trials[98]. The Directive 75/318/EEC of 20 May 1975[99] concerning the criteria and prescriptions for clinical trials is important. According to the Directive, a clinical trial is:

> a systematic study of medicinal products by human subjects, patients or healthy volunteers to get information of experimental products of their effects, to control and/or to signalise the eventual side effects, to study the absorption, the distribution, the metabolism and the secretion to define the effectiveness and the safety of products.

63. Following this definition, it is clear that the European legislator does not follow the traditional distinction, as used in Belgium[100] and in other countries[101], between a therapeutic experiment[102] and a scientific experiment[103].

---

[98] Royal Decree of 3 July 1969 concerning the market authorisation of medicinal products, The Official Law Gazette 10 July 1969.

[99] As amended by Directives 83/70/EEC and 87/19/EEC.

[100] DE DEYN, P. and CLARA, R., "Medisch experimenteel onderzoek met proefpersonen", *Welzijnsgids-Gezondheidszorg*, 1996, (20), p. 89; DELFOSSE,M.-L., *L'expérimentation médicale sur l'être humain. Construire les normes, construire l'éthique*, Brussel, De Boeck Université, 1993, p. 219; HENAU-HUBLET, C., *L'activité médicale et le droit pénal. Les délits d'atteinte à la vie, l'intégrité physique et la santé des personnes*, Brussel, Bruylant 1987, p. 50-51, No 51-52; NYS, H., *Recht, geneeskunde en medisch handelen* in A.P.R., Brussel, Story-Scientia, 1991, p. 345, No 801; RYCKMANS, X. and MEERT, R.-VAN DE PUT, *Les droits et les obligations des médecins ainsi que des dentistes, accoucheuses et infirmières*, Brussel, Larcier, I, 1971, p. 461, No 596; VANDERMEERSCH, D., "Medische fout, sterilisatie en medische experimentatie", *T.P.R.*, 1983, p. 856-861; VANSWEEVELT, T., "Medische experimenten op minderjarigen", *T.B.B.R.*, 1994, p. 330, No 3.

[101] The Netherlands: L. BERGKAMP, *Het proefdier mens. De normering en regulering van medische experimenten met mensen*, Alphen aan den Rijn, Samson Uitgeverij, 1988, p. 43; BROEKHUYSEN A.M.L.-MOLENAAR and STOLKER, C.J.J.M., *Geneesmiddelen en aansprakelijkheid*, Serie Gezondheidsrecht No18, Deventer, Kluwer, 1986, p. 62, No 22; HERMANS, H.E.G.M., *Gezondheidsrecht en minderjarigen. De rechtspositie van minderjarigen in de gzondheidszorg*, Serie Gezondheidsrecht No 24, Deventer, Kluwer, 1990, p. 101-102, No 7.3.2; LEENEN, H.J.J., "Medische experimenten op mensen in de gezondheidszorg" in *Medische experimenten met mensen. Mogelijkheden en grenzen*, W.H.G. Wolters (ed.), Utrecht, Bohn, Scheltema & Holkema, 1980, 213-217; ROSCAM H.D.C.-ABBING, "Medical research involving incapacitated persons: what are the standards?", *Europ. J. Health*, 1994, p. 147; VAN VEENENDAAL, L., *Het goede doen.*

Rightly, the legislator has preferred a uniform definition, rather than a questionable distinction. This uniform definition guarantees an equal treatment of trial subjects, regardless of the type of trial. However, some remarks have to be made . The Directive refers to the Declaration of Helsinki. This Declaration differentiates a therapeutic experiment from a scientific one. A literal application of the Helsinki Declaration can cause some insurmountable problems. Persons who participate in so-called non-therapeutic research must be healthy volunteers or patients who do not suffer from the disease studied[104]. This means concretely that research into the origin or the nature of the disease is not possible with persons who suffer from that disease.

64. Prior to the decision to test medicinal products on human beings, the researchers have already passed a long way, from literature study to labtests, including computer simulations and cultures, to elaborated animal studies. These studies are not sufficient to obtain a safe and effective drug or treatment. The results of e.g. animal studies, even with primates of a higher level, are not completely transferable to humans. There are examples where a substance has no or minimal effect to animals, but causes severe toxically and even deadly damage on humans[105]. Only research with human subjects can offer a closed judgement[106].

65. Drug research consists of different phases aimed at obtaining specific answers[107]. In the first phase, healthy volunteers are involved. The purpose of this phase is not a therapeutic one, but the preliminary wish of the safety of a new substance by means of an evaluation of the minimal active substance and the maximum tolerable doses for humans. The lack of existing valuable

---

Beschouwingen over juridische grenzen van het medisch (experimenteel) handelen, Assen, Van Gorcum, 1993, p.15-16. France: AUBY, J.-M., "Les essais de médicaments sur l'homme sain: l'état actuel du problème", R.D.S.S., 1985, p. 316; BOYER, G.,- CHAMMARD and MONZEIN, P., La responsabilité médicale, Presses Universitaires de France, 1974, p. 202; KORNPROBST, L., "Responsabilité du médecin devant la loi et la jurisprudence françaises", Flammarion, p. 504, II; PEREAU, E.H., note under Aix, 22 October 1906, E.C.R. Sirey, 1909, 322. Common Law: ANNAS, G., GLANTZ, L. and KATZ, B., Informed consent to human experimentation: the subject's dilemma, Cambridge, Massachusetts, Ballinger Publishing Company, 1977, p. 10; NICHOLSON, R.H., "Medical research with children: ethics, law and practice", p. 26; PICARD, E.I., Legal liability of doctors and hospitals in Canada, Toronto, Carswell Legal Publications, 1984, p. 117; BAUDOUIN, J.-L., "L'expérimentation sur les humains: un conflit des valeurs?" in Licéité et droit positif et références légales aux valeurs, Brussel, Bruylant, 1982, p. 172. Germany: EBERNACH, W.H., Die zivilrechtliche Beurteilung den Huamnforschung, Frankfurt am Main, Verlag Peter Lang, 1982, 8-9; FISCHER, G., Medizinischen Forschung am Menschen. Zülassigkeitsvoraussetzungen und Rechtsfolgen, Göttingen, Verlag Otto Schwartz & Co, 1979, p. 7 and p. 42.

102 Characteristic for a therapeutic experiment is the concurrence of a therapeutic and an experimental view; the enhancement of the health of the patient is sought, as the progress of knowledge.

103 The priority is the gathering of scientific data.

104 Part II Declaration of Helsinki.

105 BOYER G. CHAMARD and MONZEIN, P., o.c., p. 202-203; PENNEAU, J., La responsabilité médicale, Editions Sirey, 1977, p 161, No. 142; VOSSENAAR, T., and PAUW, H.S.P., l.c., o.c., 129-130.

106 VOSSENAAR, T. and PAUW, H.S.P., l.c., o.c. 127; WAGENER, D.J.T., "Experimenteel onderzoek in de oncologie", Ned. T. Gen., 1986, p. 814-815.

107 SCHWARTZ, D., FLAMANT, R. and LELLOUCH, J., L'essai thérapeutique chez l'homme, Paris, Flammarion Médecine-Sciences, 1980, p. 5.

"human" data turns this phase into a dangerous event. Because of this, the trials are only with a small group of subjects, who are closely monitored. The second phase[108] takes place with a small group of selected patients during a relatively short period. The proof of therapeutic effectiveness regarding the specific disorder or illness is the main purpose of this phase. At the same time, the optimal dose and the way of administration are being sought. During the third phase researchers study the tolerance of a person in combination with other medicinal products during a long middle period just as the variability in effectiveness. This phase allows for the gathering of useful information, e.g. the length of the treatment, the interaction with other medicines, the optimal administration and so forth. After closure of the third phase, all data are collected in a file, which will be presented to the competent authorities in order to obtain a registration. Finally, the fourth phase is the so-called post marketing surveillance or pharmacovigilance phase, which takes place *after* the medicinal product is registered and marketed[109]. Since the main objective is the possible discovery of (undesired) side effects, which only can be detected by means of the usage on a large scale. This phase can take several years. There is no unanimity about the question of whether phase four a real part is of drug research. Some authors[110] consider this phase as a full part, while others[111] leave this phase out entirely.

2.2.2. European Rules on Clinical Trials

2.2.2.1. Good Clinical Practices

66. In July 1990, a working group of the European Commission promulgated a guideline concerning the quality, safety and effectiveness of medicinal products, better known as *Good Clinical Practices* (GCP). A year later, the Directive 91/507/EEC of 19 July 1991 came into force on 1 January 1992. The Commission Directive 91/507/EEC requires all phases of clinical investigation to be designed, implemented and reported in accordance with *good clinical practices*. The Directive obliges Member States to adjust their regulation. The Directive also stipulates that clinical trials should be performed

---

[108] BROEKHUIJSEN-MOLENAAR, A.M.L. and STOLKER, C.J.J.M., "Geneesmiddelen en aansprakelijkheid", *Serie Gezondheidsrecht*, No18, Deventer, Kluwer, 1986, p. 62, No 22; SPRUMONT, D. *La protection des sujets de recherche notamment dans le domaine biomédicale*, Bern, Editions Staempfli, 1993, p. 41, No 2.2.1.

[109] BERRISCH, F., PALERMINI, P., STIEVENARD, J. and MOREAU, D., "Protection du citoyen et expérimentation médicale", *Programme Juridique du Citoyen*, Namur, Facultés universitaires Notre-Dame de la Paix, 1996, p. 20-21; SPRUMONT, D., *o.c.*, p.41, No 2.2.1.

[110] BROEKHUIJSEN, A.M.L.-MOLENAAR and STOLKER, C.J.J.M., *o.c.*, p. 62, No 22; CALLENS, S., *Goed geregeld? Het gebruik van medische gegevens voor onderzoek*, Antwerpen, Maklu Uitgevers, 1995, p. 243, No 268; DELFOSSE, M.-L., *Expérimentation médicale sur l'être humain. Construire les normes, construire l'éthique*, Brussels, De Boeck Université, 1993, 57; HENAU-HUBLET, C., "Les projets de réglementation de l'expérimentation sur les humains" in *Licéité en droit positif et Références légales aux valeurs*, Brussels, Bruylant, 1982, 317; NYS, H., *La médecine et le droit*, Diegem, Kluwer Editions Juridiques Belgiques, 1995, p. 315, No 816.

[111] SACKET, D.L., "Types de recherches, effectuées chez l'homme" in *Médecine et Expérimentation*, Cahiers de bioéthiques, Québec, Les Presses de l'Université Laval, 1982, 70-71, WAGENER, D.J.Th., "Experimenteel klinisch onderzoek in de oncologie", *Ned. T. Gen.*, 1986, p. 815.

in accordance with the GCP. The further development of a European procedure for the permission and the supervision of medicinal products for humans has lead to the creation of the European Agency for the Evaluation of Medicinal Products (EMEA.) (see Chapter 3)[112]. This Agency is responsible for, among others, the co-ordination of existing scientific sources and the supervision of compliance with the good manufacturing practice, the good laboratory practice and the good clinical practices. In 1996, as part of its duty, the EMEA has enacted a *Note for Guidance on Good Clinical Practice (I.C.H. GCP)*. The *ICH GCP* recommend[113] that all studies commencing after the 1st January 1997 should be undertaken in accordance with GCP. A clinical expert must ensure that this actually happens.

67. As such, both guidelines lack legal force. They are only designed to set up international ethical and scientific quality standards for conducting and reporting clinical trials that involve the participation of human subjects. Whereas the GCP (1990) only are applicable in the EU, the ICH GCP (1996) Guideline provides an unified standard for the European Union, Japan and the United States to facilitate the mutual acceptance of clinical data by the regulatory authorities in these countries. To offer a legal framework, the European Council and the European Parliament have proposed a draft directive to introduce the good clinical practice for the conduct of clinical trials. That way, the existing practice can be supported. Furthermore, the European Commission needs a delegation of competencies to edict a directive with the detailed principles and guidelines for the GCP.

2.2.2.2. Proposal for a European Parliament and Council Directive

68. Since 1997, the European Parliament, the European Commission and the European Council are preparing a draft Directive on the approximation of provisions, laid down by law, regulation or administrative action relating to the implementation of Good Clinical Practice in the conduct of clinical trials on medicinal products for human use. In the last years, it became clear that the different European initiatives with regard to drug research needed European legislative support. The standards for the performance of clinical trials are codified in the GCP Guidelines. Although the pharmaceutical industry complies with it, they lack binding legal force. Furthermore, multinational, multicentric research demands for another approach. Because this kind of research is no longer restricted to one research location and to one Member State, it falls under several national laws.

69. Council Directive 65/65/EEC requires that applications for authorisation to place a medicinal product on the market should be accompanied by a dossier containing particulars and documents relating to the result of tests and clinical trials, carried out on the product (see Chapter 3). The accepted basis for this conduct of clinical trials is founded in the current revision of the Declaration of Helsinki and the Council of Europe Convention for the protection of human rights and dignity of the human being with regard to the application of

---

112   Regulation No 2309/93 of 22 July 1993, *O.J.*, 1993, L 214.
113   I.C.H. stands for Inernational Conference on Harmonisation, held between representatives of Europe, USA and Japan.

biology and medicine. According to the Explanatory Memorandum of the proposal, the protection of human subjects is crucial, through risk assessment, based on the results of toxicological experiments prior to any clinical trial, screening by ethics committees and lastly rules on the protection of personal data. The rights of individuals who are incapable of giving their consent or who are incapable of giving a free consent must be protected. The main concern however remains the protection of the free movement of goods and a free market. The Proposal based on Article 100 A of the European Treaty aims at a rationalisation of legislation by reducing the bureaucratic and administrative requirements. It is also intended to simplify the regulatory burden for small and medium companies. Thus, the resources allocated to pharmaceutical research must not be squandered on obsolete or repetitive tests whether within the Community or in developing countries.

a. Scope

70.   The proposal deals with clinical trials, including multi-centre trials on human subjects involving medicinal products. Non-interventional clinical trials, the so-called observational studies, are excluded explicitly (Article 1,1).

71.   The principles and guidelines of the GCP will be adopted in the form of a directive, addressed to the Member States (Article 1,3). The European Commission will publish detailed guidelines, which will meet the requirements.

b. Topics

b.1 Protection of Trial Subjects

72.   The elaboration of protection of trial subjects in the proposal is rather brief. Only one Article, with four subdivisions, treats this topic (Article 3). The starting point is the respect for the measures of national legislation, which offer more protection than the provisions laid down in the draft directive, if they comply with the procedures and deadlines (Article 3,1).

73.   A clinical trial may only be undertaken if and only if the risks to the subject are not disproportionate to the potential benefits of the research (Article 3, 2, a). The right of the subject to his mental and physical integrity and the right to privacy will be respected (Article 3, 2, b). A clinical study may only be performed if the subject has given his informed consent in the proper form (Article 3, 2, c). Informed consent is the decision to take part in a clinical trial, made freely and given in writing after being duly informed of the full details, by any responsible adult trial subject or, where appropriate, by the parents, guardian or legal representative, on behalf of the minor and incapacitated adult. The subject may always withdraw his informed consent, without experiencing any disadvantages (Article 3, 2, d).

74.   An appropriately qualified healthcare practitioner will be responsible for the medical care given and the medical decisions made on behalf of the subject.

75. The promoter will be responsible for the subject having a contact point, independent of the investigator team, where he can obtain further information of the development of the trial when it can personally affect him.

b.2 Ethical Committees

76. The draft directive pays considerable attention to the existence and the working of ethical commissions (Article 4, 6). An ethics committee is, according to the proposal (Article 2, 4) an independent body, constituted of healthcare professionals and non-medical members, whose responsibility is to protect the rights, safety and well being of human subjects involved in a trial. The ethics committee also has to provide public assurance of that protection by, among other things, expressing an opinion on the trial protocol, the suitability of the investigator(s), facilities, and the methods and documents to inform trial subjects and to obtain their informed consent. An ethical commission has to give advice *before* the start of a clinical trial (Article 4, 2). In preparing its opinion, the ethics committee must consider certain information, such as:

- the relevance of the trial and the trial design;
- the protocol;
- the suitability of the investigator, the supporting staff and the facilities;
- the adequacy and completeness of the written information to be given to the subjects, their relatives, guardians and, if necessary, legal representatives;
- the provisions for compensation/treatment in the case of injury or death of a subject, attributable to a clinical trial;
- any insurance or indemnity to cover the liability of the investigator and sponsor;
- the extent to which investigators and subjects may be rewarded or compensated for participation in the trial.

77. To obtain advice from the ethical committee, the sponsor has to make an application with a complete documentation of the intended trial. Within a maximum 30 days after the official submission of the application, the ethical committee gives a advice to the sponsor and the competent authorities of the Member State (Article 4, 4). Within that period, the ethics committee may send a single request for supplementary information. In this case, the ethics committee has 30 days more, from the receipt of the supplementary information, to give definitive advice (Article 4, 5). If the directive retains those periods, every ethics committee will in the future have maximum 60 days to give advice.

78. According to the draft directive, there will be one ethics committee per Member State for multi-centre trials. If they are conducted in more than one Member State simultaneously, there will be a procedure where the opinion of one ethics committee per Member State will be given (Article 5, 1). The Member States may provide for a system, where an ethics committee of one site, involved in the multinational, multi-centred trial can advise about the installation and the capacity of that centre. This ethics committee must give advice within 15 days of receipt of the opinion of the general ethics committee. If it is negative advice, the trial may not be conducted in that single centre. The European Commission will promulgate a detailed guidance on the application format and documentation to be submitted in a request form to the ethics committee. The European Commission will also draft guidelines concerning the appropriate safeguards for the protection of personal data, in particular regarding the information that is given to trial subjects.

79. Obviously, the proposal gives the ethics committees a stronger role. Their role is no longer limited almost exclusively to the phase proceeding commencement of the clinical trial. If the sponsor wants to amend the protocol, he has to notify the ethics committee in order to obtain a favourable opinion (Article 8, 1). The responsibility of such an ethics committee will enhance, considering that their opinions are stored in an European database (see below). Members of such an ethics committee will carefully assess all the information, provided for by the sponsor, in order to avoid future claims from harmed trial subjects (see below).

b.3 Commencement of a Clinical Trial

80. The sponsor must notify the competent authorities of the Member State(s) as to where the sponsor plans to conduct the clinical trial. The sponsor may not start a clinical trial until receiving a favourable opinion of the ethics committee and when the competent authorities have notified the sponsor of no grounds for non-acceptance within 30 days of receipt of the notification.

81. If the competent authorities do not accept the conduct of the clinical trial, the sponsor may amend, only on one occasion, the content of the notification in order to take due account of the grounds given. If the sponsor fails to amend the notification accordingly, the notification will be rejected and the clinical trial may not commence.

82. The commencement of clinical trials is linked to a notification procedure, equivalent to a tacit authorisation. If the competent authorities do not give their explicit approval in time, the applicable law can consider their silence as a tacit authorisation to commence the trial. This procedure opts for simplification, which should equal speed and efficiency. The competent authorities have full power to revoke a clinical trial if they consider it unacceptable.

b.4 Conduct of the Clinical Trial

83. After the start of the clinical trial, the sponsor may make substantial amendments to the protocol, even if those amendments have an impact on the safety of the trial subjects (Article 8, 1). Of course, such amendments are strictly regulated. The sponsor must notify the competent authorities of the concerned Member States of the aims and content of these amendments. The sponsor must also inform the ethics committees concerned. The ethics committee must advise on the proposed amendments within 30 days of notification. If this opinion is unfavourable, the sponsor may not implement the amendment to the protocol. On the other hand, if the opinion is favourable and the competent authorities have raised no grounds for non-acceptance within 30 days of notification, the sponsor may proceed to conduct the clinical trial following the amended protocol. If the competent authorities raise certain grounds for non-acceptance, the sponsor must either take account of these grounds and adapt the proposed amendment to the protocol accordingly or withdraw the proposed amendment.

84. If unexpected adverse reactions or events occur, the sponsor must take appropriate urgent safety measures to protect the subjects in a clinical trial against any immediate hazard (Article 8, 2). The sponsor also must inform competent authorities and the ethics committees of these measures.

85. Within 90 days of the end of the clinical trial, the sponsor must notify the competent authorities of the Member States concerned and the ethics committees that the clinical trial has ended (Article 8, 3). If the clinical trial is terminated sooner than foreseen, this period must be reduced to 15 days and the reasons clearly explained.

b.5 Exchange of Information

86. Article 9 requires the creation of an European database, containing all notifications of clinical trials and amendments, the favourable opinion of ethics committees and the declaration of the termination of the clinical trial (Article 9, 1). It is only accessible to the competent authorities of the Member States, the European Agency of the Evaluation of Medicinal Products and the Commission.

87. The purpose of such a European database is to stimulate the exchange of information between the Member States, because most of the clinical trials are multi-centred. Further, information on the results of clinical trials is primordial for mutual recognition of national marketing authorisations for medicinal products. The centralisation of all relevant data would greatly facilitate such mutual recognition (see Chapter 3).

2.2.2.3. Biomedicine Convention

88. On 19 November 1996[114], the Committee of Ministers of the Council of Europe adopted the "Convention for the protection of human rights and dignity of the human being with regard to the application of biology and medicine: Convention on human rights and biomedicine"[115]. Meanwhile, 21 of the 40 Member States have adopted the principles of the Biomedicine Convention. The Convention shall enter into force as soon as five States, including at least four Member States of the Council of Europe, have expressed their consent to be bound by the Convention[116 117 118].

---

[114] For a short, historical overview, see HENAU-HUBLET, C., "Le projet de Convention de Bioéthique du Conseil de l'Europe: l'espoir d'une protection élevée des droits de l'homme", *T.Gez. / Rev. Dr. Santé*, 1995-1996, p. 26-27.

[115] Convention for the protection of human rights and dignity of the human being with regard to the application of biology and medicine: Convention on human rights and biomedicine, Council of Europe, Jur (1996), 14.

[116] The Biomedicine convention itself stipulates in Article 33, al. 3 that when at least five States, of which four Member States of the Council of Europe, have accepted the Bioconvention, this Biomedicine convention will apply the first day of the month after three months after the date of acceptance. "This Convention shall enter into force on the first day of the month following the expiration of a period of three months after the date on which five States, including at least four member States of the Council of Europe, have expressed their consent to be bound by the Convention (...)".

89. The scope of the Biomedicine convention is broad, because it aims at the protection of:

> *"the dignity and identity of all human beings and guarantee*
> *everyone, without discrimination, respect for their integrity and*
> *other rights and fundamental freedoms with regard to the*
> *application of biology and medicine (Article 1)".*

90. At the same time, it fixes some fundamental principles. In Article 2 of the Biomedicine convention, the States recognise the priority of the human being against society and science. The Biomedicine convention also advocates an equal access to health care of appropriate quality and respect for the dignity and identity of all human beings, and for the respect of their private life in relation to information about their health. It forbids financial gain and disposal of (a part of) the human body. The accordance with relevant professional obligations and standards is also a significant point.

91. For this topic, chapter V of the Biomedicine convention is significant because it is dedicated to scientific research. Fundamentally, the Member States recognise that scientific research shall be carried out freely. This "freedom of scientific research" is based on the right of mankind to gain knowledge and the right to progress in the field of medicines[119]. But this freedom is limited:

> *"(...) it is limited by the fundamental rights of individuals (...)"*[120].

92. Moreover, the Convention itself places several corrections. Experimentation on human beings may only take place if no alternative exists with similar effectiveness. The proportionality between possible risks and potential benefits must be respected. A competent authority, after an independent study of the scientific soundness, an evaluation of the importance of the research object and a multidisciplinary review of the ethically acceptance, must approve the study protocol. Finally, every trial subject must give an explicit, written consent, after information about his rights. He can freely withdraw this informed consent at any time. Further, Article 6 contains provisions which protect persons not able to consent. It puts forward the principle of the need of a therapeutic indication of every medical intervention. Exceptions are only allowed if a significant benefit can be expected, if the risks are minimal, if research of comparable effectiveness cannot be carried out on individuals capable of giving consent and if no alternative exists to obtain similar results.

---

[117] The Netherlands has started the procedure of ratification. The text of the Bioconvention shall be treated in the Second and First Chamber.

[118] At the moment, Belgium waits with the ratification until a public debate.

[119] Explanatory Report to the Convention for the protection of human rights and dignity of the human being with regard to the application of biology and medicine, Council of Europe, Jur (97) 1.

[120] The Explanatory Report continues: "(...) In this connection, it should be pointed out that the first Article of the Convention specifies that its aim is to protect the dignity and identity (...). Any research will therefore have to observe these principles".

93. At the moment, the Council of Europe is preparing a draft protocol on scientific research to amend the Biomedicine convention. This protocol is largely based on Recommendation R(90)3 of the Committee of Ministers of the Council of Europe[121] and wants to guarantee that only ethical and scientifically sound trials will take place, thus minimising the potential risks for human subjects[122].

2.2.3. National Legislation of Some Member States

94. In *Belgium*, two regulations govern clinical research i.e. the law on medicinal products of 25 March 1964[123] and the Royal Decree of 16 September 1985[124]. Although the Law on medicinal products does not regulate explicitly drug research, it recognises the need of such research. To prevent the unbridled and uncontrolled development of new medicinal products, the legislator imposes a system of prior authorisation. A pharmaceutical company can only market a medicinal product after obtaining an authorisation. To obtain this authorisation, the medicinal products have to meet certain minimal criteria. The ministry of Health grants the authorisation, after advice of the Commission for medicinal products (*Geneesmiddelencommissie*), which consists of university experts[125]. This Commission is based on the registration file, submitted by the pharmaceutical company, which contains the results of the different studies. The authorisation is the final piece of a slow, mostly laborious and particularly costly process. Implicitly, the legislator exerts control over the research.

95. Article 6*bis* is an important Article in the Law on medicinal products. It stipulates that the King may edict general provisions under which manufacturers, importers and distributors may conduct or may encourage the conduct of clinical trials[126]. Implicitly, this Article contains a legal authorisation of drug research[127]. It would be contrary to general legal principles to give the King the authority to regulate some matter that is *a priori* forbidden[128].

96. Royal Decree of 16 September 1985, as amended[129], has elaborated Article 6*bis*. Contrary to the Law on medicinal products, the Royal Decree is rather detailed about the concrete consequences of drug research. A file, consisting of a summary of the file, the results of the chemical, pharmaceutical and biological studies and a clinical documentation, must accompany every application for the marketing of a medicinal product. The latter, described in part 4 of the Annex of the Royal Decree, is particularly important.

---

[121] See above.
[122] HENAU-HUBLET, C.,*l.c.*, 28.
[123] *O.J.*, 17 April 1964.
[124] *O.J.*, 13 November 1985, 16.625.
[125] DEWATRIPONT, J., *l.c.*, p. 9-10, No 2.
[126] Article 6*bis*: The King may, after advice of one or more scientific authorities, appointed by him, prescribe general conditions, under which manufacturers, importers and distributors may conduct or may encourage the conduct of clinical trials.
[127] HENAU-HUBLET, C., L'activité médicale, *o.c.*, p. 43, footnote 77, NYS, H., "Medische experimenten met mensen. Juridische benadering" in *Bio-ethica in de jaren '90*, Gent, Omega Editions, 1987, p. 456, No 5.1.
[128] NYS, H., Geneeskunde, *o.c.*, p. 350, No 811.
[129] Royal Decree of 22 September 1992, *O.J.*, 5 December 1992, 25.235.

97.   Further, the regulation of the authorisation and the manufacturing of medicinal products mention drug research. Article 2 of the Royal Decree of 3 July 1969[130] contains the obligation to add the results of the clinical trials. The Royal Decree concerning the manufacturing and the distribution of medicinal products[131] enumerates a list of requirements.

98.   In *Germany*, a separate regulation of clinical trials is lacking. The legislator has only provided in the Law on medicinal products (*Artzneimittelgesetz* or *AMG)[132]* some provisions, namely the Articles 40 and 41, treat of drug trials. Article 40 contains the general conditions for research with human subjects, for the validity of the informed consent, the insurance of research (*Probandenversicherung*) and research with minors. Further, Article 41 contains a list with specific conditions for research on subjects who suffer from a disease that the experimental drugs tries to cure[133].

99.   France, thanks to the Hurriet Law of 1988, has legislation on research with human beings[134]. At first, the legislator only wanted to enact a law on drug research, but during the preparative works, it became clear that other types of research also needed regulation[135]. The dichotomy of biomedical research with direct individual benefit (recherches biomédicales avec bénéfice individuel direct) and research without direct individual benefit (recherches biomédicales sans bénéfice individuel direct) has replaced the traditional distinction between experiments with patients and those with healthy volunteers. The Hurriet Law has incorporated the ideas in the jurisprudence and the doctrine into legislation. Revolutionary is the regulation of research without any direct individual benefit: from that law, those studies are depenalised if the legal requirements are met. For this purpose, the French legislator has paid a lot of attention to the protection of the participating subjects.

100.   Only recently the Netherlands has its own specific legislation on research.

2.3. Necessary Conditions for the Legitimacy of Clinical Trial

101.   The general conditions for medical acts are also applicable to experiments. Aside from these conditions, research has to meet specific requirements[136].

---

130   *O.J.*, 10 July 1969.
131   Royal decree of 6 June 1960, *O.J.*, 22 June 1960.
132   Neurordnung des Artzeimittelgesetz of 1976, as amended.
133   See EBERNACH, W.H., *o.c.*, 229-231.
134   Loi du 20 décembre 1988 relative à la protection des personnes se prêtant à des recherches biomédicales, Code de la Santé Publique, Livre Iibis.
135   GROMB, S., Le droit de l'expérimentation sur l'homme, Parijs, Litec 1992, p.169, No98.
136   TER HEERDT, J., *Het experiment beproefd. De civielrechtelijke aansprakelijkheid voor schade ten gevolge van medische experimenten met mensen*, Maklu, Antwerpen, 2000, in press.

2.3.1. Scientific Soundness

102. First, the clinical trial must be scientifically sound[137]. This covers two aspects: the trial itself and the surroundings (staff and equipment). A clear, detailed protocol must describe the clinical trial. That protocol itself must be based on reliable lab and animal research. Furthermore, the clinical trial must be feasible and yield relevant information. Each member of the staff should be qualified by education, training and experience to perform their tasks. A physician-researcher must supervise the clinical trial[138].

2.3.2. Risk/Benefit Ratio

103. Second, the risk/benefit ratio must be respected[139]. Before a trial is initiated, foreseeable risks and inconveniences should be weighed against the anticipated benefit for the individual trial subject and the society[140]. A trial should be initiated and continued only if the anticipated benefits justify the risks. This evaluation is not a static process but a dynamic one. The researcher must abstain from a once-only risk assessment. Instead, the evaluation must consider newly available information[141]. Only in this way can the researcher can abort the trial prematurely, if continuation will lead to damages[142], death or other serious complication when the risks exceed the advantages[143]. One border cannot be crossed. Namely, if prior reason exists that death or disability will occur, the trial may not be performed. Most (inter)national documents mention this prohibition[144].

2.3.3. Subsidiarity

104. Starting-point with drug research is that only persons who can give a free and informed consent will be involved in the trial. This fundamental rule is the subsidiarity-rule. If the clinical trial can take place with healthy, competent and independent subjects, it is preferable instead of the enclosure of subjects of vulnerable groups.

---

[137]   Declaration of Helsinki, basic principles 1 and 2; NYS, H., *o.c.*, p. 352-353, No 816-821.
[138]   Declaration of Helsinki, Basic Principle No 3.
[139]   NYS, H., *o.c.*, p. 354, No 823; VAN OEVELEN, A. and DE BOECK, A., *l.c.*, p. 347, No 75; Declaration of Helsinki, Basic principle 4.
[140]   NYS, H., Geneeskunde. Recht en medisch handelen, Brussels, E. Story-Scientia, 1991, p. 354, No 823; VAN OEVELEN, A. and DE BOECK, A., *"De begrenzing van de contractuele vrijheid t.a.v. het menselijk lichaam"* in *Over zichzelf beschikken? Juridische en ethische bijdragen over het leven, het lichaam en de dood,* Antwerp, Maklu Uitgevers, 1996, p. 347, No 75; Declaration of Helsinki, basic principle 4.
[141]   BERGKAMP, L., *o.c.*, p. 153, No 7.2.4.
[142]   Declaration of Helsinki, Chapter III, Non-therapeutic biomedical research involving human subjects, Article 3; Nuremberg Code, principle 10.
[143]   Declaration of Helsinki, Chapter I, basic principle 7.
[144]   Principle 5 of the Nuremberg Code: *"No experiment should be conducted where there is an a priori reason to believe that death or disabling injury will occur (...)".*

2.3.4. Free and Informed Consent

2.3.4.1. Content

105.   Last but not least, subjects should give their free and informed consent. The Draft Directive does not provide a strict regulation concerning the informed consent of human subjects. Instead, it refers to the measures in the Member States. But, the free and informed consent is essential for the legitimacy of clinical trials. Without it, the clinical trial is theoretically forbidden. Different national and international documents confirm this fundamental claim[145]. This consent should be preferable in writing.

106.   Consent alone, moreover, is not enough. It must meet certain conditions. First, the subject has to be capable to give consent. Further, the consent must be informed[146]. In short, sufficient information must be given on the purpose of the clinical trial, the nature, the length, the used methods and the foreseeable, relevant risks. Furthermore, the information should be given in a language understandable for layman[147].

2.4. Review by Ethical Committees

2.4.1. Formation

107.   According to the ICH GCP (1996), the EC should consist of a reasonable number of members, who collectively have the qualifications and experience to review and evaluate the science, medical aspects and ethics of the proposed trial. The ICH GCP recommends that the EC should include at least five numbers, whereunder at least one member whose primary area of interest is in the non-scientific area and at least one member who is independent of the institution/trial site[148]. Only those EC members who are independent of the investigator and the sponsor of the trial may vote and may provide opinion on a trial-related matter[149].

108.   Apparently, only members who participate in the review and discussion, may vote and provide their opinion. The investigator may provide information on any aspect of the trial, but should not participate in the deliberations of the EC or in the vote of the EC[150]. If the investigator is a

---

[145]   See for instance: Declaration of Helsinki (Articles 9, 10 and 11 Basic Principle); Recommendation R(90)3 of the Committee of Ministers of the Council of Europe, principle 3; Biomedicine convention, Article16.

[146]   VAN LIL, M., NYS, H. and SEGAL, L., "Regulering door middel van deontologische regels" in Bio-ethica, *o.c.*, p. 471, No4; VAN OEVELEN, A. and DE BOECK, A., "De begrenzing van de contractuele vrijheid t.a.v. het menselijk lichaam" in *Over zichzelf beschikken? Juridische en ethische bijdragen over het leven, het lichaam en de dood*, Antwerpen, Maklu Uitgevers, 1996, p. 313, No 9-11.

[147]   BROEKHUIJSEN-MOLENAAR, A.M.L. and STOLKER, C.J.J.M., Geneesmiddelen, *o.c.*, 64; VAN LIL, M., NYS, H. and SEGAL, L., *l.c.*, *o.c.*, p. 472, No 4.

[148]   Article 3.2.1 ICH GCP (1996).

[149]   Article 3.2.4 ICH GCP (1996).

[150]   Article 3.2.5 ICH GCP (1996).

member of the EC, he should abstain from voting. An EC member may invite non-members with expertise in special areas for assistance[151].

2.4.2. Tasks

109. It is generally agreed that research on humans should not be carried out unless some form of independent ethical review body has scrutinised the proposals. Their function is dual. On the one hand the ethical committee has to guarantee that only those trials that correspond to the criteria. On the other hand the ethical committee has to control the development of the trial. The Draft Directive focuses on the functions of the ethical committee. According to the ICH GCP (1996) an EC should safeguard the rights, safety and well being of all trial subjects. Special attention should be paid to trials that may include vulnerable subjects[152]. The Belgian legislation obliges hospitals to create an independent ethics committee. Besides an accompanying and advising function concerning the ethical aspects of individual health matters, the ethics committee must also evaluate research protocols[153].

2.4.2.1. A Priori Approval

110. Before a trial can start, the EC should review it, within a reasonable time (3.1.2 ICH GCP 1996) and give advice. The Draft Directive indicates the time within which the EC should advise. The actual text prescribes that the EC should give motivated advice within maximum of 30 days after the official introduction of the application[154]. The EC can ask for more information, only once, in addition to the give information and posses than over an additional period of 30 days to give the final advice.

111. To evaluate the trial, the EC must obtain several documents: trial protocol(s), amendment(s), written informed consent forms and consent form updates that the investigator proposes for use in the trial, subject recruitment procedures (e.g. advertisements), written information to be provided to subjects, the investigator's brochure, available safety information, information about payments and compensation available to subjects, the investigator's current curriculum vitae and other documentation evidencing qualifications, and any other documents that the EC may need to fulfil its responsibilities[155].

112. The Belgian Royal Decree demands a written opinion of the EC. The phrases of this decree create a legal obligation for researchers to ask for an opinion. Although the Royal Decree does not provide in any sanction, a breach of this obligation can lead to a refusal of authorisation. Further, researchers have a deontological duty to ask the EC for advice.

---

[151]   Article 3.2.6 ICH GCP (1996).
[152]   Article 3.1.1 ICH GCP (1996).
[153]   PALERMINI, P. and DELFOSSE, M.-L., "L'expérimentation médicale sur l'être humain. Propositions pour un cadre législatif", *T. Gez. / Rev. Dr. Santé*, 1996-97, p. 339, No 3; TER HEERDT, J., *l.c.*, p. 211-212, No 9.
[154]   Article 4, 4 Draft Directive.
[155]   Article 3.1.2 ICH GCP (1996).

113. According to the Royal Decree, the advice is not binding. The researcher has the freedom (theoretically) to start the experiment regardless, despite the fact that he has received a negative opinion. In reality however, negative advice implies the amendment of the protocol or leads to a rejection. Two cases of advice by the National Council of the Order of Physicians have stimulated this practice. The first case of advice[156] as well as the second one[157] determines expressly that it must be positive.

114. In *France* the researcher is legally obliged to ask the EC prior to the research for an opinion. If not, he risks penal sanctions. If the EC gives a negative opinion, the research may only start after the expiration of two months, after notification of the minister of Health[158].

2.4.2.2. Control

115. The task of the EC does not end with the opinion, prior to the start of the research. It has also the duty to follow up the trial. This allows the EC to check if the researchers comply with the protocol. Indirectly it is a guarantee that unwanted turns of the trial are notified in advance so that premature suspension is not theoretical possibility. According to the ICH GCP (1996) the EC should conduct continuing review of each ongoing trial at intervals appropriate to the degree of risk to human subjects, that is at least once per year (3.1.4).

2.4.3. Responsibility

116. Whereas in the past, little attention was paid to the liability of EC for their opinions, nowadays, the awareness grows that EC's can make mistakes too. For their negligent and harmful conduct, the possibility has to exist to address the EC.

2.5. Confidentiality

117. Members of the EC obtain necessary confidential information about clinical research: information about new drugs, data about patients and subjects and more in general about the health situation of persons. Are these members bound by a duty of confidentiality? In general, the heterogeneous composition of the EC can cause problems. Only if physicians or specialists are members of the EC, then they are bounded by their medical secret. In most European countries, the non-appliance with the duty to respect this medical secret leads to criminal sanctions. But what about non-physicians: are they in the same way bounded by

---

[156]   "Klinische proeven met geneesmiddelen", *T. Orde Gen.*, 1984, (32), 48: *"Every biomedical research must be subject of a protocol, that a EC has evaluated and has given positive advice, prior to the performance"*.

[157]   "Bio-ethiek en de Nationale Raad van de Orde der Geneesheren", *T. Orde Gen.*, 1992 (55), 35-36: *"1. Biomedical research on human beings needs the presentation of a draft of the trial to an EC"* and *"6. A physician who participates in biomedical research, must check if an EC has approved the protocol"*.

[158]   Article L.209-12 Code de la Santé Publique: *"Avant de réaliser une recherche sur l'être humain, tout investigateur est tenu d'en soumettre le projet à l'avis d'un comité consultatif (...). Les projets ayant fait l'objet d'un avis défavorable ne peuvent être mis en oeuvre avant un délai de deux mois à compter de leur réception par le ministre"*.

this medical secret? Neither the GCP (1990) nor the ICH GCP (1996) contain any provisions about confidentiality. This means that the national regulations apply. In France, the Law of 20 December 1988 stipulates that all the members of the EC fall within the scope of the medical secrecy[159].

2.6. Practical Suggestions for an Investigation Agreement

2.6.1. Form

118. A first question that arises is with whom the investigation agreement is closed. Is it between the pharmaceutical company and the investigator or with the hospital where the clinical trial will be performed or are both parties implicated? In general, the agreement is closed between an investigator and a sponsor, a pharmaceutical company, and must contain some general provisions: the agreement must indicate the place where the trial will be conducted. Further, a schedule has to be set up, so that there is a clear ending of the trial. Because the investigator, in most cases, necessarily uses hospital staff and equipment, the investigator and the hospital must draft or a specific contract or amend the already existing contract with an annex so that their relationship becomes transparent. This annex or contract can regulate things such as the remuneration of the use of hospital staff and equipment, the use of hospital space, and so on.

2.6.2. Content

119. An important aspect of the investigation agreement is the provisions about the ownership of the trial results and the confidentiality of the trial (results). To avoid interpretation problems, the investigation agreement can indicate that the trial know-how, results, case report forms and/or notebooks, documents, and products are the exclusive property of the sponsor. Concerning the discoveries, as a result of the trial, the agreement should mention that the investigator might not claim or have any intellectual or industrial property rights.

120. Also, the agreement must state that the investigator has the duty to professional secrecy concerning the trial, and in particular, the nature of the products studies, the trial, the persons taking part herein, the know-how and the results obtained. The investigator is obliged to provide information regarding the trial only to the sponsor, the monitor, the hospital administration, the EC and the competent services within the Ministry of Health. If the investigator wants to produce publications, presentations or communications regarding the trial, he needs to have the prior written agreement of the sponsor, who shall have the right to examine the content of said publications, presentations and communications.

2.6.3. Payment

121. The investigator agreement clearly has to indicate which fee will be paid and what procedure must be followed. There is a preference to pay per subject instead of per trial. To avoid the case that the investigator only includes

---

[159]   Article L.209-11 of the Law No 88-1138 of 20 December 1988.

subjects to receive payment, without ensuring that they will complete the trial, it is preferable to pay in parts. Thus, it is not uncommon to pay the fee in two instalments. A first part will be paid when the subject is enrolled in the trial, a second part when the case report form notebook for the subject has bee completed and furnished to the sponsor. If the case report form notebook is incomplete, the second instalment of the fee shall not be paid. Further, to ensure that the investigator follows the directives of the sponsor and complies with the clinical investigation plan, the legal regulations and the European GCP, a guarantee can be build in, e.g. the sponsor can in the light of non-compliance suspend payment of the fee.

122. Normally, the amounts provided for in the investigation agreement represent the total cost to the sponsor for the trial. No additional charges can be invoiced to the sponsor by the investigator or the hospital where the trial takes place. An exception can be made for travel and lodging expenses, arising from or relating to the conduct of the trial, e.g. meetings with co-investigators, consultations with the monitor, on condition that the investigator produces receipts and that the investigator has previously approved such expenses.

2.6.4. Responsibility

123. Normally, the duty to obtain a liability insurance coverage rests upon the sponsor. But, most agreements contain a provision that the investigator remains liable for any damage, caused directly or indirectly by his acts or acts of persons, acting partially or entirely under his supervision. This means that it is important for the investigator to be fully covered by his insurance policy. The moment a physician wants to perform clinical research, he must warn his insurance company. Often, the policy excludes compensation for damages caused by clinical research or considers it as a severe fault. However, the most fair clause in an investigation agreement is the clause stipulating that the promoter will pay the insurance fee and will bear all costs for damages caused by clinical research. If the investigator commits a severe fault, the promoter always can recover his loss from the responsible investigator.

2.7. Conclusions

124. In several Member States, separate legislation concerning clinical trials exists already. But also on the European level, the concern for the welfare and protection of clinical subjects, despite the urge of simplification and the need of cost reducement, is growing. Such European project must be encouraged. Too often, pharmaceutical researchers are confronted with different regulations. In some countries, Belgium for example, researchers, hospitals, ethics committees and pharmaceutical companies must fall back on legally not binding documents, such as the deontological code of physicians, the Declaration of Helsinki and the Good Clinical Practices. These explain several aspects of research, but in some areas, especially when clinical research is performed on vulnerable groups, they reveal blatant contradictions.

As soon as the draft directive of the European Parliament and Council will be adopted, further steps can be made to harmonise the different regulations of the Member States. This will be a significant improvement, especially for international multi-centric clinical research, now the same procedures will apply in the different Member States.

3. MARKETING AUTHORISATION OF A MEDICINAL PRODUCT

3.1. Introduction

125. EU regulators first ventured into the area of pharmacy with Directive 65/65/EEC of 26 January 1965 on the approximation of provisions laid down by law, regulation or administrative action relating to medicinal products (hereinafter Directive 65/65/EEC)[160]. The driving force behind this regulatory co-operation has been the better protection of public and animal health, and ensuring free circulation of medical products in the EU. So, the Directive 65/65/EEC pursued two objectives: the protection of public health and the free movement of products (see also Chapter 1). Medicinal products are indeed special products that cannot merely be manufactured and put on the market[161]. The problem of thaliomyde showed regulators and the public that the public health might be at stake in the marketing of medicinal products. Therefore, Directive 65/65/EEC provided that an authorisation must be issued by the competent authorities before the medicinal product can be put on the market[162].

126. Directive 65/65/EEC that provided for a national marketing authorisation procedure was only a first step into the harmonisation of the pharmaceutical sector. In this chapter we analyse other steps of harmonisation such as the introduction of the Community procedures, i.e. the Centralised Procedure (see under 3.3.1.), the Mutual Recognition Procedure (see under 3.3.2.) and the Community Referral Procedure (see under 3.3.3.). This chapter deals also with the abridged marketing procedure (see under 3.4.), the problem of variations to the terms of a marketing authorisation (see under 3.5.) and some other authorisations (see under 3.6).

3.2. The National Marketing Authorisation Procedure

3.2.1. Standard Procedure to place Medicinal Products on the Market

127. No medicinal product may be placed on the market of a Member State unless a marketing authorisation has been issued[163]. In order to obtain this authorisation, the person responsible for placing that product on the market[164] must apply to the competent authority of the Member State concerned[165]. This person has to provide several particulars and documents. These include among others the package, the leaflet of the medicinal product, the mock-ups of the sales presentation of the proprietary product (see Chapter 7), the results of e.g.

---

[160] *O.J.*, No 22, L 369, 9 February 1965.

[161] CASSIA,, P. and SAULNIER, E., "L'autorisation de mise sur le marché des médicaments à usage humain dans l'union européenne", *Rev. Du Marché commun et de l'Union européenne*, 1996, p. 750; recital 2 of Directive 65/65/EEC.

[162] With regard to the issue whether an authorisation is required when a medicinal product is not intended to be put on the market, see BOGAERT, P., *EC Pharmaceutical Law*, Chancery Law Publishing, No 3.9.

[163] Article 3 of Directive 65/65/EEC. The authorisation to market a medicinal product is different from an authorisation to manufacture medicinal products (see below).

[164] This person must be established in the within the EEA. Which encompasses the European Economic Area, i.e. the European Union plus Norway, Iceland and Liechtenstein.

[165] Article 4 of Directive 65/65/EEC.

clinical trials (see Chapter 2), the document showing that the manufacturer of the product is authorised to produce proprietary products (see below), the summary of the product characteristics (SPC), etc.

128. According to Article 5 of Directive 65/65/EEC, national authorities grant marketing authorisations based on safety, quality and efficacy. An authorisation shall be refused if it proves that the medicinal product is harmful in the normal conditions of use, that its therapeutic efficacy is lacking or is insufficiently substantiated by the applicant, or that its qualitative and quantitative composition is not as declared[166] or have not been amended or when the controls on the finished product have not been carried out[167].

129. With regard to contraceptives or abortifacients, Member States have also the opportunity to refuse a medicinal product to be put on the market for other reasons[168].

130. The authorisation is valid for five years and is renewable for five-year periods[169] on application by the holder at least three months before the expiry date and after consideration by the competent authority of a dossier containing, in particular, details of the data on pharmacovigilance and other information relevant to the monitoring of the medicinal product[170].

131. According to Article 21, the authorisation to market a medicinal product shall not be refused, suspended or revoked except on the grounds set out in the Directive[171].

3.2.2. The Progress towards the Harmonisation of Pharmaceutical Law

3.2.2.1. Standards to Perform Clinical Trials

132. Directive 65/65/EEC was only a first step in the approximation of the laws of Member States relating to medicinal products. It was necessary that this approximation was continued in view of the existing disparities related to the control of medicinal products[172]. The Directive 65/65/EEC provided, for example, that applications for authorisation to place a medicinal product on the market should be accompanied by particulars and documents relating to the

---

[166]   The authorisation shall likewise be refused if the particulars and documents submitted in support of the application do not comply with Article 4 of the Directive.

[167]   Article 11 of Directive 65/65/EEC.

[168]   Article 6 of Directive 65/65/EEC; see DEBOYSER, P., p. 114.

[169]   Article 7 of Directive 65/65/EEC.

[170]   Article 10 of Directive 65/65/EEC.

[171]   See also E.C.J., Pierrel v Ministero della Santa, Case C-83/92*E.C.R.*, 1993, I-6419. According to the Court, Directive 65/65 precludes national authorities not only from introducing grounds for suspension or revocation other than those laid down by Community law, but also from providing for the lapse of authorizations to market medicinal products. See also E.C.J., Clin-Midy v Belgium, Case C-310/82, *E.C.R.*, 1984, 251: The Court decided that Article 21 of Directive 65/65 must be interpreted as meaning that authorisation to market a proprietary medicinal product may not be refused, suspended or revoked, save on the ground of the protection of public health as referred to in the Directive.

[172]   See VAN DER VLIES, R. and CALLENS, S., "Protection of innovation in the Pharmaceutical Industry", *BSLR*, 1998, p. 90-96.

results of tests and trials carried out on the product. However, standards and protocols to perform these tests and trials were lacking in the original text of the Directive 65/65/EEC. Directive 75/318 of 20 May 1975 on Member States' harmonisation of the rules relating to analytical, pharmacotoxicological and clinical standards and protocols in respect of the testing of medicinal products, had to harmonise the rules on analytical, pharmacotoxicological and clinical standards and protocols in respect of the testing of medicinal products[173]. So, this Directive was an important step to remove the hindrances of the free movement of medicinal products.

3.2.2.2. The Committee for Proprietary Medicinal Products

133. Another step towards a free movement of medicinal products was achieved by Directive 75/319/EEC of 20 may 1975[174]. A Committee for Proprietary Medicinal Products (CPMP) was set up in order to facilitate the adoption of common decisions by Member States on the authorisation of medicinal products on the basis of the scientific criteria of quality, safety and efficacy, and the achievement thereby of the free movement of medicinal products within the Community[175].

134. The opinions of the CPMP were, however, not binding. Therefore, differences in decision-making between Member States were still present. In order to find a first solution for this problem, Directive 83/570/EEC[176] gave a new role to the Committee. If several applications have been made for marketing authorisation on a particular medicinal product, and Member States have adopted divergent decisions concerning the authorisation of the medicinal product or its suspension or withdrawal from the market, a Member State, or even the person responsible for placing the medicinal product on the market, could refer the matter to the Committee. Even before a decision was made, a Member State could refer the matter to the Committee before reaching a decision on a request for a marketing authorisation or on the suspension or withdrawal of an authorisation[177].

---

[173] *O.J.*, L 175, 9 June 1975, p. 1.

[174] Directive 75/319/EEC on the approximation of provisisions laid down by law, regulation or administrative action relating to medicinal products, *O.J.*, L 147, 9 June 1975, p. 13.

[175] Article 8, 1 of Directive 75/319/EEC.

[176] Direcitve 83/570/EEC of 26 October 1983 amending Directives 655/65/EEC, 75/318/EEC and 75/319/EEC on the approximation of provisions laid down by law, regulation or administrative action relating to proprietary medicinal products, *O.J.*, L 332, 28 November 1983, p. 1.

[177] Article 12 of the modified Directive 75/319/EEC.

3.2.2.3. From a Multi-state and Concertation Procedure to a Community Procedure

135. Directive 75/319/EEC and in particular Directive 83/570/EEC enabled the holder of an authorisation in one Member State to request the extension of that authorisation in at least two other Member States. In order to obtain recognition in one or more of the Member States of an authorisation issued by a Member State in accordance with Article 3 of Directive 65/65/EEC (see above), the holder of an authorisation had to submit an application to the competent authorities. He had to ensure that the original Member State and any subsequent Member State was in possession of identical information upon which to base their decisions[178].

136. So this Multi-State Procedure aimed to give a marketing procedure if the product was already authorised in the initial Member State according to harmonised rules[179]. The Member States for which a new authorisation was being applied had 90 days to deliver an authorisation or to formulate reasons to oppose to the authorisation. In the latter case, the matter was referred to the CPMP. This Committee could deliver an opinion that had no binding effect since the Directive provided merely that the Member States must decide (within 60 days after the opinion of the Committee) what action to take on the Committee's opinion[180].

137. The further step towards harmonisation was via the 87/22/EEC Directive[181]. This Directive provided for some high-technology medicinal products in an obligatory Community mechanism for concertation. Member states were obliged to consult the CPMP for products on List A (i.e. products developed by means of biological processes). Products on List B (i.e. other high technology medicinal products) had only to be referred to the CPMP at the request of the applicant.

3.3. Community Procedures for a Marketing Authorisation

138. In the process towards harmonisation it was important to create a community marketing authorisation that was valid throughout the Community. This was achieved by the Council Regulation (EEC) No 2309/93 of 22 July 1993 laying down Community procedures for the authorisation and supervision of medicinal products for human and veterinary use and establishing a European Agency for the Evaluation of Medicinal Products (see under 3.3.1)[182]. To facilitate access to the Community market, Council Directive 93/39/EEC of 14 June 1993 amending Directives 65/65/EEC, 75/318/EEC and 75/319/EEC in respect of medicinal products[183], established an alternative route, the

---

[178]   Article 9 of Directive 75/319/EEC.

[179]   DEBOYSER, l.c., p. 124.

[180]   BOGAERT, P.K., o.c., No 3.80.

[181]   Council Directive 87/22/EEC of December 22nd 1986 on the approximation of national measures relating to the placing on the market of high-technology medicinal products, particularly those derived from biotechnology, O.J., L 15/38.

[182]   O.J., L..214, 24 August 1993, p. 1.

[183]   O.J., L 214/22.

"decentralised procedure", which was inspired by the Multi-State procedure (see above), and was based on the principle of Mutual Recognition (see under 3.3.2). Besides the Centralised Procedure and the Decentralised or Mutual Recognition Procedure, Community decisions are taken to resolve community referrals (see under 3.3.3).

3.3.1. The Centralised Procedure

3.3.1.1. In General

139. . Council Regulation (EEC) No 2309/93 of 22 July 1993 creates a centralised community procedure for the authorisation of medicinal products, for which there is a single application, a single evaluation and a single authorisation allowing direct access to the single market of the Community[184].)[185]. Instead of 15 applications to each Member State's national authority, companies with an innovative product have the 'possibility' of a single application and scientific evaluation[186] leading to the granting of a marketing authorisation. The Regulation No 2309/93 came into force 1 January 1995. The Regulation decreases the power of individual Member States in authorising a product to be commercialised[187]. The 'centralised procedure' was inspired by the concertation procedure of Directive 87/22/EEC (see above).

140. Regulation No 2309/93 is an important step towards standardising authorisation at the Community level for the marketing of medicinal products[188]. It sets common Community standards of quality, safety and efficacy of pharmaceutical products[189].

141. Regulation No 2309/93 establishes also a European Agency for the Evaluation of Medicinal Products (EMEA). The EMEA has as a primary task to provide scientific advice of the highest possible quality to the Community institutions and the Member States[190]. The exclusive responsibility for preparing the opinions of the Agency is entrusted to CPMP[191]. In fact, the Agency

---

[184] Article 12, 1 of Regulation No 2309/93. Also, Article 12, 2 states that 'The refusal of a Community marketing authorisation shall constitute a prohibition on the placing on the market of the medicinal product concerned throughout the Community'.

[185] See above.

[186] SAUER, F., "Accelerating Drug Approach in Europe", *BSLR*, 1997, p. 3.

[187] CASSIA, P. and SAULNIER, E., "L'autorisation de mise sur le marché des médicaments à usage humain dans l'Union Européenne", *Rev. Du Marché commun et de l'Union européenne*, 1996, p. 753.

[188] The Council and the European Parliament is revising a draft codification of pharmaceutical legislation. The adoption of the final text will probably not take place before the beginning of 2001.

[189] KON, S. and SCHAEFFER, F "Parallel Imports of Pharmaceutical Products: A New Realism, or Back to Basics", *ECLR*, 1997, p. 125; GEDDES, A., "Free Movement of Pharmaceuticals within the Community: The Remaining Barriers", *EHR*, 1991, p. 296.

[190] Article 51 of Regulation No 2309/93. Some organisations, like the European Federation of Pharmacuetical Industries and Associations (EFPIA) are asking for the appointment of an 'ombudsman' to facilitate the resolution of issues wtihin the centralised (and mutual recognition procedures) (see EFPIA, *Regulation 2000. An EFPIA PERSPECTIVE ON THE FUTURE OF MEDICINES'REGULATION IN EUROPE*, 1999, p. 3).

[191] Recital 13 of Regulation No 2309/93.

comprises the CPMP[192], which is responsible for preparing the opinion of the Agency on any question relating to the evaluation of medicinal products, a secretariat, an executive director and a management board[193].

3.3.1.2. Scope of the Regulation

142. The Community issues and supervises the marketing authorisation for medicinal products falling within the scope of Regulation No 2309/93[194]. The medicinal products for which this centralised Community procedure is *obligatory*[195] are the products[196] developed by means of one of the following biotechnological processes:

- recombinant DNA technology;
- controlled expression of genes coding for biologically active proteins in prokaryotes and eukaryotes including transformed mammalian cells;
- hybridoma and monoclonal antibody methods[197].

143. Applications for medicinal products containing a new, active substance *may* use the centralised procedure[198]. In addition, applications for innovative medicinal products with novel characteristics as defined in part B of the Annex to Council Regulation No 2309/93 may also, at the request of the applicant, be accepted for consideration under the centralised procedure. The following

---

[192] This Committee consists of two members nominated by each Member State (Article 52 of Regulation No 2309/93). In addition to their task of providing objective scientific opinions to the Community and Member States on the questions which are referred to them, the members of the Committee must ensure that there is appropriate co-ordination between the tasks of the Agency and the work of competent national authorities (Article 52, 2 of Regulation No 2309/93).

[193] Article 50 of Regulation No 2309/93.

[194] Article 4, 1 of Regulation No 2309/93.

[195] This is critiqued because the obligation to comply with the centralised procedure is equally imposed for products that may have only a local interest or even if the intention is to market the product only on the territory of one Member state, see WAELBROECK, D. and COUNYE, D., "Vers une libre circulation des médicaments grâce à l'harmonisation des procédures d'authorisation de mise sur le marché", *Journal des Tribunaux Droit Européen*, 1997, p.98.

[196] Article 3 of the Regulation. As written above, this system of compulsory and optional use of the procedure is based on the Annex of Directive 87/22; Part A of the Annex is identically worded to Part A of the Annex to Directive 87/22. Part B of the Regulation as described above however, differs from Part B of Directive 87/22.

[197] See part A of the Annex to Regulation No 2309/93.

[198] A new chemical, biological or radiopharmaceutical active substance includes a chemical, biological or radiopharmaceutical substance not previously authorised as a medicinal product in the European Union, an isomer, mixture of isomers, a complex or derivative or salt of a chemical substance previously authorsied as a medicinal product in the European Union, but differing in properties with regard to safety and efficacy from that chemical substance previously authorised, a biological substance previously authorised as a medicinal product in the European Union, but differing in molecular structure, nature from the source material or manufacturing process, a radiopharmaceutical substance which is a radionucleide, or a ligand not previously authorised as a medicinal product in the European Union, or a ligand not previously authorised as a medicinal product in the European Union, or the coupling mechanism to link the molecule and the radionuclide has not been previously authorised in the European Union (EUROPEAN COMMISSION, *Notice to Applicants*, p. 53).

categories of medicinal products for human use are, for example, eligible for Part B status:

- new medicinal products derived from human blood or human plasma;
- medicinal presented for an entirely new indication which, in the opinion of the Agency, is of significant therapeutic interest;
- medicinal products developed by other biotechnological processes which, in the opinion of the Agency, constitute a significant innovation.

144. It should be noted that Regulation (EC) No 141/2000 of 16 December 1999 on orphan medicinal products has introduced also a Community marketing authorisation for orphan medicinal products (see below) in accordance with Regulation (EEC) No 2309/93. Moreover, the applicant has not to justify that the product qualifies under Part B of the Annex to Regulation No 2309/93.

3.3.1.3. Filing an Application to Market

145. An application for authorisation must be accompanied by the particulars and documents referred to in Articles 4 and 4a of Directive 65/65/EEC as well as with the documents listed in Article 6 of Regulation No 2309/93. The application must also be accompanied by the fee payable to the EMEA for the examination of the application[199].

146. The EMEA ensures that the opinion of the CPMP is given within 210 days. The CPMP opinion, which may be favourable or unfavourable, is, wherever possible, reached by scientific consensus.

147. The authorisation shall be refused if it appears that the quality, the safety or the efficacy of the medicinal product has not been adequately or sufficiently demonstrated by the applicant[200]. Authorisation shall also be refused if the particulars and documents are incorrect or if the labelling and package leaflets are not in accordance with Directive 92/27/EEC (see Chapter 7).

148. In accordance with Article 9, 3 of Regulation No 2309/93, the Community Decision on the marketing must include details of any conditions or restrictions that could be imposed on the supply or use of the medicinal product concerned, including the conditions under which the medicinal product may be available to patients, with regard to the criteria laid down in Council Directive 92/26/EEC of 31 March 1992 concerning the classification for the supply of medicinal products for human use. Therefore, the Community Decision may include the notion that the medicinal product is subject to medical prescription.

149. A marketing authorisation that has been granted shall be valid throughout the Community[201] for five years and shall be renewable for five-year

---

[199]   The amount of these fees is regulated by Council Regulation No 297/95 of 10 February 1995 on fees payable to the European Agency for the Evaluation of Medicinal Products, *O.J.*, L 35, 15 February 1995, p. 1).

[200]   Article 11 of Regulation No 2309/93.

[201]   Article 12 of Regulation No 2309/93.

periods[202]. The authorised medicinal products must be entered in the Community Register of Medicinal Products[203]. Notification of marketing authorisation is published in the Official Journal of the European Communities[204].

3.3.1.4. A Community Decision

150. If the Committee is of the opinion

-   that the application does not satisfy the criteria for authorisation set out in the Regulation, or
-   the SPC should be amended, or
-   the labelling or package leaflet of the product is not in compliance with Council Directive 92/27/EEC of 31 March 1992 on the labelling of medicinal products for human use and on package leaflets, or
-   the authorisation should be granted subject to certain specific obligations,

the EMEA shall inform the applicant[205]. Within 15 days of receipt of the opinion, the applicant may provide written notice to the Agency that he wishes to appeal. If he does not appeal within 15 days, he shall be deemed to have agreed with the opinion, and the opinion becomes final. The grounds for appeal must be forwarded to the EMEA within 60 days of receipt of the opinion. Within 60 days of receipt of the grounds for appeal, the CPMP will consider whether its opinion should be revised. Once the CPMP issues a final opinion, it is forwarded within 30 days of its adoption, to the Commission, the Member States, and the applicant together with an assessment report and the reasons for its conclusions[206]. Within 30 days of receipt of the opinion, the Commission shall prepare a draft of the decision to be taken in respect of the application, taking account of Community law. The draft decision shall be forwarded to the Member States and the applicant.

151. The Commission is assisted by a Standing Committee on Medicinal Products for Human Use. The representative of the Commission shall submit to the Committee a draft of the measures to be taken. The opinion of the Committee is delivered by the majority laid down in Art. 205 of the Treaty in the case of a decision that the Council is required to adopt on a proposal from the Commission. The Commission is not bound by the opinion of the Committee[207].

---

202   Article 13, 1 of Regulation No 2309/93. In exceptional circumstances an authorisation may be granted subject to certain specific obligations, to be reviewed annually by the EMEA.

203   According to Article 13, 4 medicinal products that have been authorised by the Community shall benefit form the ten-year period of protection referred to in point 8 of the second paragraph of Article 4 of Directive 65/65/EEC (see below).

204   Article 12, 3 of Regulation No 2309/93.

205   Article 9, 1 of Regulation No 2309/93.

206   Article 9, 2 of Regulation No 2309/93.

207   The Member States may forward written observations on the draft decision of the Commission (Article 10.3. of Regulation No 2309/93). Regualation No 1662/95 lays down detailed arrangements for impleming the Community decision-making procedure (*O.J.*, L 158, 8 July 1995, p. 4).

152. The Commission adopts the measures envisaged if they are in accordance with the opinion of the Committee. If the measures envisaged are not in accordance with the opinion of the Committee, or if no opinion is delivered, the Commission shall, without delay, submit to the Council a proposal relating to the measures to be taken. The Council shall act by a qualified majority. If on the expiry of a period of three months from the date of referral to the Council, the Council has not acted, the proposed measures shall be adopted by the Commission, save where the Council has decided against the said measures by a simple majority.

3.3.2. The Mutual Recognition Procedure or the Decentralised Procedure

3.3.2.1. The Marketing Authorisation Holder initiates the Procedure

153. Directive 93/39/EEC[208] establishes an alternative route, the "decentralised procedure", which is inspired by the Multi-State procedure, and is based on the principle of mutual recognition[209]. The authorisation to place a medicinal product on the market in one Member State ought, in principle, to be recognised by the competent authorities of the other Member States. This procedure will be used for medicinal products that are not subject to the centralised procedure and that the applicant wants to circulate throughout the Community[210]. Before 1998, the second Member State had the option to ignore the first Member State's assessment. With the new Article 7a of Directive 65/65/EEC, that came into force January 1st 1998, any second Member State asked to grant an authorisation subsequent to that granted by the first Member State, is obliged to demand the other member states' assessment report. A decision to recognise the original marketing authorisation granted by the first Member State must take place within 90 days of receipt of the application.

154. So, for marketing authorisations in more than one Member State, the person responsible for placing the product on the market may either make an application in one of the Member States and once the marketing authorisation has been granted make applications in other Member States concerned requesting them to mutually recognise the marketing authorisation already granted or make (parallel) applications in each of the Member States concerned and request a national authorisation in each.

155. In order to obtain the recognition in one or more of the Member States of an authorisation issued by a Member State, within 90 days[211], the holder of the authorisation must submit an application to the competent authorities of the Member State(s) concerned[212]. He has to testify that the dossier is identical to the one accepted by the first Member State, or he must identify any additions and amendments it may contain. The holder of the marketing authorisation must

---

[208]   Council Directive 93/39/EEC of June 14th 1993 amending Directives 65/65/EEC, 75/318/EEC and 75/319/EEC in respect of medicinal products, *O.J.*, L 214/22.

[209]   This principle is adopted in Case C-120/78 Rewe-Zentral , *E.C.R.*, 1979, 649.

[210]   Products that are only to be marketed in one Member state can be authorised through the national procedure.

[211]   EUROPEAN COMMISSION, *Notice to Applicants*, 1998, p. 15.

[212]   Article 9, 1 of Directive 75/319/EEC.

also notify the CPMP of this application, inform it of the Member States concerned and of the dates of submission of the application, and finally send it a copy of the authorisation granted by the first Member State (as well as of the other granted authorisations)[213].

156. Where a Member State is informed that another Member State has authorised a medicinal product that is the subject of an application for authorisation in the Member State concerned, that Member State must forthwith request the authorities of the Member State that has granted the authorisation, to forward to it the assessment report[214].

157. After all the concerned Member States have confirmed receipt of the valid application and the Reference Member State's assessment report, the Reference Member State notifies all concerned Member States and the marketing authorisation holder of the start of the 90-day period referred to in Article 9, 4 of Directive 75/319/EEC. Each Member State shall normally recognise the marketing authorisation and the summary of product characteristics granted by the first Member State within 90 days of receipt of the application and the assessment report.

158. A marketing authorisation is valid for five years. The marketing authorisation holder may apply for a renewal of the authorisation[215]. For a variation of the marketing authorisation, see below.

3.3.2.2. Member State asks for the Procedure

159. Member States may benefit from the assessment of another Member State by mutual recognition even in cases where the applicant has not requested mutual recognition. The same period of 90 days applies.

160. So, where a Member State notes, for example, that an application for authorisation is already under active examination in another Member State in respect of that medicinal product, the Member State concerned may decide to suspend the detailed examination of the application in order to await the assessment report prepared by the other Member State[216]. The Member State concerned must inform the other Member State and the applicant of its decision to suspend the detailed examination of the application in question. As soon as it has completed the examination of the application and reached a decision, the other Member State shall forward a copy of its assessment report to the Member State concerned.

161. Within 90 days of the receipt of the assessment report, the Member State concerned shall normally recognise the decision of the Reference Member State and the SPC as approved by it (by granting a marketing authorisation with

---

213   Article 9, 2 of Directive 75/319/EEC.
214   Article 7a of Directive 65/65/EEC.
215   For a good overview of the renewal process, see EUROPEAN COMMISSION, *Notice to Applicants*, p. 32.
216   Article 7 of Directive 65/65/EEC.

an identical summary of the product characteristics, or in the case of a negative assessment, by refusing the application).

162. In exceptional cases only, where a Member State is of the opinion that there are grounds for supposing that the authorisation of the medicinal product concerned may present a risk to public health[217], it may refer the matter for arbitration (see below).

3.3.3. Community Referrals

3.3.3.1. Grounds for Referral

163. An authorisation to place a medicinal product on the market in one Member State ought in principle to be recognised by the competent authorities of the other Member States unless there are serious grounds for supposing that the authorisation of the medicinal product concerned may present a risk to public human safety[218]. In the event of a disagreement between Member States about the quality, the safety or the efficacy of a medicinal product, a scientific evaluation of the matter would be undertaken by the CPMP in the EMEA, leading to an opinion arising from which the Commission would prepare a single decision on the area of disagreement, binding on the Member States.

164. The instances where a disagreement could arise are, for example:

- where a Member State notes that an application for authorisation is already under active examination in another Member State and the Member State concerned decides to suspend the examination of the application in order to await the assessment report prepared by the other Member State[219],
- where a Member State is informed by the applicant that another Member State has authorised a medicinal product that is the subject of an application for authorisation in the Member State concerned[220],
- where a Member State considers that there are grounds for supposing that the authorisation of the medicinal product concerned may present a risk to public health[221],
- if the Member States have adopted divergent decisions concerning the authorisation of the medicinal product[222] (e.g. where one Member State authorises and another refuses the same medicinal product or where the same medicinal product has been authorised in two or more Member States but the authorisations, particularly the indications, differ significantly) or where a medicinal product, with a current marketing authorisation in some or all Member States is suspended or withdrawn from the market,

---

217   The expression 'risk to public health' refers to quality, safety and efficacy of the medicinal product.
218   EUROPEAN COMMISSION, *Notice to Applicants*, p. 39.
219   Article 7 of Directive 65/65/EEC.
220   Article 7a of Directive 65/65/EEC.
221   Article 10 of Directive 75/319/EEC.
222   Article 11 of Directive 75/319/EEC.

- where the interests of the Community are involved[223],
- where a Member State considers that the variation of the terms of a marketing authorisation which has been granted or its suspension or withdrawal is necessary for the protection of public[224],

3.3.3.2. The Arbitration Procedure

165. The CPMP shall issue a reasoned opinion within 90 days of the date on which the matter was referred to it[225].

166. Where the opinion of the Committee is that:

- the application does not satisfy criteria for authorisation, or
- the SPC should be amended, or
- the authorisation should be granted subject to conditions for its safe and effective use, or
- a marketing authorisation should be suspended, varied or withdrawn,

the EMEA shall forthwith inform the person responsible for placing the medicinal product on the market[226].

167. This person has 15 days to notify the EMEA of his intentions to appeal. In that case, he shall forward the detailed grounds for appeal to the Agency within 60 days of receipt of the opinion. Within 60 days of receipt of the grounds for appeal, the Committee shall consider whether its opinion should be revised[227].

3.3.3.3. Commission and Council Decision and its implementation by Member States

168. After the completion of the appeal or if after 15 days the applicant did not appeal, the opinion of the CPMP becomes final. Once the final CPMP opinion is received at the Commission, the European Commission shall prepare a draft of the decisions that will be forwarded to the Member Sates and the applicant. The Commission shall be assisted by a Standing Committee on Medicinal Products for Human Use. The representative of the Commission shall submit to the Committee a draft of the measures to be taken. The Committee shall deliver its opinion on the draft[228].

---

[223] Article 12 of Directive 75/319/EEC.

[224] Article 15a of Directive 75/319/EEC. In this case, the Member State *must* refer the matter to the CMPM. Referral is, in other words, not merely a possibilty.

[225] Article 13, 1 of Directive 75/319/EEC. In exceptional cases, this period may be extended by a further 90 days.

[226] Article 13, 4 of Directive 75/319/EEC.

[227] Article 13, 4 of Directive 75/319/EEC.

[228] The opinion shall be delivered by the majority laid down in Art. 205 of the Treaty in the case of decisions which the Council is required to adopt on a proposal from the Commission. The votes of the representatives of the Member States within the Committee shall be weighted in the manner set out in that Article. The Chairman shall not vote.

169. The Commission shall adopt the measures envisaged if they are in accordance with the opinion of the Committee. If the measures envisaged are not in accordance with the opinion of the Committee, or if no opinion is delivered, the Commission shall submit to the Council of Ministers a proposal relative to the measures to be taken. The Council shall act by a qualified majority. If on the expiry of a period of three months from the date of referral to the Council, the Council has not acted, the proposed measures shall be adopted by the Commission[229].

170. The decision shall be addressed to the Member States concerned by the matter and to the person responsible for placing the medicinal product on the market[230].

171. The Decision is binding on all Member States, which will have to withdraw, grant or vary the marketing authorisations as necessary to comply with the Decision.

172. The Member States shall either grant or withdraw marketing authorisation, or vary the terms of a marketing authorisation as necessary to comply with the decision within 30 days of this notification[231].

3.4. The Abridged Procedure[232]

3.4.1. The Emergence of the Abridged Procedure

173. Article 4 of Directive 65/65/EEC defines the procedures and documents required in order to obtain a marketing authorisation. A communication of the results of three categories of tests[233], conducted in order to establish the quality, safety and efficacy of the medicinal product, is also required (see Chapter 2).

174. Particulars and documents required to accompany the application must be submitted. However, in certain circumstances the application can be exempted from the submission of all the data of Article 4 of Directive 65/65. This is the case in 'abridged procedures' for marketing authorisations. The abridged procedure allows an applicant, under certain conditions, to obtain a marketing authorisation by referring to the authorisation of the original manufacturer.

---

[229] Article 37a of Directive 75/319/EEC.

[230] Other Member States not directly concerned at the time of the Decision are also bound as soon as they receive an application for marketing authorisation for the same medicinal product.

[231] Article 14, 4 of Directive 75/319/EEC.

[232] This section is based on VAN DER VLIES, R. and CALLENS, S., "Protection of innovation in the Pharmaceutical Industry", *BSLR*, 1998, p. 90-96.

[233] These tests concern: physio-chemical, biological or microbiological tests; pharmacological and toxicolergal tests and clinical trials. Clinical trials will be subject to a specific Directive, see for the proposal of this Directive *O.J.*, C306/9, October 18th 1997.

3.4.2. Article 4, 8 of Directive 65/65/EEC and Exemptions to the Principle of Providing Full Test Results

175. Article 4, 8 of Directive 65/65/EEC reunites two conflicting policy considerations, namely 'ensuring that innovative firms are not placed at a disadvantage' on the one hand, and on the other hand 'not conducting repetitive tests on humans or animals without overriding cause'[234]. It was acknowledged that where a well-known ingredient in a conventional formulation is indicated for well-established therapeutic uses, it would be unnecessary and indeed unethical to expect companies to repeat all the pharmaceutical and toxicological tests in animals or the clinical trials in humans. Directive 65/65/EEC therefore allows for abridged applications for marketing authorisation, omitting some or all of the original animal data or human clinical trials data[235]. So Article 4, 8 of directive 65/65/EEC aims to balance the interests of the generic suppliers in obtaining access to the market for products which no longer enjoy complete intellectual property protection (in particular on the expiration of relevant patents), with the interests of innovative firms in the reasonable protection of their investments in research and development[236].

176. Article 1 of Directive 87/21 distinguishes three cases (Article 4, 8, a, i, ii, and iii in which the manufacturer is not required to provide the results of pharmacological, toxicological tests and clinical trials. In each case, a qualified expert[237] must provide scientific evidence to justify the use of the abridged procedure[238].

177. In the first case (art. 4, 8, a, i), the applicant is not required to provide full test results if he can demonstrate that the medicinal product is 'essentially similar' to a product already authorised in the Member State concerned and if the original holder of the marketing authorisation has consented to the use of his documents[239].

178. The second case (art. 4, 8, a, ii) gives an extremely precise and highly restrictive definition of the conditions to be satisfied in order to use the abridged procedure by reference to published scientific literature[240]. It is the legislature's

[234] Recitals 5-7 of Directive 87/21.
[235] ANDERSON, P., "Data exclusivity under EC Law" in *The European Pharmaceutical Law Forum*, Amsterdam, 1997.
[236] See THOMPSON, R., *The single market for pharmaceuticals*, London, Butterworths, 1994, p. 55. The abridged procedure is not to prejudice the law relating to the protection of industrial and commercial property; Article 1 Directive 87/21: "However, and without prejudice to the law relating to the protection of industrial and commercial property".
[237] Within the meaning of Directive 75/319, as amended by Directive 83/570.
[238] Article 2, c of Directive 75/319. In case of new medicinal products containing known constituents not hitherto used in combination for therapeutic purposes, the results of pharmacological and toxicological tests and of clinical trials relating to that combination must be provided, but it shall not be necessary to provide references relating to each individual constituent (Art. 4, 8, b of Directive 65/65/EEC). This abridged procedure is not analysed in this chapter.
[239] Article 4, 8, a, i of Directive 65/65/EEC.
[240] Only experts for the purpose of Directive 75/319 who are required to take account of scientific and technical progress (see Article 9 of Directive 65/65) are entitled to demonstrate by detailed references to published scientific literature presented in

intention that minimal use should be made of this possibility. Since in practice only a medicinal product that has been used for decades, and whose constituent(s) have been subject to detailed tests at length and commented on in scientific literature would satisfy those requirements, the scope of the exemption to the general principle has been narrowed. Since innovative firms are reviewing each article that an investigator is willing to publish, chances are very low that the published article on a clinical trial will contain sufficient information to allow a generic applicant to be exempted from full test results on the basis of Article 4, 8, a, ii. This is confirmed by the *Scotia* case[241].

179. In this case, Scotia obtained marketing authorisations for evening primrose oil products indicated for atopic eczema and mastalgia. A generic company succeeded in obtaining marketing authorizations for its product "Unigam" from authorities in the UK, Ireland and Germany on the basis of the abridged procedure. The Licensing Authority in the UK was considered to have power of discretion in granting an authorization for "Unigram", by derogating from the requirements of the second case of application of Article 4,8, namely the reference to published literature.

180. The Advocate General (AG) in this case said the rationale behind the legislation was to reach the ultimate objective: an expanded single market in quality medicinal products. The protection of innovation is essential in order to attain this ultimate objective[242]. Granting a discretion to the licensing authorities would jeopardize it. To support this, the AG referred to *Clin-Midy*[243] and the *Pierrel* cases[244] in which strict compliance with Community marketing authorizations is required[245]. Thus, no discretion was granted.

181. The European Court of Justice (ECJ) upheld the opinion of the AG[246] and has required published literature to be introduced in support of an abridged application with the same degree of detail needed in the presentation of original tests and trials. So, for example, information relating to clinical trials should include details such as the individual patients' age, sex, criteria for admission to the trial and so on[247].

---

accordance with the second paragraph of Article 1 of Directive 75/318 that the constituent or constituents of the medicinal product have a well-established medicinal use, with recognized efficacy and an acceptable level of safety' (see point 8, ii second paragraph, Article 4 of Directive 65/65 amended by Directive 87/21.

[241] Case C-440/93, Scotia, *E.C.R.*, 1995, I-2851.

[242] See points 18 to 23 of the Opinion.

[243] Case C-310/82 Clin-Midy v Belgium, *E.C.R.*, 1984, 251.

[244] Case C-83/92, Pierrel v Ministero della Santa, *E.C.R.*, 1993, I-6419.

[245] Judgement in Clin-Midy: Article 21 of Directive 65/65 must be interpreted as meaning that authorisation to market a proprietary medicinal product may not be refused, suspended or revoked, save on the ground of the protection of public health as referred to in the Directive. Judgement in Pierrel: Directive 65/65 precludes national authorities not only from introducing grounds for suspension or revocation other than those laid down by Community law, but also from providing for the lapse of authorizations to market medicinal products (see above).

[246] See point 21-23 of the judgment.

[247] ANDERSON, D., "Data Exclusivity under EC Law", *The European Pharmaceutical Law Forum*, Amsterdam, 1997.

182. Finally, a second applicant is exempted from providing full test results if he can demonstrate the essential similarity of his product (so-called generic product) to a product that has been authorised within the Community for six years in accordance with Community provisions at force and has been marketed in the Member State of application[248].

183. The period of six years is automatically extended to 10 years for medicinal products submitted through the centralised procedure of Regulation No 2309/93, or where the consultation procedure has been followed for products that have been authorised following an opinion of the CPMP[249]. Further, the individual Member States have the option to extend the protection to 10 years for all products marketed in their territory, or to limit the period to that of a patent protection, i.e. less than six years[250].

184. However, where the medicinal product is intended for a different therapeutic use from that of the other proprietary medicinal products marketed or is to be administered by different routes or in different doses, the results of appropriate pharmacological and toxicological tests and/or of appropriate clinical trials must be provided[251].

3.4.3. Article 4, 8, a, iii of the Directive 65/65 EEC and Confidential Information

185. The question of whether authorisation can prevent licensing authorities a marketing authorisation from using test results for competitors of generic products was discussed in the so-called "Tagamet"-case. Smith Kline, manufacturer and original holder of the first UK marketing authorisation of "Tagamet", sought to prevent generic competitors to use the abridged procedure under Article 4, 8, a, iii to obtain product licenses under the English Medicine Act of 1968 for products containing cimetidine, the sole active ingredient of the product "Tagamet"[252]. The generic competitors argued that "Tagamet" had been on the market for more than 10 years and that they could rely on material in hands of the UK Licensing Authority.

186. Smith Kline argued that such information (submitted as part of their original application) was confidential and could only be used by the Licensing Authority for the purpose of assessment of the original application and supervision of the authorised product on the market.

---

248 Article 4, 8, a, iii.
249 Article 4 of Directive 87/22.
250 Ireland and Luxembourg have opted for a six year protection, whereas Belgium, France, Germany, Italy, the Netherlands, Sweden, Austria and the United Kingdom have opted for ten years. In Spain, Portugal and Greece the rules were not applicable before 1992. They, and Denmark and Greece opted to deny protection beyond the life of the patent (Notice to Applicants III/5944/94, January 1995).
251 The provision on data exclusivity was necessary since patent law does not always protect medical innovation. A patent is not always possible or effective, as in the case of a natural substance or of a substance that is already known but on which additional research has been carried out with a view to a new therapeutic use.
252 R. v. Licensing Authority, ex. P. Smith, Kline & French Laboratories Ltd, 2 CMLR, 1988, 883. Reversed on appeal, 3, CMLR, 1988, 301, Affirmed, Smith, Kline & French ltd. v. Licensing Authority, 2, CMLR, 1989, 137.

187. This was accepted in the first instance. According to the judge, the burden of proof is on the generic applicant, even after the expiration of the 10-year period and ruled that data submitted in support of the original product were confidential and could not be used to validate a second application[253].

188. The generic manufacturers appealed and the Court of Appeal reversed the Court of first instance, stating that the Licensing Authority was expected to play an active role and that it was entitled to look at the original file. After the product has been used for 10 years, the confidential data of the original marketing authorisation holder can be used without their consent in establishing the essential similarity of a generic applicant's product.

189. The House of Lords, on appeal from the Court of Appeal, found that the term 'without prejudice to law relating to the protection of intellectual property rights' of Article 4, 8 includes the principle of confidentiality of English law. Nevertheless, this does not prevent the Licensing Authority from making use of the information to ensure similarity. It is the right and duty of the Licensing Authority to make use of all the information supplied by any applicant for a product license that assists the licensing authority in considering whether to grant or reject any other application[254].

3.4.4. Article 4, 8, a, iii of the Directive 65/65/EEC and Impact of Original Authorisation on Me-too Applicant

190. The question of the impact of original authorisation on me-too applicants is dealt with in the Monsanto case in 1980[255]. In this case, a marketing authorisation under Directive 65/65/EEC was granted to Grunenthal in Germany for "Tramadol". In 1990 Monsanto applied for marketing authorisation for "Tramadol" in the UK. Since this was the first application for authorisation in the UK the application included not only data submitted by Grunenthal to the German authorities but also additional data. The authorisations were granted in 1994.

191. Galen applied for marketing authorisations for "Tramadol" in the UK under the abridged procedure of Article 4,8, iii. The English licensing authority accepted without further inquiry that the original marketing authorisation granted in 1980 by the German authorities had been 'in accordance with Community provisions' and accordingly granted the marketing authorisation under the abridged procedure to Galen in 1996. Monsanto challenged the grant of the authorisation arguing that the original German authorisation had not been granted 'in accordance with Community provisions in force' so that Galen should not have been permitted to use the abridged procedure. The English High Court held that the licensing authority was not obliged to investigate whether the original authorisation was in accordance with Community provisions in force at

---

253   "This interpretation would have considerably extended the scope of the protection of the original applicant's data to an indefinite period; if the licensing authority were forbidden from consulting the original file then it would be impossible for a second applicant to demonstrate similarity" (HANCHER, L., *o.c.*, p. 31).

254   See recitals 28-29 of the case before the House of Lords.

255   R.v. Licensing Authority, ex parte Monsanto, *CMLR*, 1997, 402

the time of the original authorisation, but could rely on the official record of such authorisations[256].

3.4.5. Article 4, 8, a, iii of the Directive 65/65 EEC and interpretation of Essential Similarity

192. Disputes arose about the interpretation of Article 4, 8, a, iii of Directive 65/65/EEC and in particular whether the authorisation for a general medicinal product should extend to all the indications and dosage schedules authorised for the original medicinal product up to that time, or whether the protection period for the original medicinal product should also be applied to the indications and dosage schedules for that subsequently authorised medicinal product[257][258].

193. The Court of Justice decided that Article 4, 8, a, iii of Directive 65/65/ must be interpreted as meaning that a medicinal product is essentially similar to an original medicinal product where it satisfies the criteria of

- having the same qualitative and quantitative composition in terms of active principles,
- having the same pharmaceutical form and
- being bioequivalent, unless it is apparent in the light of scientific knowledge that it differs significantly from the original product as regards safety or efficacy[259].

---

[256]   See Case C5/94 Hedley Lomas of May 23rd 1996 where the UK attempted to prevent the export of meat from Spain into their territory on the motif that the UK feared that Spain did not apply the Community Directive 74/577. The E.C.J. stated that Member states should have mutual confidence concerning the correct application of the Community law by the other Member states and that they cannot take unilateral measures to correct the alleged incorrect application of Community law by other Member states (points 19 and 20).

[257]   Questions on the interpretation of Article 4, 8, a, iii have been raised in three connected cases pending before the English High Court of Justice, Queens Bench Division. Each one is connected with a different medicinal product, namely "Captopril", "Aciclovir" and "Randitidine". In each of the cases there are three parties: the respondent, the applicants and innovative companies.

[258]   In the Captopril-case, Generic applied under Article 4, 8, a, iii of Directive 65/65 for a marketing authorisation for Captopril tablets on January 20th 1993. The MCA refused several applications and dispute arose between Generic and the MCA about those refusals.

In the second case, Wellcome became aware of five marketing authorisations granted by MCA for different indications and dosage forms of Aciclovir tablets and intravenous infusion, granted under the abridged procedure. Wellcome lodged an application for judicial review of the MCA's decision to grant the marketing authorisations under the abridged procedure without prior consent of Wellcome in respect of therapeutic indications, routes of administration and dosage forms for Aciclovir tablets and intravenous infusion that had been approved in the Community in earlier authorisations granted less than ten years previously on the basis of data submitted by Wellcome.

In the Rantidine proceedings, Generics applied for marketing authorisation for Rantidine tablets using the abridged procedure. The MCA first refused to grant marketing authorisations for indications that had not been approved in the Community for ten years. Then it changed its position and granted all requested marketing authorisations. Glaxo commenced proceedings for judicial review of the MCA's decision

[259]   E.C.J., 3 December 1998, C-368/96.

194. The competent authority of a Member State may not disregard the three criteria set out above when it is required to determine whether a particular medicinal product is essentially similar to an original medicinal product. According to the Court, having the same therapeutic indications is not one of the criteria which, according to what is decided above, must be satisfied in order that two medicinal products may be regarded as essentially [260]similar. It follows that an applicant for marketing authorisation for a medicinal product that is essentially similar to a product that has been authorised for not less than 6 or 10 years in the Community and is marketing in the Member State for which the application is made, is not required to supply pharmacological, toxicological and clinical documentation, regardless of the therapeutic indications to which the documentation for the original medicinal product relates. Consequently, the applicant may receive marketing authorisation *for all therapeutic indications* covered by the latter documentation, including those indications authorised for less than 6 or 10 years. A medicinal product that is essentially similar to a product that has been authorised for not less than 6 or 10 years in the Community and is marketed in the Member State for which the application is made may according to the Court be authorised under the abridged procedure provided for in Article 4, 8, a, iii of Directive 65/65, as amended, for all *dosage forms, doses and dosage schedules* already authorised for that product. The Court's decision poses concerns for the research-based pharmaceutical companies. They are indeed concerned about the Court's apparent acceptance that the generic industry should be entitled to benefit at an early stage from the substantial amounts of work undertaken by them in obtaining approval for the new indication and the new dosage forms[261].

3.5. Variations to the Terms of a Marketing Authorisation

195. A medicinal product may be changed. These changes or variations may involve administrative changes and/or more substantial changes. With the implementation of new systems of marketing authorisation (see e.g. the centralised procedure or the mutual recognition procedure) it became necessary to codify variations and to set out common procedures. These procedures must on the one hand facilitate the task of both industry and authorities and on the other hand, guarantee that changes to the medicinal product do not give rise to public health concerns[262]. Two Regulations are adopted to provide for procedure to examine the variations, i.e. a Regulation (EC) No 541/95 of 10 March 1995 concerning the examination of variations to the terms of a marketing authorisation granted by a competent authority of a Member State in a mutual recognition procedure[263]) and a Regulation No 542/93 concerning the examination of variations to the terms of a marketing authorisation falling within the scope of h Council Regulation (EEC) No 2309/93[264].

196. Any application by the person responsible for placing the medicinal product on the market to vary a marketing authorisation that has been granted on

---

[260]   E.C.J., 3 December 1998, C-368/96, r. 43.
[261]   JONES, N. and NITTENBERG, R., "'Essentially similar' despite being different: the Squibb case", *BSLR*, 1998-1999, p. 152.
[262]   EUROPEAN COMMISSION, *Notice to Applicants*, p. 73.
[263]   *O.J.*, L 55, 11 March 1995, p. 7.
[264]   *O.J.*, L 55, 11 March 1995, p. 15.

the basis of a mutual recognition procedure or for which there has been a Community referral must be submitted to all the Member States that have previously authorised the medicinal product concerned. Regulation (EC) No 541/95 includes a notification system or an administrative procedure for minor variations to the terms of a marketing authorisation and an approval procedure for major variations. Variations to the terms of a marketing authorisation are described as amendments to the documents introduced by the marketing holder at the moment of the decision on the marketing decision[265] except where a new application for a marketing authorisation must be presented[266]. Changes to a marketing authorisation requiring a new application are listed in Annex II to the Regulation No 541/95 and include for example changes to the active substance(s), changes to the therapeutic indications, such as an addition of an indication in a different therapeutic area, changes to the pharmaceutical form and route of administration.

197. Minor variations include, for example, changes in the content of the manufacturing authorisation, changes in the name of the medicinal product, changes in the name and/or address of the marketing authorisation holder[267], deletion of an indication, batch size of the active substance[268].

198. To obtain a minor variation (or type I variation), a notification procedure has to be followed. First, an identical application must be submitted simultaneously to the national competent authorities of the different Member States where the medicinal product has been authorised. If within 30 days of the date of the start of the procedure, the national competent authority of the reference Member State has not been sent to the marketing authorisation holder, who submitted the application, the notification provided for in Art. 5, 2 of Regulation No 541/95, the variation requested is deemed accepted by all Member States that have received the application. If a national competent authority cannot accept the request for variation, the procedure of art. 5, 2 of Regulation No 541/95 must be followed.

199. To obtain a major variation (or type II variation), an approval procedure has to be followed. An identical application must be submitted simultaneously to the national competent authorities of the different Member States where the medicinal product has been authorised. Within 60 days following the date of the start of the procedure, the national competent authorities of the Reference Member State shall prepare an assessment report and a draft decision that must be addressed to the other national competent authorities concerned. Within 30 days following receipt of the draft decision and the assessment report, the other national competent authorities concerned shall accept[269] the draft decision and inform the national competent authority of the Reference Member State to this

---

[265] Or after approval of any previous variation.

[266] Art. 2 of Regulation (EC) 541/95.

[267] Transfer of marketing authorisation to a new holder is not considered as a variation to the terms of a marketing authorisation, except for the situation of changes in name and/or address of the marketing authorisation holder.

[268] For the entire list of minor variations, see Annex 1 to the Regulation (EC) No 541/95.

[269] If mutual recognition by one or more national competent authorities of the draft decision of the national competent authority of the Reference Member State is not possible, the procedure of Community referral (see above) will be applied.

effect[270]. Each national competent authority concerned by the application for the variation must adopt a decision in conformity with the draft decision.

200. The procedures for approval of variations to the terms of a marketing authorisation that have been granted in accordance with Regulation No 2309/93 are set out in Regulation No 542/95. This Regulation makes also a distinction between minor variations (type I variations) (listed in Annex I to this Regulation) and major variations (type II variations). To obtain a Type I variation, a notification procedure must be followed. The holder of the marketing authorisation must submit to the EMEA an application. If the EMEA has not sent within 30 days of receipt of a valid application, the holder of the marketing authorisation a notification of its negative opinion, the variation applied for shall be deemed to have been accepted. To obtain a type II variation, the approval procedure of Articles 6, 7 and 8 of the Regulation No 542/95 must be followed.

3.6. Other authorisations

3.6.1. Marketing authorisations for specific products

206. In addition or as an exception to the rules laid down in Directive 65/65/EEC specific legislation is enacted for specific medicinal products such as for immunological medicinal products consisting of vaccines, toxins or serums and allergens or for radiopharmaceuticals[271], for radiopharmaceuticals[272], for homeopathic medicinal products[273] or for orphan medicinal products[274], etc. Already in the recital 8 of the Directive 75/319/EEC it was argued that the provisions of Directive 65/65/EEC as well as of Directive 75/319/EEC were inadequate for such products. Below we present briefly the legal basis of the marketing authorisation procedure for these specific medicinal products.

3.6.1.1. Homeopathic medicinal products

207. Because the provisions of Directive 65/65/EEC and Directive 75/319/EEC were not always appropriate for homeopathic medicinal products, specific provisions have been adopted for these products. It was argued that having in regard to the particular characteristics of these medicinal products, such as the very low level of active principles they contain and the difficulty of applying to them the conventional statistical methods relating to clinical trials, a special simplified registration procedure was required. Council Directive 92/73/EEC of 22 September 1992 widening the scope of Directives 65/65/EEC and 75/319/EEC on the approximation of provisions laid down by law, regulation or administrative action relating to medicinal products and laying down additional provisions on homeopathic medicinal products[275] provides for

---

270   Art. 7, 3 of Regulation (EC) No 541/95.
271   Directive 89/342/EEC of 3 May 1989, *O.J.*, L. 142, 25 May 1989, p. 14.
272   Directive 89/343/EEC of 3 May 1989, *O.J.*, L. 142, 25 May 1989, p. 16.
273   Directive 92/73/EEC of 22 September 1992, *O.J.*, L. 297, 13 October 1992, p. 8.
274   Regulation (EC) No 141/2000 of 16 December 1999, *O.J.*, L. 18, 22 January 2000, p. 1.
275   *O.J.*, 13 October 1992, L 297/8.

such a procedure. Proof of therapeutic efficacy must not be required for homeopathic medicinal products.

3.6.1.2. Radiopharmaceuticals

208. The classic provisions on medicinal products, as provided, for example, in Directive 65/65/EEC and Directive 75/319/EEC seemed to be inadequate for radiopharmaceuticals. In the case of radiopharmaceuticals in their finished form, which are made up exclusively from authorised kits, generators or precursor radiopharmaceuticals in health care establishments, a specific authorisation is not required[276]. The Directive 89/343/EEC provides that a marketing authorisation remains required for generators, kits, precursor radiopharmaceuticals and industrially prepared radiopharmaceuticals.

3.6.1.3. Medicinal products derived from human blood or human plasma

209. It was argued that the provisions laid down in e.g. Directive 65/65/EEC and Directive 75/319/EEC were inadequate with regard to medicinal products derived from human blood or human plasma. Moreover, the Community wanted to support the efforts of the Council of Europe to promote voluntary unpaid blood and plasma donation to attain self-sufficiency throughout the Community in the supply of blood products, and to ensure respect for ethical principles in trade in therapeutic substances of human origin[277]. The Commission wanted also to achieve that a manufacturer can demonstrate his ability to guarantee batch-to-batch consistency and the absence of specific viral contamination[278]. Therefore, Council Directive 89/381/EEC of 14 June 1989 extending the scope of Directives 65/65/EEC and 75/319/EEC on the approximation of provisions laid down by law, regulation or administrative action relating to proprietary medicinal products and laying down special provisions for medicinal products derived from human blood or human plasma[279] was enacted. This Directive 89/381/EEC does not apply to whole blood, to plasma or to blood cells of human origin[280]. According to Art. 3, 4 of Directive 89/381/EEC, Member States must take the necessary measures to promote Community self-sufficiency in human blood or human plasma. For this purpose, they must encourage the voluntary unpaid donation of blood and plasma and must take the necessary measures to develop the production and use of products derived from human blood or human plasma coming form voluntary unpaid donations.

---

[276] Council Directive 89/343/EEC of 3 May 1989 extending the scope of Directives 65/65/EEC and 75/319/EEC and laying down additional provisions for radiopharmaceuticals, *O.J.*, 25 May 1989, L 142/16.
[277] Recital 5 of Directive 89/381/EEC.
[278] Recital 7 of Directive 89/381/EEC.
[279] *O.J.*, 28 June 1989, L 181/44.
[280] Article 1, 2 of Directive 89/381/EEC.

3.6.1.4. Orphan medicinal products

210. A medicinal product shall be designated as an orphan medicinal product if its sponsor can establish:
- that it is intended for the diagnosis, prevention or treatment of a life-threatening or chronically debilitating condition affecting not more than five in 10 thousand persons in the Community when the application is made or that is intended for the diagnosis, prevention or treatment of a life-threatening, seriously debilitating or serious and chronic condition in the Community and that without incentives it is unlikely that the marketing of the medicinal product in the Community would generate sufficient return to justify the necessary investment, and
- that there exists no satisfactory method of diagnosis, prevention or treatment of the condition in question that has been authorised in the Community or, if such method exists, that the medicinal product will be of significant benefit to those affected by that condition[281].

211. Within the EMEA a Committee for Orphan Medicinal Products being set up. This Committee must, for example, examine any application for the designation of a medicinal product as an orphan medicinal product and advise the Commission on the establishment and development of a policy on orphan medicinal products for the European Union[282]. The person responsible for placing on the market an orphan medicinal product may request that authorisation to place the medicinal product on the market be granted by the Community in accordance with the provisions of Regulation (EEC) No 2309/93 without having to justify that the medicinal product qualifies under Part B of the Annex to that Regulation (see above).

3.6.1.5. Parallel Imports

212. We refer to Chapter 6 for the issue of (national) marketing authorisations and parallel imported medicinal products. We emphasise that under the centralised procedure for marketing authorisation, the only changes which may be made are changes in the language of the labelling and package leaflet and/or, more rarely, changes in the size of the package (repackaging). Provided none of these changes has been made, the parallel distributor may under Community pharmaceutical law place directly on the market the medicine which has been distributed in parallel[283], provided that the distributor notifies the national and where appropriate, Community authorities that such distribution has taken place. Where any of the above mentioned changes have been made, the distributor must send the authorities more specific information, for example one or more samples or mock-ups of the medicines as they will be marketed in

---

281   Art. 3 of Regulation (EC) No 141/2000 of the 16 December 1999 on oprhan medicinal products (*O.J.*, L 18, 22 January 2000, p. 1; see also Commission Regulation (EC) No 847/2000 of 27 April 2000 laying down the provisions for implementation of the criteria for designation of a medicinal product as an orphan medicinal product and definitions of the concepts 'similar medicinal product' and 'clinical superiority' (*O.J.*, L. 103, 28 April 2000, p. 5).

282   Art. 4 of Regulation (EC) No 141/2000.

283   EUROPEAN COMMISSION, *Notice to Applicants*, p. 128.

the Member State of distribution, including the package leaflets. This will enable the competent authority to check that the medicine distributed in parallel is indeed covered by the marketing authorisation already issued, as regards the contents of the labelling and package leaflet or the size of the package[284]. The competent authority must respond within 30 days[285].

3.6.2. Labelling changes

213. Changes to an aspect of the labelling or package leaflets of medicinal products connected with the SPC follow the procedure for variations (see above). Changes to an aspect of the labelling or the package leaflet covered by the Directive 92/27/EEC on the labelling of medicinal products and not connected with the SPC are examined in accordance with art. 10, 3 of Directive 92/27/EEC (see Chapter 6)[286].

3.6.3. Application for renewal of an authorisation

214. An authorisation is only valid for a period of time. Renewal of the authorisation is allowed. The marketing authorisation holder must make an application for renewal. We refer to the relevant paragraphs above for the renewals.

3.6.4. Manufacturing authorisation

215. An applicant for a marketing authorisation of a medicinal product is obliged to demonstrate that the manufacturer is authorised to produce proprietary products[287]. According to Article 16 of Directive 75/319/EEC Member States must take all appropriate measures to ensure that the manufacture of medicinal products is subject to the holding of an authorisation[288]. The authorisation is required notwithstanding that the medicinal products manufactured are intended for export and for the various processes of dividing up, packaging or presentation[289]. The authorisation is required for both total and partial manufacture. The authorisation is also required for imports coming from third countries into a Member State. In order to obtain the manufacturing authorisation, the applicant must provide particulars in support of the application and:

- specify the medicinal product and pharmaceutical forms which are to be manufactured or imported and also the place where they are to be manufactured and/or controlled;

---

[284] EUROPEAN COMMISSION, *Notice to Applicants*, p. 128.
[285] *Ibid.*
[286] EUROPEAN COMMISSION, *Notice to Applicants*, p. 13.
[287] Art. 4, 10 of Directive 65/65/EEC.
[288] For the authorisation to distribute and sell medicinal products, see Chapter 4 and Chapter 11).
[289] Art. 16, 2 of Directive 75/319/EEC. However, such authorisation is not required for preparation, dividing up, changes in packaging or presentation where these processes are carried out, solely for retail supply, by pharmacists in dispensing pharmacies or by persons legally authorised in the Member States to carry out such processes.

-        have at his disposal, for the manufacture or import, suitable and sufficient premises, technical equipment and control facilities complying with the legal requirements,

-        have at his disposal the services of at least one qualified person within the meaning of Article 21 of Directive 75/318/EEC[290].

216.   Directive 91/356/EEC of 13 June 1991 laying down the principles and guidelines of good manufacturing practice for medicinal products for human use[291] contains principles and guidelines of good manufacturing practice. These guidelines primarily concern personnel, premises and equipment, documentation, production, quality control, contracting out, complaints and product recall, and self-inspection[292].

---

[290]   Art. 17 of Directive 75/319/EEC.
[291]   *O.J.*, L 193, 17 July 1991, p. 30.
[292]   According to Article 3 of Directive 91/356/EEC the competent authorities shall in interpreting the principesl and guidelines of good manufacturing pracice refer to the guidelines publshed by the Commission in the *Guide to good manufacturing practice for medicinal products. (The rules governing medicinal products in the European Community*, Office for Offical Publications of the European Communities, Vol. IV).

4. DISTRIBUTION OF MEDICINAL PRODUCTS

4.1. Introduction

217. In practice, medicinal products reach the end-user through an international distribution chain from manufacturer to distributor, to pharmacist or hospital.

218. Generally, a distribution agreement between a manufacturer and a distributor is a vertical agreement between undertakings performing activities at different levels of an industry. So generally the parties to a vertical agreement do not compete with each other as their activities are confined to different levels of the markets on which they meet: the product of one is input for the other.

219. Medicinal products are usually distributed through exclusive distribution agreements, exclusive customer allocation agreements or a combination of both. In an exclusive distribution agreement, the supplier limits its sales in a certain area to one particular exclusive distributor for that territory and the distributor is usually limited in its active selling outside its territory. Exclusive customer allocation agreements differ from exclusive distribution agreements as they replace the territorial restriction with a restriction to a particular class of customer.

220. Such vertical agreements often contain selling or purchasing restrictions, territorial restrictions, export bans, price restrictions, minimum order requirements (combined with rebates), customer restrictions or restrictions on the use of the products ("vertical restraints"). They may therefore prevent, restrict or distort competition.

221. These vertical restraints may negatively affect the market by:

- keeping other suppliers or other buyers out by raising barriers to entry;
- reducing inter-brand competition between the companies currently operating in a market by the collusion of suppliers or buyers;
- reducing intra-brand competition between distributors of the same brand; and
- creating obstacles to market integration, including limitations on consumers' freedom to purchase goods or services in any Member State they choose.

222. Despite these negative effects, it is important to recognise that vertical restraints often have positive effects including:

- the protection of investments by both the supplier and the buyer (e.g. through territorial restrictions, exclusivity or non-competition agreements);
- the protection of the know-how one party provides to the other (e.g. through exclusivity and non-competition agreements);
- the exploitation of economies of scale in distribution. Better co-ordination between the participating companies can reduce transaction

and distribution costs and optimise investments and sales (e.g. through exclusive distribution or purchasing, quantitative restrictions or selective distribution);

-       imposing a certain degree of uniformity and quality standardisation on the distributors (e.g. in selective distribution).

223.   This Chapter examines to what extent these vertical restraints are permitted under EC competition law.

224.   Session 1 highlights some important aspects of EC Competition Law on product distribution and their specific application by the European Commission (the "Commission"), the European Court of Justice (the "Court") and the Court of First Instance to the distribution of medicinal products.

225.   Council Directive 92/25 of 31 March 1992 on the wholesale distribution of medicinal products for human use prescribes some important requirements for any wholesaler of medicinal products.   Chapter 2 examines how those requirements must also be taken into account when drafting an agreement for distributing medicinal products.

4.2. Distribution of Medicinal Products and EC Competition Law

4.2.1. Article 81, 1 of the EC Treaty

4.2.1.1. Article 81, 1 of the EC Treaty: the Principle

226.   Article 81, 1 of the EC Treaty (the "Treaty") prohibits agreements between undertakings, decisions by associations of undertakings and concerted practices that appreciably prevent, restrict or distort competition within the Common Market, affecting trade between Member States. Article 81, 2 provides that such agreements, decisions or practices are automatically void.

4.2.1.1.1. The Notion "agreement"

227.   The notion "agreement" must be interpreted broadly.   It not only includes all legally binding arrangements (written or oral), but can also include correspondence, general sales conditions, announcements, guidelines or instructions.

228.   However, Article 81, 1 does not apply to agreements between a parent company and its subsidiary or between two subsidiaries of the same parent company, if they form a single economic unit.

229.   In the *Viho* case, the Court confirmed that Article 81, 1 does not apply to an agreement between a parent company and its subsidiaries forming a single economic unit:

"within which the subsidiaries do not enjoy real autonomy in determining their course of action in the market, but carry out the instructions issued to them by the parent company which wholly controls them"[293].

230. This holds true even if the parent company's policy of essentially dividing national markets between its subsidiaries produces effects outside the group's ambit, which could affect the competitive position of third parties. The Court did however confirm that such conduct could fall under Article 82 of the Treaty.

4.2.1.1.2. Agreements of Minor Importance

231. The Court has recognised that agreements of minor importance are not caught by Article 81, 1[294]. The Commission's *De Minimis* notice[295] of 1997 reflects this.

232. This Notice provides that the Commission will not bring proceedings under Article 81 for agreements between small and medium sized enterprises with an annual turnover of less than EUR 40 million.

233. It also provides that larger companies may rely on the Notice regardless of their turnover, if they are party to a vertical agreement under which the combined turnover of the parties does not exceed the market share threshold of 10 %[296].

234. However, fundamental restrictions or other restraints that blatantly distort competition due to their cumulative effects cannot benefit from the Notice, irrespective of the parties' market shares.

4.2.1.2. An Appreciable Restriction under Article 81, 1 of the Treaty

235. In its *Guidelines on vertical restraints*, the Commission describes the main factors to consider when establishing whether a vertical restraint constitutes an appreciable restriction of competition under Article 81, 1 of the Treaty:

- The supplier's market position:
  This is first established by assessing the supplier's market share of the relevant product and of the geographic market[297]. Competitive advantages such as a cost advantage, a first-mover advantage and the supplier holding essential patents further influence that position.

- Competitors' market position:
  The same indicators apply to establishing competitors' market position. The more competitors and the stronger their market position, the lower the risk that (a) a supplier or a buyer can individually foreclose the market and (b) that inter-brand competition can be reduced.

---

[293] Case C-73/95, Viho Europe BV v Commission, *E.C.R,.*, 1996, I-5457.
[294] Case C-22/71, Béguelin Import v GL Import Export, *E.C.R.*, 1971, 949.
[295] Notice on agreements of minor importance of 9 December 1997, C. 372, p. 13.
[296] See below for a discussion of market share and the relevant market.
[297] In principle, the markets for medicinal products are national.

- Entry barriers:
  Vertical links and vertical integration of sunk costs[298] may operate as an entry barrier by making access more difficult and by keeping out potential competitors.

- Buying power:
  This is the buyer's market share on the up-stream purchase market, reflecting the importance of its demand for its possible suppliers and on the down-stream market.

- Maturity of the market:
  Mature markets are markets that have existed for some time where the technology is widespread and stable and where no major brand innovations are occurring. The demand is also relatively stable or declining. In such markets, negative effects are more likely than in more dynamic markets.

- Level of trade:
  Negative effects are less likely at the intermediate product level than at the final product level and less likely at the wholesale level than at the retail level of final products.

- The nature of the products:
  In general, the more heterogeneous and inexpensive a product and the more it resembles a one-off purchase, the more likely vertical restraints will have a negative effect.

- Other factors:
  Other factors may be important in assessing particular vertical restraints, including the coverage of the market by similar agreements between different parties, the duration of the agreement, the extent and duration of a non-competition obligation[299] and so on.

4.2.2. Article 81, 3 of the EC Treaty and the Block Exemption Regulations

4.2.2.1. Article 81, 3 of the Treaty: the Principle

236. Article 81, 3 permits vertical agreements caught by Article 81, 1 to be exempted if they provide sufficient benefits. They must:

- contribute to improving production or distribution or to promoting technical or economic progress;
- allow consumers a fair share of these benefits;

---

[298] Sunk costs are the costs necessary for entering or being active in a market (like advertising to build customer loyalty). They are (partly) lost when exiting the market.

[299] Non-competition agreements for less than one year between non-dominant companies do not usually give rise to appreciable anti-competitive effects or to net negative effects. Agreements from one to five years usually require a proper balancing of pro- and anti-competitive effects, while agreements longer than five years are considered unnecessarily long to obtain efficiencies for most types of investments.

- not impose restraints that are not indispensable to attaining these benefits on the undertakings concerned;
- not allow such undertakings to eliminate competition for a substantial portion of the products in question.

237. Competition concerns only arise if there is insufficient inter-brand competition, i.e. if a degree of market power exists at the level of the supplier or the buyer or both. In case of insufficient inter-brand competition, the protection of inter- and intra-brand competition becomes important.

238. The Commission normally grants exemptions on a case-to-case basis, after notification of the contemplated agreement.

239. However, the Commission has adopted regulations containing block exemptions for several categories of agreements. These regulations list which clauses may and may not be inserted in agreements and which may only apply if the conditions of the regulations are fulfilled. In such event, the agreement must not be notified individually to the Commission to be exempted from the application of Article 81, 1 of the Treaty. The most important block exemption regulations are those governing exclusive distribution[300], exclusive purchase[301] and franchise agreements[302].

4.2.2.2. Commission Regulation No 2790/1999[303]

240. This Regulation concerns the application of Article 81, 3 of the Treaty to categories of vertical agreements and concerted practices (the "Regulation") and provides a block exemption for vertical restrictions. This exemption only applies in limited circumstances.

4.2.2.2.1. Scope of the Regulation

241. The Regulation applies to:

1. Agreements or concerted practices:
- between two or more undertakings;
- at different levels of the production or distribution chain;
- concerning the conditions under which undertakings may purchase, sell or resell the contract goods or services.

2. Vertical agreements between an association of distributors selling to final consumers and its members or between an association and its suppliers if

---

[300]   Regulation No 1983/83 of 22 June 1983.
[301]   Regulation No 1984/83 of 22 June 1983.
[302]   Regulation No 4087/88 of 30 November 1988.
[303]   EC Regulation No 2790/1999 of 22 December 1999 on the application of Article 81, 3 of the Treaty to categories of vertical agreements and concerted practices, *O.J.*, L 336, 29 December 1999, p. 21.

the total annual turnover[304] of individual members of the association and connected undertakings[305] does not exceed EUR 50 million[306].

3. Provisions of vertical agreements concerning the assignment or use of intellectual property rights for using or reselling goods or services supplied if the provisions:
-       are not the primary object of the agreement but are necessary for the agreement[307], and
-       do not contain restrictions on competition with the same object or effect as vertical restraints not exempted under the Regulation.

4. Non-reciprocal vertical agreements between competing undertakings[308] if:
-       the buyer's total annual turnover does not exceed EUR 100 million[309]; or
-       the buyer is a distributor and not a manufacturer of competing goods or services. This means that the buyer only competes with the supplier at the distribution level.

242.   Article 81, 1 does not generally apply to vertical agreements between parties to a vertical agreement whose market share on the relevant market is 10 % or less.

4.2.2.2.2. The Regulation's Relationship with Existing Block Exemptions

243.   Existing block exemption regulations are effective until 31 May 2000. The Regulation applies as of 1 June 2000.

244.   However, Article 12 of the Regulation provides that Article 81, 1 of the Treaty does not apply from 1 June 2000 until 31 December 2001 for agreements that entered into force on or before 31 May 2000 if these agreements:

---

[304]   This means the turnover of the last financial year of the relevant party to the agreement and its connected undertakings for all goods and services, excluding dealings between the relevant party and its connected undertakings or between its connected undertakings.

[305]   Connected undertakings are undertakings in which a party to the agreement:
-       owns more than 50 % of the capital or business assets; or
-       may exercise more than half the voting rights; or
-       may appoint more than half the members of the supervisory board, board of management or bodies legally representing the undertaking; or
-       may manage the undertaking's affairs;
Connected undertakings includes, undertakings that directly or indirectly, have these rights or powers over a party to the agreement or undertakings having those rights or powers over the first undertakings. Undertakings in which the parties to the agreement or undertakings connected with them jointly have such rights or powers are also considered connected undertakings.

[306]   If the exemption applies, it will continue to apply unless total annual turnover is exceeded by more than 10 % for two consecutive financial years.

[307]   Trademarks, copyright and know-how are generally considered necessary for the distribution of goods or services.

[308]   Article 1 of the Regulation defines competing undertakings as actual or potential suppliers of goods or services, which are identical or which are considered by users as interchangeable or substitutable given their characteristics, price and intended use. The same applies if these goods or services are supplied by an undertaking connected to a party to the agreement.

[309]   See above.

- do not comply with the conditions of the Regulation; and
- do comply with the conditions of an existing block exemption.

245. Therefore agreements entered into force before 31 May 2000 must conform to the Regulation at the latest on 31 December 2001.

4.2.2.2.3. The Exemption

246. The likelihood that the positive effects of vertical restraints outweigh possible anti-competitive effects depends on the degree of market power of the undertakings. It therefore depends on the extent to which these undertakings face competition from other suppliers of goods or services that users consider identical or similar by reason of their characteristics, price and intended use.

247. The parties' market share on the relevant market is the key issue under the Regulation.

248. Article 3 of the Regulation provides that Article 81, 1 of the Treaty does not apply to restrictions in vertical agreements if the market share[310] of the supplier and undertakings connected to the supplier on the relevant market does not exceed 30 %. For exclusive supply obligations, the threshold of 30 % applies to the buyer's market share[311].

249. The exemption based on the market share continues to apply for the two calendar years following the year in which the market share threshold is crossed, provided that it does not exceed 35 %. The exemption continues to apply for one calendar year if (a) the relevant market share exceeds 35 % or (b) the two-year period expires. This means that if the market share threshold is 32 % in 2001, the exemption will continue to apply until the end of 2003, unless the relevant market share exceeds 35 % before the end of 2002.

250. Moreover, Article 8 of the Regulation provides that the Commission may[312] by regulation declare that, where parallel networks of similar vertical restraints cover more than 50% of a relevant market, the Regulation shall not apply to vertical agreements containing such restraints and relating to that market.

---

[310] The market share is calculated on the basis of the total market sales value of the goods or services under the contract (and those considered identical or equivalent) sold by the supplier or a connected undertaking. If this information is not available, other reliable market information (like market sales volumes) can be used to establish the market share. The figures concern the preceding year or the average of the three preceding calendar years in markets where it takes on average more than one year to produce on order, depending on the nature of the goods or services.

[311] Including the market share held by undertakings connected to the buyer in the market where it purchases the goods or services.

[312] Pursuant to Article 1 bis of Regulation No 19/65/EC.

4.2.2.2.3.1. The Relevant Product and Geographic Markets

251. To assess the application of the Regulation and the *De Minimis* Notice, it is important to determine the relevant product market and geographical market of the supplier or buyer.

252. As a general rule, the relevant product market includes any goods or services the buyer regards as interchangeable by reason of their characteristics, prices and intended use. The relevant geographic market is the area:

- in which the undertakings supply the products or services;
- where the conditions of competition are sufficiently homogeneous; and
- which can be distinguished from neighbouring geographic areas because conditions of competition are appreciably different in those areas.

253. Demand substitution is the most important factor for distribution agreements. An assessment of demand substitution entails a determination of the range of products, which end-users consider substitutes. The question is whether the parties' customers would switch to readily available substitutes or to suppliers located elsewhere in response to a hypothetically small but permanent relative price increase (in the range of 5% to 10%)[313].

4.2.2.2.3.2. The Relevant Product Market for Medicinal Products

254. The manufacture of medicinal products generally takes place in two separate processes: the manufacture of the active substances (raw materials and intermediates) and the manufacture of the medicinal products. During the manufacture of the medicinal products the active substances are mixed with other substances and produced in galenic form such as capsules or tablets.

255. Active substances are manufactured for in-house purposes and are also traded. There are therefore separate product markets for active substances upstream from the markets for medicinal products.

256. *(i) Market for raw materials and market for finished products*
In *Commercial Solvents* the Court distinguished between the market for the raw materials for the manufacture of a medicinal product and the market on which the medicinal product is sold:

> "Contrary to the arguments of the applicants, it is in fact possible to distinguish the market in raw material necessary for the manufacture of a product from the market on which the product is sold. An abuse of dominant position on the market in raw materials may thus have effects restricting competition in the market on which the derivatives of the raw materials are sold and these effects must be taken into account in

---

[313] Commission Notice on the definition of the relevant market for the purposes of Community competition law, *O.J.*, C. 372, 9 December 1997, p. 5.

considering the effects of an infringement, even if the market for the derivative does not constitute a self-contained market"[314].

257. The markets for raw materials or intermediates must essentially be assessed on the basis of the demand substitutability of each of the products for the buyers, who are the manufacturers of the medicinal products[315].

258. *(ii) Segmented market according to ATC classification*
The Commission subdivided medicinal products into therapeutic classes following the "Anatomical Therapeutic Classification" (ATC), which the World Health Organisation recognises and uses. This classification allows medicinal products to be grouped together by reference to their composition and their therapeutic properties[316].

259. Under the third level of the ATC classification, medicinal products are grouped in terms of their therapeutic indications (their intended use). This classification can therefore be used as an operational market definition. Third-level medicinal products generally serve the same treatment purpose and are not interchangeable with products from other classes. Medicinal products may also be subdivided into different segments on the basis of different criteria. This may lead to distinctions essentially on the basis of demand-related criteria.

260. We can distinguish between medicines that may only be issued on prescription and those that may be sold over the counter and between medicines that are wholly or partially reimbursed under the health insurance system and medicines that are not reimbursed. However, these segments partly overlap: most medicines issued only on prescription are reimbursed and most medicines sold over the counter are not. Also, placing a medicine in a particular segment is not permanent, as it is based on decisions of national authorities, which can lead to changes between these segments.

261. A definition of a product market based on a third level ATC classification is not appropriate for all cases and may be either too narrow or too wide. Sometimes it may be appropriate to analyse a product at other levels of the ATC classification or to group third-level categories together. An example of this is when products from different ATC classes compete as possible treatments for a specific diagnosed medical condition.

262. *(iii) Market divided according to medical use*
In principle, the interchangeability of medicinal products depends not only on their physical, technical or chemical properties but also on their functional

---

[314] Joined cases 6 and 7-73, Instituto Chemioterapico Italiano S.p.A. and Commercial Solvents Corporation v EC Commission, *E.C.R.*, 1974, 223.

[315] See e.g. Commission decision, 7 May 1998, Case IV/M.1143 – DSM/Koninklijke Gist-Brocades, *O.J.*, C 353, 19 November 1998, p. 9.

[316] Commission decision, 3 April 1995, Case IV/M.495 – Behringwerke AG/Armour Pharmaceutical Co, *O.J.*, C. 134, 1 June 1995, p. 4; Commission decision, 28 September 1995, Case IV/M.631 – Upjohn/Pharmacia, *O.J.*, C. 294, 9 November 1995, p. 9; Commission decision, 30 July 1998, Case IV/M.1245 – Valeo/ITT Industries, *O.J.*, C. 288, 16 September 1998, p. 5; Commission decision, 28 February 1995, Case IV/M.555 – Glaxo/Wellcome, *O.J.*, C. 065, 16 March 1995, p. 3.

substitutability as viewed by those supervising their consumption. This means medical practitioners for medicines available on prescription only. Their knowledge of active properties and similarities of medicines will of course influence their prescription practice.

263. Therefore, whether different medicines are prescribed for the same illness cannot be the only criterion. The main criterion is that the prescription is based on fundamentally the same medical criteria, taking into account whether the medicines correspond to each other in terms of tolerance, toxicity and side effects[317].

264. It might also be appropriate to apply a narrower market definition where the medicines in question have obviously different indications. The use of medicinal products may also vary nationally.

265. Products that are not yet on the market but that are at an advanced stage of development have not yet been allocated an ATC classification. Hence to assess their potential to compete with other products, either in development or when already on the market, can only be assessed by reference to their characteristics and intended use[318].

266. The Commission sometimes considers that if a buyer purchases a portfolio of products from the same supplier the entire portfolio may determine the product market. Given the specificity of the medicinal products, it seems difficult to apply this concept to vertical agreements under which a manufacturer grants a distributor the right to distribute many products with different therapeutic properties. In this case, it seems appropriate to assess competition for every single type of product in the portfolio with different therapeutic properties.

4.2.2.2.3.3. The Relevant Geographic Market for Medicinal Products

267. The common market programme for the scientific and technical requirements applying to medicines was completed through the harmonisation of technical legislation on medicinal products within the Community and the new marketing authorisation procedures for medicinal products that entered into force on 1 January 1995.

268. However for assessing competition, the relevant geographic market for the sales of medicinal products remains essentially national[319].

---

[317] Commission decision, 30 July 1998, Case IV/M.1245 – *Valeo/ITT Industries, O.J.,* C. 288, 16 September 1998, p. 5.

[318] Commission decision, 21 September 1995, Case IV/M.632 – Rhône Poulenc Rorer/Fisons, *O.J.,* C. 263, 10 October 1995, p. 4.

[319] Commission decision, 30 July 1998, Case IV/M.1245 – Valeo/ITT Industries, *O.J.,* C. 288, 16 September 1998, p. 5; Commission decision, 21 September 1995, Case IV/M.632 – Rhône Poulenc Rorer/Fisons, *O.J.,* C. 263, 10 October 1995, p. 4; Commission decision, 28 September 1995, Case IV/M.631 – Upjohn/Pharmacia, *O.J.,* C. 294, 9 November 1995, p. 9; Commission decision, 3 April 1995, Case IV/M.495 – Behringwerke AG/Armour Pharmaceutical Co, *O.J.,* C. 134, 1 June 1995, p. 4; Commission decision, 28 February 1995, Case IV/M.555 – Glaxo/Wellcome, *O.J.,* C. 065, 16 March 1995, p. 3.

269. This is mainly because of the administrative procedures or purchasing policies that national health authorities have introduced in the different Member States. This includes measures influencing price mechanisms and different levels of reimbursement by the social security system for different categories of medicines. Prices of medicinal products may differ substantially from one Member State to another. Branding and sizing strategies and distribution systems differ widely further indicating the national character of the geographic market for medicinal products[320].

270. The markets for active substances, which are upstream from the pharmaceutical markets, are international markets that have to be examined at the Community level. They may even have to be examined at a broader level[321], given the lack of customs barriers and the frequent mutual recognition of product licences between the United States and the European Economic Area[322]. The same applies to future product markets, whose main characteristic is that no products have yet been registered[323].

4.2.2.2.4. Blacklist Clauses

271. Article 4 of the Regulation is a "blacklist" of the fundamental restrictions that are excluded from the scope of the Regulation and for which individual exemption is unlikely. This covers the following vertical restrictions:

272. *(a) Vertical price fixing clauses*
These clauses restrict a distributor's ability to determine the selling price for its customers. A manufacturer may only impose a maximum or a recommended re-sale price. In other words, he may not impose a fixed or minimum re-sale price.

273. *(b) Territorial or customer exclusivity clauses*
These clauses limit a distributor's territory or the customers to whom a distributor may sell goods or services. The Commission has found that these restrictions are blacklist clauses. It has, however, permitted a restriction on:

-       *active* sales into the exclusive territory or to an exclusive customer group reserved to the manufacturer or allocated by the manufacturer to another dealer;
-       sales to end-users by a distributor operating at the wholesale level of trade;

---

[320]   Commission decision, 30 July 1998, Case IV/M.1245 – Valeo/ITT Industries, *O.J.*, C. 288, 16 September 1998, p. 5; Commission decision, 21 September 1995, Case IV/M.632 – Rhône Poulenc Rorer/Fisons, *O.J.*, C. 263, 10 October 1995, p. 4; Commission decision, 28 September 1995, Case IV/M.631 – Upjohn/Pharmacia, *O.J.*, C. 294, 9 November 1995, p. 9; Commission decision, 3 April 1995, Case IV/M.495 – Behringwerke AG/Armour Pharmaceutical Co, *O.J.*, C. 134, 1 June 1995, p. 4.
[321]   Commission decision, 7 May 1998, Case IV/M.1143 – DSM/Koninklijke Gist- Brocades, *O.J.*, C.353, 19 November 1998, p. 9.
[322]   Commission decision, 30 July 1998, Case IV/M.1245 – Valeo/ITT Industries, *O.J.*, C. 288, 16 September 1998, p. 5.
[323]   Commission decision, 30 July 1998, Case IV/M.1245 – Valeo/ITT Industries, *O.J.*, C. 288, 16 September 1998, p. 5.

- sales to unauthorised distributors by members of a selective distribution network;
- a distributor's ability to sell components, supplied for incorporation, to customers who may use them to manufacture the same type of goods as those produced by the manufacturer.

274. *c) Restrictions on direct or indirect sales to end-users by distributors of a selective distribution system operating at the retail level.*

275. *d) Restrictions on cross supplies between all levels of distributors within a selective distribution system.*

276. *e) Restrictions between a supplier of components and a buyer*
are meant restrictions agreed between a supplier of components and a buyer who incorporates these components, which limit the supplier to selling the components as spare parts to end-users or other service providers not entrusted by the buyer with the repair or servicing of its goods.

277. The Regulation only exempts non-competition clauses of a fixed duration of five years or less[324]. If a non-competition obligation is renewable, it is only exempted if no obstacles exist that may hinder the distributor from effectively terminating the obligation[325].

278. After termination of the agreement, an ongoing obligation that causes a distributor not to manufacture, purchase, sell or resell goods or services is only exempted if it is limited to one year after termination of the agreement and if the obligation:

- concerns goods or services that compete with the goods or services under the contract;
- is limited to the place from where the distributor operated during the contract; and
- is necessary to protect know-how transferred by the supplier to the distributor[326].

279. However, parties to a vertical agreement may impose a restriction, which is unlimited in time on the use and disclosure of know-how that has not entered the public domain[327].

4.2.3. Article 82 of the EC Treaty

280. Article 82 prohibits an abuse by an undertaking or undertakings of a dominant position within the Common Market (or in a substantial part of it) if the abuse may affect trade between Member States.

---

[324] Article 5 of the Regulation.
[325] Guideline No 48 of the Guidelines on vertical restraints.
[326] Article 5, b of the Regulation.
[327] Article 5, b of the Regulation.

4.2.3.1. Dominant Position

281. Article 82 does not define the concept of "dominant position". It has been clarified through decisions of the Commission and judgements of the Court. A dominant position means a degree of market control, which enables an undertaking to behave independently of its competitors and customers to an appreciable extent.

282. To determine whether an undertaking has a dominant position, the relevant product and geographical market[328] must be established on the basis of the criteria set out above.

4.2.3.2. Abuse of a Dominant Position

283. Article 82 of the Treaty does not define what constitutes "abuse", but lists examples of abusive conduct:

- directly or indirectly imposing unfair purchase or selling prices or other unfair trading conditions;
- limiting production, markets or technical developments to the detriment of consumers;
- applying dissimilar conditions to equivalent transactions with other trading parties and placing them at a competitive disadvantage;
- making contracts subject to the other party accepting supplementary obligations, which by their nature or according to commercial usage are not connected to the subject of a contract.

284. Both Articles 81 and 82 require that trade between Member States must be "affected".

285. In *Hoffmann-La Roche* the Court ruled that the concept of abuse in Article 82 concerns:

> "the behaviour of an undertaking in a dominant position which is such as to influence the structure of a market where, as a result of the very presence of the undertaking in question, the degree of competition is weakened and which, through recourse to methods different from those which condition normal competition in products or services on the basis of transactions of commercial operators has the effect of hindering the maintenance of the degree of competition still existing in the market or the growth of that competition"[329].

286. Article 82 of the Treaty does not require a causal relationship between the market power resulting from the existence of a dominant position and the abuse. A finding of abuse cannot be objected to because non-dominant

---

[328]   The geographical market is the market within which the market power of the undertaking is measured.

[329]   Case 85/76, Hoffmann-La Roche v EC Commission, *E.C.R.*, 1979, 541.

undertakings have acted in the same way or because the conduct is normal practice in the relevant market[330].

4.2.4. Vertical Restraints in Distribution Agreements for Medicinal Products

287. What is the Commission's and the Court's position on the application of Articles 81 and 82 of the Treaty and the Regulation to the pharmaceutical industry?

4.2.4.1. Export Restrictions

288. The Court has consistently held that by their very nature, clauses prohibiting exports restrict competition as their purpose is to try to prevent parallel imports into other Member States and to partition national markets[331]. This is so whether the clauses stem from the supplier or the customer. Article 81, 1 of the Treaty prohibits these clauses if they affect trade between Member States.

289. Therefore, what is important is whether an agreement (or decision or concerted practice) prohibiting export:

- may influence the pattern of trade between Member States; and
- is capable of hindering the objectives of a single market between Member States[332].

290. That influence must also be appreciable. A vertical agreement according absolute territorial protection escapes Article 81, 1 if it only "insignificantly" affects the market considering particularly the position and the importance of the parties in the market for the products concerned[333].

291. Even if a distributor does not implement a clause prohibiting export, this does not prove that is has had no effect. Its very existence may create a "visual and psychological" effect, which contributes to a partitioning of the

---

[330]   VAN BAEL, I. and BELLIS, J.-F., *Competition law of the EEC*, Oxfordshire, CCH Editions Limited, 1990, p. 393; VAN GERVEN, W., GYSELEN, L., STUYCK, J., MARESCEAU, M. and STEENBERGEN, J., *Beginselen van Belgisch privaatrecht, Handels- en economisch recht*, Part 2, Mededingingsrecht, Antwerp, E. Story-Scientia, 1996, 479 ff.

[331]   Cases C-89/85, C-104/85, C-114/85, C-116/85, C-117/85 and C-125/85 to C-129/85, Ahlstroem Osakeyhtioe and Others v EC Commission *E.C.R.*,1993, I-1307.

[332]   Case T-77/92, Parker Pen Ltd v EC Commission, *E.C.R.*, 1994, II-549; Case T-66/89, Publishers Association v EC Commission, *E.C.R.*, 1992, II-1995; generally, Article 81, 1 of the Treaty does not apply to bans on exports to countries outside the EEA: VAN BAEL, I. and BELLIS, J.-F., *Competition law of the EEC*, Oxfordshire, CCH Editions Limited, 1990, 107.

[333]   Joined cases 100/80 and 103/80, Musique diffusion française and Others v EC Commission, *E.C.R.*, 1983, 1825; Case 99/79, Lancôme v ETOS, *E.C.R.*, 1980, 2511; Commission decision of 25 November 1980, Case IV/29.702 – Johnson & Johnson, *O.J.*, L 377, 31 December 1980, p. 16. See above for the definition of the relevant product and geographical market of medicinal products. See, however, also the *De Minimis* Notice which does not exclude that agreements entered into between parties having a combined market share of less than 10 % may still infringe Article 81, 1 of the Treaty if they have as their object to confer territorial protection on the participating undertakings or third undertakings.

market[334]. Therefore, Article 81, 1 will still apply. It is sufficient that an agreement has an anti-competitive object; it does not need to have an actual effect on the market[335].

292. Clauses prohibiting export may also be prohibited under Article 82 of the Treaty, if the undertaking imposing the clause has a dominant position on the relevant market.

4.2.4.2. Dual Pricing Systems and Discount Practices

293. The Commission has always objected to parties rejecting economic considerations and charging different prices or granting different discounts depending on the destination of a product. The Commission has held this has the same effect as formal export restrictions and could therefore lead to a partitioning of markets.

294. The Commission has challenged surcharges placed on parallel traders and price reductions granted by a supplier to help its exclusive distributor to compete with parallel imports[336].

295. In the recent *Organon* case, the Commission challenged a discount granted by Organon under the British Pharmaceutical Price Regulation Scheme. The scheme governed how much pharmaceutical companies operating in the UK may earn on capital returns and aims to secure effective medicines at reasonable prices. The discount applied only to sales to pharmaceutical wholesalers of products sold under a British National Health Service prescription.

296. Although the difference in pricing was obviously directly attributable to differences in national reimbursement regimes, the Commission found that the new price regime formed part of a continuous business relationship between Organon and its wholesalers. It was therefore an agreement falling under the Article 81 (1) prohibition as the prices of products varied according to their geographical destination. The agreement thus affected parallel trade to other Member States. Organon decided to withdraw the new price regime and the Commission stopped its proceedings[337].

297. Granting unfair fidelity or loyalty rebates or imposing similar pricing schemes may also breach Article 82 if for example they have the object or effect of obliging the buyer to purchase its requirements from the dominant supplier[338].

4.2.4.3. Resale Price Maintenance

298. Resale price maintenance occurs in agreements or concerted practices whose object is to establish a fixed or minimum resale price level[339] that the

---

334   Case T-77/92, Parker Pen Ltd v EC Commission, *E.C.R.*, 1994, II-549.

335   Case C-277/87, Sandoz prodotti farmaceutici SpA v EC Commission, *E.C.R.*, 1990, I-45.

336   VAN BAEL, I. and BELLIS, J.-F., *Competition law of the EEC*, Oxfordshire, CCH Editions Limited, 1990, p. 108-110.

337   KON, S. and SCHAEFFER, F., "Parallel imports of pharmaceutical products: a new realism, or back to basics", *ECLR*, 1997, p. 128-129.

338   BOYCE, J., "Commercial agreements revisited", *European Counsel*, 2000, V(1), 45.

buyer must apply to its customers. Resale price maintenance is a fundamental restriction that is excluded from the scope of application of the block exemption (Article 4 of the Regulation) and for which individual exemption is unlikely. Only recommended (non-binding) resale prices and maximum resale prices are permitted.

299. Resale price maintenance can be achieved directly through contractual provisions or concerted practices. However, it can also be achieved indirectly by:

-      signing an agreement fixing the maximum discount the distributor can grant beyond a certain prescribed level;
-      subordinating the payment of rebates or sharing promotional costs to a particular price level; and
-      taking measures aimed at identifying price-cutting distributors, such as implementing a price monitoring system or requiring retailers to report other members of the distribution network who deviate from the standard price level.

300. These methods may also be used so that recommended prices function like resale price maintenance mechanisms.

4.2.4.4. Resale Restrictions

301. Resale restrictions (including territorial restrictions) are also fundamental restrictions under Article 4 of the Regulation, except for restrictions on:

-      active re-sales into an exclusively allocated territory or customer group where these restrictions are imposed by the supplier on its direct buyers[340];
-      re-sales to unauthorised distributors by the members of a selective distribution system; and
-      re-sales by a buyer of intermediate goods or services, which are supplied for incorporation.

302. These restrictions may be achieved directly in a contractual clause prohibiting a buyer from reselling to certain customers or to customers in certain territories or in a clause requiring a buyer to refer orders from these customers to other distributors.

303. Restrictions may also be achieved through indirect measures including:

-      a refusal to grant or a reduction of bonuses or discounts, and
-      a refusal to supply or a reduction of supplied volumes.

---

[339]   Or, for example, obliging a distributor to set its prices between a minimum and maximum price level and requiring the supplier's consent for prices outside the band.

[340]   The use of Internet to advertise or to sell products is generally considered a form of passive sales if a website is not clearly designed to primarily reach customers inside the territory or customer group exclusively allocated to another distributor. Unsolicited e-mailing to individual customers are considered active selling.

304. If a supplier imposes these restrictions in conjunction with a monitoring system aimed at verifying the effective destination of the supplied goods (for example the use of differentiated labels or serial numbers), these practices are even more likely to be seen as a ban on re-sales.

4.2.4.5. Restrictions on Use

305. Generally, a restriction imposed by a supplier on a customer's use of a product is considered a breach of competition law.

306. *Beecham Pharma-Hoechst*[341] concerned a supply agreement for bulk ampicillin. The supplier required the buyer to only resell the product:

- in a form packaged as medicine for consumers rather than in bulk form; and
- for human consumption (not for veterinary use).

307. The Commission objected to these requirements stating that restrictions on the form in which a raw material may be resold or on the uses to which it may be put are as detrimental to free competition in the Community as geographical market-sharing.

308. In *Bayer Dental*, the Commission objected to a supplier's prohibiting its buyers from supplying originally packaged products (carrying registered trade marks) to a third party in an opened form. The Commission reasoned that this excluded forms of repackaging that do not affect the original state of the products. Therefore, this prohibition would restrain buyers from reselling repacked products and thus restrict competition[342].

309. Restrictions on the resale of a product in its raw form would prevent purchasers from buying the product in an unprocessed form from anyone other than the original supplier. In the same way the Commission objected to UBC's restricting its buyers from selling any UBC bananas when green. Based on Article 82 of the Treaty, the Commission considered this restriction as a prohibition on exports[343].

310. It seems that a supplier may only impose restrictions on the use of its products if:

- justified by government health regulations requiring specific approval for such uses of the product[344]; or

---

[341]   See VAN BAEL, I. and BELLIS, J.-F., *Competition law of the EEC*, Oxfordshire, CCH Editions Limited, 1990, p. 117.

[342]   Commission decision, 28 November 1990, IV/32.877 – Bayer Dental, *O.J.*, L 351, 15 December 1990, p. 46.

[343]   Case 27/76, United Brands Company and United Brands Continental v EC Commission, *E.C.R.*, 1978, 207.

[344]   Notice under Article 19 (3) of Council Regulation No 17 concerning an application for a negative clearance, Kathon Biocide, *O.J.*, 1984, C 59/6.

-       objectively justified by the possible "danger-to-health" nature of the product.

4.2.4.6. Refusal to Supply

311.   A refusal to supply a potential buyer may breach both Articles 81 and 82 of the Treaty.

312.   A leading case in this respect is the *Bayer AG (Adalat)* case. For several years, Bayer AG, the parent company of the Bayer group manufactured and marketed a range of medicinal preparations under the trade name Adalat. Adalat is a leading high-profile product with a Community market share of 8 %. In most Member States, the national health authorities directly or indirectly fix the price of Adalat.

313.   Between 1989 and 1993, the prices fixed by the Spanish and French health services averaged 40 % lower than prices in the United Kingdom. Because of these significant price differences, wholesalers in Spain and France exported Adalat to the United Kingdom. Bayer UK's sales of Adalat fell by almost half because of the parallel imports. Bayer Spain and Bayer France decided to no longer meet orders from wholesalers in Spain and France.

314.   The Commission held that Article 81, 1 prohibits a refusal to supply a medicinal product to prevent an increase in parallel exports from Member States where the product is marketed at a significantly lower price than in the Member State of importation[345]. Hence, a refusal to supply a distributor is an export prohibition imposed by a supplier.

315.   Bayer contested the Commission's decision and applied for interim relief measures. It maintained that it unilaterally determines its business policy on the basis of a monitoring system not designed to dissuade wholesalers from exporting. The President of the Court suspended the Commission's decision given the serious risk of damage to Bayer[346].

316.   Unless objectively justified, a dominant undertaking's refusal to supply may also constitute an abuse within the meaning of Article 82, as it limits the product's distribution channels and may eliminate distributors.

317.   In *Commercial Solvents* the Court held that a dominant manufacturer of raw materials for the industrial production of ethambutol controlled the supply of derivatives to manufacturers. It could not therefore refuse to supply these raw materials if the refusal would eliminate all competition from major manufacturers of derivative products. The dominant manufacturer's decision to start producing these derivatives itself did not justify the refusal[347].

---

[345]   Commission decision, 10 January 1996, IV/34.279/F3 – Adalat, *O.J.*, L 201, 9 August 1996, p. 1; Commission decision, 18 March 1992, IV/32.290 – Newitt/Dunlop Slazenger International and Others, *O.J.*, L 131, 16 May 1992, p. 32.

[346]   Case T-41/96 R, Bayer AG v EC Commission, *E.C.R.*, 1996, II-381.

[347]   Joined cases 6 and 7-73, Instituto Chemioterapico Italiano S.P.A. and Commercial Solvents Corporation v EC Commission, *E.C.R.*, 1974, 223.

4.3. Good Distribution Practice of Medicinal Products

4.3.1. Quality Control

318. The wholesale distribution of medicinal products often covers several Member States simultaneously. Therefore, it is important that the products maintain an appropriate level of quality throughout the entire distribution network. This is so that licensed medicinal products are distributed to retail pharmacists and to other persons entitled to sell medicinal products to the general public without altering their properties.

319. The Council issued Directive 92/25/EEC on the wholesale distribution of medicinal products for human consumption (the "Council Directive")[348] to guarantee control over the entire distribution chain of medicinal products, from leaving the factory to being sold to the public.

320. The Commission has also published Guidelines on good distribution practice in which it sets out requirements that wholesalers must comply with (the "Guidelines")[349].

4.3.2. Wholesale Distribution of Medicinal Products

4.3.2.1. Authorisation for Wholesale Distribution of Medicinal Products

321. The Council Directive defines the wholesale distribution of medicinal products as all activities to procure, hold, supply or export medicinal products apart from supplying medicinal products to the public.

322. Wholesale distribution of medicinal products is subject to a specific licence[350]. Applicants and holders of this specific licence must fulfil the following minimum requirements[351]:

- keep accounts with details of entry and withdrawal transactions; records must be verified at least once a year and kept for five years;

---

[348] Council Directive 92/25/EEC of 31 March 1992 on the wholesale distribution of medicinal products for human consumption, *O.J.*, L 113, 30 April 1992, p. 1. In Belgium, the Council Directive was implemented by a Royal Decree of 31 December 1992 amending the Royal Decree of 6 June 1960. The Guidelines were implemented by a Ministerial Decree of 17 October 1995. In France, the Council Directive was implemented by Articles L596-600 and R5105-5116 of the *Code de la Santé publique & Pharmacie* and the Decree No 98-79 of 11 February 1998. In the United Kingdom, the Council Directive was implemented by the Medicine Act 1968 (Amendment) Regulations 1993, the Medicine (Applications for Manufacturer's and Wholesale Dealer's Licences) Regulations 1993 and the Medicine (Standard Provisions for Licences and Certificates) Regulations 1993.

[349] Guidelines on good distribution practice of medicinal products for human use, *O.J.*, C 63/4, 1 March 1994, p. 171.

[350] Persons expressly authorised to supply medicinal products to the public are exempted from the requirement to hold a licence if they do not perform a wholesale activity in a principal or secondary role.

[351] Under the Belgian Royal Decree of 6 June 1960 (as amended several times), the wholesaler has the significant obligation of always maintaining a stock that is sufficient to provide its buyers daily with the products they usually need.

- submit proof of the qualifications of personnel;
- provide suitable premises for storage, which are available for inspection; and
- draft an emergency plan for the removal of a product from the market if the authorities so instruct.

323. The procedure for granting the licence must not exceed 90 days from the receipt of the application. Any refusal, suspension or withdrawal must be notified to the party concerned. The Member States and the Commission must be informed of any withdrawal or suspension of a license.

324. A wholesaler wanting to distribute products in a Member State other than the Member State in which the licence was granted must provide the competent authorities of that Member State with all information concerning the licence issued by the first Member State. The authorities must inform the wholesaler of any public service obligations[352] imposed on wholesalers operating on their territory.

325. Holders of the licence may only supply medicinal products to other authorised wholesalers or to persons authorised to supply those products to the public. However, in an emergency the licence holders may also supply to the public[353].

4.3.2.2. Personnel

326. Under Article 5 of the Council Directive, a wholesaler of medicinal products must have staff (and in particular a qualified manager (the "management representative")) who meet the conditions of the legislation of the Member State concerned.

327. The Guidelines further specify that personnel should be trained in their duties and that training sessions should be recorded[354]. Key personnel involved in warehousing medicinal products must have the appropriate ability and experience to guarantee that the products or materials are properly stored and handled.

4.3.2.3. Documentation

328. Orders, written distribution procedures and records must be available to the competent authorities for inspection[355].

329. The written procedures should clearly describe the different operations that may affect the quality of the products or the distribution activity. These include:

---

[352]   Article 1 of the Council Directive requires wholesalers to permanently guarantee an adequate range of medicinal products to meet the requirements of a specific geographical area and to deliver the supplies requested within a very short time to the whole area concerned.

[353]   Article 19 of the Guidelines.

[354]   Articles 1-3 of the Guidelines.

[355]   Article 6 of the Council Directive and Articles 6-8 of the Guidelines.

- receipt and checking deliveries,
- storage,
- cleaning and maintaining the premises (including pest control),
- recording the storage conditions,
- maintaining security for on-site stock and consignments in transit,
- withdrawing products from saleable stock,
- keeping records (of client orders, returned products, recall plans, etc).

330. These procedures must be approved, signed and dated by the persons responsible for the quality system[356]. It may be important to describe these procedures in detail in a distribution contract.

331. Each operation, purchase and sale should be clearly traceable in the records that must be retained for at least five years. The records must specify the date of the operation, the name of the medicinal product, the quantity received or supplied and the name and address of the supplier[357].

4.3.2.4. Premises and Equipment

332. Premises, installations and equipment must be suitable and adequate to ensure the proper preservation and distribution of the medicinal products[358].

333. As with the transportation of medicinal products[359], their receipt is subject to strict conditions[360]. Distributors must have a reception area separate from the storage area, which protects deliveries from bad weather during unloading. Deliveries should be examined in this reception area. Products with broken seals or damaged packaging or products that are suspected of possible contamination must be immediately withdrawn from saleable stock and destroyed or kept in a separate area.

334. Medicinal products must be stored apart from other goods and under the conditions prescribed by the manufacturer to protect them from deterioration from light, moisture and temperature. Some medicinal products may require specific storage conditions[361].

335. Distributors of medicinal products should use the "first in, first out" stock rotation system and withdraw products beyond expiry date or shelf life[362].

4.3.2.5. Returns and Recalls

336. Non-defective medicinal products that have been returned to the distributor may only be added to the saleable stock after:

---

[356]   Article 6 of the Guidelines.
[357]   Articles 6, e and 8 of the Council Directive and Article 8 of the Guidelines.
[358]   Articles 5 and 6 of the Council Directive.
[359]   Article 20 of the Guidelines.
[360]   Articles 10 and 11 of the Guidelines.
[361]   Articles 12 and 13 of the Guidelines.
[362]   Article 15 of the Guidelines.

- a favourable examination by a duly authorised person; and
- a decision of the management representative.

337. They must consider the nature of the products, their shelf life, compliance with their required storage conditions and the time elapsed between the products' supply and return[363]. The products must be in their original unopened containers and all returns must be recorded.

338. Distributors of medicinal products must also produce a written procedure for urgent and non-urgent recalls on the basis of the delivery records[364]. A person must be specifically designated as responsible for carrying out and co-ordinating recalls. The distribution contract may describe those procedures, indicating the name of the person responsible.

339. In a recall message, the distributor requests that the recalled products be removed immediately from the saleable stock and stored separately in a secure area until they are sent back according to the instructions of the holder of the marketing authorisation. The holder must first approve the recall message.

340. Any return, recall operation or receipt of counterfeit products (to be labelled as "not for sale") must be recorded at the time it is carried out. The records must be available to the competent authorities. In each case, a formal decision must be taken on the disposal of these products.

4.4. Conclusion

341. Medicinal products are generally distributed through international vertical agreements between a manufacturer and several distributors located in different countries.

342. When drafting an international distribution agreement for medicinal products the parties must take account of EC Competition Law (and the Regulation in particular) and of how the Commission and the Court have applied the Law to the pharmaceutical industry.

343. The key issue of the Regulation is the supplier or the buyer's share on the relevant market. The relevant market must be carefully assessed on a case-by-case basis. Attention must also be paid to the fundamental restrictions of the Regulation.

344. When drafting a distribution agreement for medicinal products, it is also important to follow Council Directive 92/25/EEC and the Guidelines on that Directive (and their implementing provisions in national law). These Guidelines concern the supply, staffing, premises and equipment required for storing and returning or recalling medicinal products.

---

[363] Articles 22-24 of the Guidelines.
[364] Articles 25-30 of the Guidelines.

5. GENERAL INTELLECTUAL PROPERTY ASPECTS AND MEDICINAL PRODUCTS

5.1. Overview

345. In this chapter we intend to give an overview of the intellectual property rights relevant to the pharmaceutical industry. Intellectual property rights and especially patent rights are important in this very competitive sector and, in view of the immense investments necessary for marketing new medicinal products, we can expect them to continue to grow in importance.

346. The issues concerning free movement of goods and the exhaustion of intellectual property rights will be discussed in Chapter 6.

5.2. Patent Law

5.2.1. Definition and Context

347. Patent Law is designed to protect inventions. It grants the holder of the patent an exclusive right to prevent third parties from exploiting the patented invention for a limited period.

348. Patent law is important for the pharmaceutical industry in general since it grants the pharmaceutical companies the time they need to exploit and commercialise their medicinal products without competition. This enables them to recover the major investment connected with the long and costly process of research and development that necessarily precedes the marketing of each medicinal product. Below, we give a short, non-exhaustive overview of the key features of patent protection in general and certain specific problems, and we address issues related to patents in the pharmaceutical industry. The overview focuses on the European situation and is based more particularly on the European Patent Convention of Munich (EPC) and the relevant European Union legislation.

5.2.2. Patentable Inventions

5.2.2.1. What is a Patentable Invention?

349. For an invention to be patentable, it must:

1. be new;
2. involve an inventive step; and
3. be capable of industrial application[365].

350. An invention is considered new if it is not part of the state of the art[366]. The state of the art is everything available to the public, in whatever form or manner, before the date the patent application is filed. If the patent applicant

---

[365] Article 52, 1 EPC.
[366] Article 54 EPC see §3 on the so-called "collision".

discloses anything about the invention during the six months before the patent application is filed, only in certain specific circumstances will the invention still be considered new[367].

351. Second, an invention is considered to have met the inventiveness requirement if, again taking into account the state of the art at the date of filing, the invention was not obvious to a person skilled in the art concerned[368]. This condition is the most difficult and most disputed issue in almost all patent cases. A considerable amount of case law and legal literature is devoted to this problem.

352. Third, an invention is considered capable of industrial application if it can be made or used in any kind of industry, including agriculture[369].

5.2.2.2. Different Types of Patents

353. Generally speaking, two types of patents are distinguished. Product patents, grant a "monopoly right" to the patentee to make, offer, commercialise, import or store the specific product covered by the patent. Process/method patents grant a monopoly right to the patentee to use the specific process/method covered by the patent and to commercialise the products obtained through the patented process/method. It is clear that product patents usually offer broader protection since third parties must have the patentee's consent to commercialise and even to use the product as such. A process patent, however, does not prohibit to commercialise the product if obtained by a different process. Of course, if technically a product can only be obtained by the patented process, a process claim also offers a broad protection.

5.2.2.3. Legal Exclusions and Exceptions

354. Discoveries, scientific theories, mathematical methods, aesthetic creations, schemes, rules and methods for performing mental acts, playing games or doing business, and programs for computers as well as presentations of information are as such[370] explicitly excluded from patent protection[371].

355. More relevant for the pharmaceutical industry is that under Article 52 (4) of the EPC, methods for treating the human or animal body by surgery or therapy and diagnostic methods practised on the human or animal body are also excluded since they are not regarded as inventions capable of industrial application. The exclusion of treatment and diagnostic methods as inventions capable of industrial application was introduced because a number of countries were of the opinion that allowing them to be patentable would result in higher costs for patients and national health insurance schemes and would unacceptably limit the freedom of the medical community.

---

[367] Article 55 EPC.
[368] Article 56 EPC.
[369] Article 57 EPC.
[370] There is much case law on these exclusions. Generally speaking, they are interpreted narrowly and limited to inventions that consist only of these subject-matters.
[370] Article 52 EPC.

356. However, paragraph (4) of Article 52 EPC expressly states that products, in particular substances or compositions for use in any of the methods, are not covered by that exclusion. Therefore, (active) substances, medicinal products or medical devices can obtain patent protection as long as they fulfil the three requirements of patentability. The medical purpose for which the substance or product can be used may and must not be mentioned.

357. In some cases however, a substance or composition is already known (and therefore no longer novel) before people first become aware of its medical use. For this reason, Article 54, 5 of the EPC contains an exception to the novelty requirement. A substance or composition may be patentable despite not fulfilling the novelty requirement, if:

- it is comprised in the state of the art and is for use in a method of treatment or diagnosis; and
- its medical use for that method is not part of the state of the art.

358. This exception is the "first medical use/application" exception that allows already known substances or compositions to be patented, but only for their (new and inventive) medical application.

359. Further medical applications of products of which one medical application is already known seemed therefore not to benefit from the exception to the novelty requirement in Article 54, 5. The research into new medical applications of known pharmaceutical substances is very important for the pharmaceutical industry as a whole. Therefore attempts were made to patent the outcome of that research by claiming "the use of a known substance for a (novel) treatment of disease X". The European Patent Office (EPO) rejected those claims, deeming them to fall under the exclusion in Article 52, 4 EPC on methods of treatment. However, the European pharmaceutical industry faced a considerable competitive disadvantage because countries like the United States allow methods of treatment to be patented. Therefore, many further attempts have been made to avoid this exclusion by creatively writing the patent claims. In Switzerland, the Swiss Patent Office accepted claims directed to the use of a substance or a composition for the manufacture of a medicinal product for a specified new therapeutic application. Finally, in 1984, the enlarged Board of Appeal of the EPO held that these claims do not fall under the exclusion in Article 52, 4 EPC. This specific kind of claim is now widely known as the "Swiss claim" in the industry.

360. A Swiss claim allows second (and further) medical applications to be patented. The enlarged Board of Appeal recognised that:

(i) the process of manufacture as such is not different from known processes using the same substance or composition, and

(ii) the medicinal product obtained by the process is similar to a known medicinal product.

361. However, the novelty may be found in the sense of the medicinal product having novel technical features (e.g. a new formulation, dosage or synergistic combination) or may derive from the medicinal product's new therapeutic use[372].

362. Finally, under Article 53 EPC no patent is granted for inventions whose publication or exploitation would be contrary to public order "*ordre public*" or morality. A plant or animal variety or essentially biological process for producing plants or animals is also not patentable. However, this provision does not apply to microbiological processes or their products.

363. Another category of invention which deserves a special mention is biotechnological inventions. Biotechnological inventions, including inventions concerning genes, are notoriously considered to be of crucial importance to the future development of medicinal products. Biotechnological research offers essential insights into the causes of certain diseases (dysfunction of genes) and is used to create new and more efficient drugs. Biotechnological inventions are in principle patentable under the EPC and to date, the EPO has received around 15,000 biotechnology-related patent applications while around 3,000 patents have already been granted in this field. The European Community is aware that biotechnology and genetic engineering are playing an increasingly broad role in a wide range of industries and that the protection of biotechnological inventions will be of fundamental importance for the Community's industrial development. It therefore enacted Directive 98/44/ECC of 6 July 1998 on the legal protection of biotechnological inventions[373]. Member States were obliged to implement the Biotech Directive in their national laws before 30 July 2000. In several Member States, however, there is huge political opposition to its implementation. The EPO is not legally obliged to implement the Directive since it is not part of the formal structure of the European Union. However, because its Contracting States are mainly composed of EU Member States, it revised the EPC implementing regulations (the Rules) to bring them into line with the Directive[374].

364. The Biotech Directive first acknowledges that biotechnological research requires a considerable amount of high-risk investment and therefore only adequate and harmonised legal protection can maintain and encourage investment in this field. It confirms that biotechnological inventions must fulfil the same basic requirements as other inventions. The recitals of the Biotech Directive are long and reflect the political opposition that had (and still has - at national level) to be overcome.

365. The Biotech Directive regards as patentable any invention of a product consisting of biological material or a process by which biological material is produced, processed or used[375]. Biological material which is isolated from its natural environment or produced by means of a technical process may be

---

[372]   Eisai Co. Ltd. 5/83 {1985}, *O.J.*, EPO 64, 21.
[373]   *O.J.*, L 213, 30 July 1998 p. 13.The Netherlands are challenging the validity of the Biotech Directive before the E.C.J. on several grounds, including the legal basis of the Directive, the principle of subsidiarity, breach of international law and breach of fundamental human rights.
[374]   The revised Rules (Chapter VI: Biotechnological inventions) came into force on 1 September 1999.
[375]   Article 3, 1 Biotech Directive.

patentable even if it previously occurred in nature. Biological material is defined in Article 2 of the Biotech Directive as any material containing genetic information and capable of reproducing itself or being reproduced in a biological system.

366. Genes and partial sequences of a gene are patentable, provided that the industrial application of the sequence or partial sequence is disclosed in the patent application. Recital 24 states that compliance with the industrial application criterion requires specification of which protein or part of a protein is produced and what function it performs in cases where a sequence or partial sequence of a gene is used to produce a protein or part of a protein. This requirement will undoubtedly be important in the controversy over the patentability of ESTs (Expressed Sequence Tags).

367. Certain biotechnological inventions are considered not patentable and are therefore excluded.

368. Article 6 of the Directive excludes inventions which are contrary to morality or public order, and lists examples of such inventions:

–   processes for cloning human beings;
–   processes of modifying the germ line genetic identity of human beings;
–   use of human embryos for industrial or commercial purposes; and
–   processes for modifying the genetic identity of animals which are likely to cause them suffering without any substantial benefit to man or animal; and
-    animals resulting from such processes.

369. Article 5 expressly excludes the human body, at the various stages of its formation and development, as well as the simple discovery of one of its elements, including the sequence or partial sequence of a gene. However, an element isolated from the human body or otherwise produced by means of a technical process, including the sequence or partial sequence of a gene, may constitute a patentable invention, even if the structure of that element is identical to that of a natural element.

5.2.3. Filing and Prosecution

370. To obtain a patent, the inventor or his assignee must file a patent application with the competent patent authority. The authority will decide whehter to grant the patent, after examining the merits of the application, the extent of which may vary under the applicable legislation.

371. Before the mid-seventies, a patent applicant who wished to file his patent in several European countries needed to file a separate patent application in each country. This "national route" still exists but is nowadays, especially in the pharmaceutical industry, used only exceptionally. Where the first patent application is filed by a Convention applicant in one of the Contracting States of the 1883 Paris Convention, a right of priority is given (during the 12 months from filing of the first application) to file patents in the other Contracting

States[376]. The priority sets aside state of the art later than the first application and prevents any third party from acquiring competing rights in the other countries concerned.

372. Currently, several other international conventions exist which facilitate the filing and prosecution of patent applications in more than one country. Two of these must be mentioned and are briefly discussed below.

373. The Patent Cooperation Treaty (PCT) of Washington of 19 June 1970 is an international treaty, with approximately 100 signatories, which facilitates the task of applicants in filing and prosecuting the same patent application in many countries. Instead of having to immediately file the patent application in each of the designated PCT member States separately, an applicant, may elect to operate a PCT filing, irrespective of whether he made a first "priority application" less than 12 months earlier. This amounts to a filing in each of the national patent offices of the designated PCT member States. The possible priority date of the initial patent application will apply for all patents obtained under the PCT and a single international search report is established on the novelty and inventiveness requirements. However, after that, the patent application will have to be prosecuted further in each designated member State, or in the regional established structures such as the European Patent Office (EPO), separately. These remain autonomous in deciding whether to grant the patent.

374. Another convention of major importance is the European Patent Convention (EPC) of 5 October 1973 which further harmonises the procedure of granting a European patent. A European patent is a patent granted by the EPO in Munich and covers those contracting states designated by the applicant. The contracting states include all the countries of the European Union, and some other European countries. The main characteristics of the EPO procedure are its centralised character (one single procedure for all countries concerned) and the substantive examination (patentability, novelty, inventive steps, industrial application). The EPO also offers a centralised opposition procedure, which remains open for nine months from the date the patent is issued. However, enforcement and cancellation generally remain a matter for each of the different national laws, and are thus often referred to, since, after being granted, a European patent becomes a bundle of national patents.

375. The European Commission is currently pushing to bring into force a Community patent, a single patent covering all the Member States and having equal effect throughout the Community. There is now a proposal for a regulation. This would improve and replace the Community Patent Convention of 15 December 1975, which a substantial number of Member States never ratified, indicating that unification will not be an easy task. The main hurdles are the languages issue and jurisdictional matters.

---

[376]   Article 4 of the Paris Convention for the Protection of Industrial Property (revised in Stockholm, 1967).

5.2.4. Duration

376. In Europe and many other countries the duration of a patent is 20 years, commencing on the date the application is filed, providing of course that all costs and renewal fees arc paid in time.

377. For patents of medicinal products a special system exists. In certain cases, special extended protection is allowed to compensate for the loss of effective protection due to the regulatory approval process that delays the marketing of medicinal products. This will be discussed in detail below under Supplementary Protection Certificates.

5.2.5. Costs and Fees

378. The costs related to filing and prosecuting a patent application are considerable. As patent applications must be carefully drafted, they are usually prepared by a specialist patent attorney, at great expense. There are also the costs of filing, searching, examining, and last but not least translating the European patent into the national languages of the designated countries. To obtain a European patent in around 15 countries for a relatively simple invention can therefore cost around BEF 1.5 million (around EUR 37,500). These costs are of course a lot higher if a PCT application is made, designating additional countries such as the United States and Japan.

379. Furthermore, once a patent is granted, renewal fees must be paid each year, usually starting after the third year and gradually increasing until the 20th year. Since the payment of renewal fees in each country where the invention is patented can be burdensome for inventions whose protection is no longer worthwhile, renewal fees are sometimes not paid until the 20th year in all countries concerned.

380. The high costs and fees are forcing companies to be selective in their choice of countries. Protection is therefore usually sought only in major markets and countries where competitors are based.

5.2.6. Rights and Infringement

381. Patent law is designed to grant the patent holder, within certain limits, a monopoly over the patented invention. We give hereinafter an overview of the scope of this monopoly as generally defined in Europe.

382. Therefore, the patent holder has the right to prevent all third parties who do not have his consent from:

- making, offering, putting on the market or using a product which is the subject matter of the patent, or importing or stocking the product for these purposes;
- using a process which is the subject matter of the patent or, when the third party knows, or it is obvious in the circumstances, that the use of the process is prohibited without the consent of the owner of the patent,

from offering the process for use within the territory for which the patent is valid;

- offering, putting on the market, using, importing or stocking for these purposes the product obtained directly by a process which is the subject matter of the patent.

383. These are all direct infringements of the patent against which the patent holder can take legal action. The extent of protection conferred by a specific patent is of course determined by the subject matter terms of the patent claims, for which the description and drawings will be used to interpret the claims.

384. In addition, the patent holder can also take action against indirect or contributory infringement. He can therefore prevent all persons, who do not have his consent, from supplying or offering to supply on the territory for which the patent is valid, to a person other than parties entitled to exploit the patented invention certain means, relating to an essential element of the invention, for putting it into effect, when the third party knows, or it is obvious in the circumstances, that those means are suitable and intended for putting that invention into effect. This does not apply when the means are staple commercial products, except when the third party induces the person supplied to commit direct infringements.

385. Most European patent laws also expressly exclude a number of acts from the rights granted to the patent holder. For the pharmaceutical industry, the most important exclusions are:

- experimental acts relating to the subject matter of the patented invention, and
- the extemporaneous preparation of a medicine for individual cases, in a pharmacy in accordance with a medical prescription or acts concerning the medicine so prepared.

386. The experimental use exception has given rise to a lot of legal discussion and disputes. First, it is clear that submitting samples of a patented product to obtain a marketing authorisation which implies the product's manufacture beyond experimental use does not fall under this exception and constitutes a patent infringement in most European countries (or an infringement of the supplementary protection certificate). For clinical trials the legal situation is less clear. It was long argued that only trials made with a purely non-commercial purpose could benefit from this exception. Recently however, there seems to be a shift towards allowing clinical trials (and their results) to enjoy the experimental use exception in so far as they also serve an experimental purpose and are not made purely for obtaining a marketing authorisation[377].

5.2.7. Overview of International Jurisdictional Issues

387. Patent cases in general and patent litigation in the pharmaceutical industry in particular tend to be very complex. This is not only because of the

---

[377]   German Federal Supreme Court in Clinical Trials I and II (RPC 1997, 623 and RPC 1998, 424).

nature of patents, but also because of the international jurisdictional issue involved, especially when a European patent is involved with alleged infringement in several European countries by one or more alleged infringers. For both the plaintiff and the defendant, such cases call for a carefully devised strategy taking into account the basic principles set out below.

388. The following rules only apply if the provisions of the Brussels or Lugano Convention on jurisdiction and enforcement of judgements in civil and commercial matters govern the patent dispute in question[378]. The general principle (Article 2) of jurisdiction is that persons domiciled in a contracting State must be sued in the courts of that State. For European patent litigation, this means that a patent infringement action can be brought in the courts of the defendant's domicile for infringing activities taking place in all the countries where the national parts of the European patent are in force. Depending on the reputation of the courts of that contracting State for patent litigation, a plaintiff may or may not want to do that.

389. This approach however is rather theoretical because Article 16 provides for the exclusive jurisdiction of the courts of the State in which the (part of the European) patent is in force as soon as its validity is questioned. This, together with Articles 21 and 22, means that almost all cases are brought separately in the courts of each State concerned.

390. This widespread practice also complies with the rule that a plaintiff may sue a defendant in tortious matters in the courts of the place where the harmful event occurred (Article 5, 3°). The place where the harmful event occurred is considered to be the place where the defendant carried out tortious activities (e.g. the infringement) as well as the place where the damages occur. If based on the place of the damages, the jurisdiction is limited to the damages that occurred in the State of the court seized.

391. In cases where there are multiple defendants domiciled in different contracting States, all of the defendants may be sued at the domicile of a co-defendant if the claims involved are sufficiently related, i.e. making it necessary to deliver a single, joint decision and consequently avoid the risk of conflicting decisions[379]. This rule is usually seen as allowing a plaintiff broad forum shopping in cases of joint infringement by more than one party of different national parts of a European patent. The Court of Appeal of The Hague recently held that this rule may only be used if the co-defendant used for establishing jurisdiction is "the spider in the web", i.e. holds the leading position in the

---

[378] The jurisdictional rules of the Brussels Convention of 27 September 1968 and Lugano Convention of 16 September 1998 on jurisdiction and the enforcement of judgments in civil and commercial matters apply if the defendant is domiciled in a contracting state (Article 2). All member states of the European Union are contracting states of the Brussels Convention.

[379] Some argue that since the EPC did not address issues of infringement and consequently referred these issues to the national laws of the member States, diverging decisions on infringement in different member States are possible under the convention, so there is no need for a single, joint decision.

infringement scheme[380]. The European Court of Justice has yet to address this issue.

392.   Defendants have also found rules in the Brussels and Lugano Convention, which they try to use to their advantage. They find the rules on *lis pendens* (pending proceedings) and related actions particularly useful.

393.   *Lis pendens* (Article 21) occurs when proceedings, involving the same cause of action and between the same parties, are brought in the courts of different contracting States. In such cases, any court other than the court first seized must stay its proceedings until the jurisdiction of the court first seized is established. Once that jurisdiction is established, any court other than the court first seized must decline jurisdiction in favour of that court. On the basis of this rule, defendants fearing a claim for infringement have tried to initiate an action for a declaration of non-infringement[381] (sometimes combined with an action for invalidity) before the patent holder could bring his action. By doing so, they try not only to force the patent holder to litigate before a court deemed more favourable to the defendant but also and essentially to have any other proceedings suspended in other countries, in particular with the aim of avoiding cross-border injunctions[382]. Practitioners refer to such actions as "*Italian torpedos*" although other jurisdictions such as Belgium have been considered by some to be attractive in that respect[383]. The future of such tactics is dubious.

394.   When related actions (Article 22) are pending, at least while the actions are pending at first instance, the courts may stay their proceedings but there is no obligation to do so. Related actions are defined as actions which are so closely connected that it is expedient to hear and determine them together to avoid the risk of irreconcilable judgements resulting from separate proceedings. Therefore, neither the same parties nor the same cause of action need be involved.

395.   Another sort of torpedo is an invalidity torpedo, which is based on the rule in Article 16 that, regardless of domicile, the courts of the contracting State in which the patent was delivered has exclusive jurisdiction. Any other court seized which is principally concerned with a matter over which the courts of another contracting State have exclusive jurisdiction must declare itself without jurisdiction. There is some discussion as to whether invalidity and infringement are so closely linked that if the defendant brings such an action in the court of a different contracting State for that (part of the European) patent, that other court must declare itself without jurisdiction over both the invalidity issue and the

---

380   Court of Appeal of The Hague, Expandable Graft / Boston Scientific, IER, 1998, 170.
381   In the cases Gubisch and Tatry, the E.C.J. held that a claim for non-infringement and a claim for infringement must be considered to concern the same cause of action (Cases No 144/86 and No 406/92).
382   A cross-border injunction is an injunction which extends beyond the territory of the country in which the court is established and is in cases of European patent litigation based on the infringement under foreign law of the foreign national parts of the European patent.
383   This is likely to change in view of the decision of 12 May 2000 of the court of first instance of Brussels, which denied any jurisdiction of the Belgian courts under the Convention to determine any infringement issue outside Belgium and considered the torpedo an abuse of process.

infringement issue. The general view is that the other court must stay its proceedings until the question of invalidity is resolved (related actions: Article 22). The advantage of the invalidity torpedo is that unlike the non-infringement torpedo it need not be initiated before another court is seized by the patent owner since it concerns exclusive jurisdiction which prevails at all times.

396. Finally, the Brussels and Lugano Conventions allow the courts of a contracting State to take provisional measures in applying the rules of the Convention, provided they are possible under that State's national laws, even if the courts of another contracting State have jurisdiction over the substance of the matter.

5.2.8. Remedies

397. The main remedies a patent holder may seek are injunctions, which can be preliminary or permanent depending on whether the action is in summary proceedings or on the merits, and actions for compensation for the actual damage suffered. These remedies are also available to a patent holder's licensee where a third party infringes one of the exclusive rights mentioned earlier. Some countries also allow recovery of the infringer's turnover or profits if the infringement was made in bad faith. Several countries have a special fast track procedure on the merits.

398. We must specifically mention discovery proceedings in patent litigation. Discovery is often a key element in patent litigation since it may provide the potential plaintiff with the necessary evidence of not only the existence but also the scope of the infringement. Sometimes a potential plaintiff cannot obtain the necessary evidence of the infringement by himself and needs legal authorisation to gather the evidence where it can be found. Discovery proceedings take many forms and vary according to national laws. However, as Belgian lawyers, we feel it appropriate to briefly describe the main features of the descriptive seizure proceedings under Belgian law ("*saisie-description*" or "*beslag inzake namaak*") since this procedure is very effective in patent litigation and can even, in the right circumstances, combine discovery and injunctive relief. Despite some important differences, this procedure is rather close to the French "*saisie-contrefaçon*".

399. Articles 1481 to 1488 of the Belgian Code of Civil Procedure set out the descriptive seizure procedure. The holder of a patent (or another IP right, except trademark rights) who knows or suspects that his patent is being infringed may file an *ex parte* request for measures of descriptive seizure.

400. The plaintiff will either seek a description of the alleged infringing activities or, besides such description and subject to further requirements, injunctive relief.

401. For the first remedy, the judge of seizures can appoint an expert, authorising him to simply describe the alleged infringing activities. This description relates to both the alleged infringing objects or methods and all documents, drawings, or invoices which are relevant to prove the existence and the scope of the alleged infringing activities. The expert, who in some circumstances can be accompanied by a representative of the plaintiff, may enter all places indicated in the order by the judge of seizures and may take all steps he considers appropriate to ensure maximum discovery of relevant information. These findings, together with copies of the relevant documents, are then compiled in a report which the expert files with the court and sends to the patentee and to the alleged infringing party.

402. Second, the judge of seizures may issue an injunction, ordering the enjoined party to no longer dispose of the alleged infringing goods. The judge can also appoint a sequestrator and allow an attachment of the goods resulting from the infringing activities.

403. Case law has introduced certain necessary conditions for obtaining the relief mentioned above. As the main purpose of the descriptive measure in the framework of descriptive seizure proceedings is to enable a patent owner to determine whether an infringement of his patent is actually taking place, this remedy is granted fairly readily. Indeed all that is required is that a valid patent is invoked and that the owner of this patent has apparently reasonable grounds to suspect that an infringement is occurring.

404. However, when considering a request for an injunction, the judge of seizure must establish whether *prima facie* (i.e. at first view): (i) the patent rights which are invoked cannot reasonably be contested (ii) the patent infringement cannot reasonably be contested and (iii) the injunction is reasonably justified in the circumstances of the case. These circumstances have included consideration of public health concerns, such as availability of a substitute medicine.

405. Finally, an important feature of the descriptive seizure procedure is its unilateral nature ("*non audita altera parte*"), namely the party against whom the descriptive seizure measures are sought is not heard by the judge of seizures who is handling the request. Indeed, the alleged infringer (or retailer, etc.) will only be informed of the order against him immediately before it is carried out by receiving then a copy of the order of the judge of seizure, a process which warrants the "surprise effect" of the whole operation.

5.2.9. Supplementary Protection Certificates

406. In view of the novelty requirement and consequently the need to be the first to file a patent application, most patent applications covering a new medicine are filed at the very beginning of the lengthy research and development process. As seen in Chapter 2, it takes many years (on average 7 to 13 years) before the medicine is thoroughly tested and has received the necessary marketing authorisations.

407. Therefore, unlike in most other industries, a pharmaceutical patent holder cannot start commercialising its products under the patent from the date of filing or shortly thereafter. Instead it must wait a number of years. As the lifetime of pharmaceutical patents is, like for all patents, 20 years starting from the filing date, the effective patent protection, i.e. the protection from the date the medicinal product becomes available on the market, would therefore be seriously reduced. Further, as not much time or investment is needed to copy pharmaceutical products, producers of generic products can usually enter the market rather quickly after the patent lapses.

408. Therefore, after years of lobbying by the pharmaceutical industry, the European Union decided to remedy what was viewed as detrimental to the research-based pharmaceutical companies. It was feared that without action, research centres in the European Union would relocate to countries offering greater protection, especially since major trading partners such as the United States and Japan offered such extended protection. As a result, Council Regulation 1768/92 of 18 June 1992 concerning the creation of a supplementary protection certificate for medicinal products was enacted and came into force on 1 January 1993[384].

409. Although intimately linked with patent protection, the protection granted by a supplementary protection certificate is not merely an extension of the patent but constitutes protection *sui generis* (protection with its own legal regime). It tries to strike a fair balance between competing interests such as those of public health and those of the patent holder. As an objective, the holder of both a patent and a certificate should be able to enjoy an overall maximum of fifteen years of exclusivity from the time the medicinal product in question first obtains authorisation to be placed on the market in the Community[385].

410. Under the Regulation, any medicinal product, protected by a patent in a member State and subject to an administrative authorisation procedure before being placed on the market, may be the subject of a certificate[386]. A product is defined as meaning the active ingredient or a combination of active ingredients of a medicinal product. A medicinal product is:

-    any substance or combination of substances presented for treating or preventing disease in humans or animals; or
-    any substance or combination of substances which may be administered to human beings or animals with a view to making a medical diagnosis or to restore, correct or modify physiological functions.

411. A certificate will be granted in a member State if the following conditions are fulfilled[387]:

-    the product is protected by a basic patent in force[388];

---

384   The European Court of Justice rejected an attempt by Spain, where many generic companies are based, to challenge the power of the European Council to enact the Regulation with referral to Article 100a of the Treaty, in the case C-350/92 {1995}, *Kingdom of Spain vs. Council of the European Union.*

385   Recital 8.

386   Article 2.

387   Article 3.

388   Basic patent under the Regulation means a patent which protects a medicinal product as defined, a process to obtain a product or an application of a product and which is designated by its holder for the purpose of the procedure for grant of a certificate. In the case C-181/95 {1997}, the European Court of Justice held that when a medicinal product is covered by more than one basic patent, a certificate can be granted to each basic patent holder.

- a valid authorisation to place the product on the market as a medicinal product has been granted[389];
- the product has not already been the subject of a certificate; and
- the authorisation referred to above is the first authorisation to place the product on the market as a medicinal product.

412. The application for a certificate must be made with the competent industrial property office of the Member State[390] within six months from the date on which the authorisation to place the product on the market was granted. By exception, in the rare circumstance that the authorisation to place the product on the market is granted before the basic patent is granted, the application for a certificate must be made within six months of granting the patent[391]. The exact content of the application for a certificate is described in Article 8 of the Regulation[392].

413. Only the original basic patent holder or his successor in title will be granted a certificate[393].

414. Within the limits of the protection conferred by the basic patent, the subject matter of the protection conferred by a certificate only extends to the product covered by the authorisation to place the corresponding medicinal product on the market and for any further use of the product as a medicinal product subsequently authorised before the expiry of the certificate[394].

415. Subject to the above, a certificate confers the same rights as the basic patent and is subject to the same limitations and the same obligations[395]. These rights come into force on the expiry of the basic patent. There is no set period during which these rights remain valid. Their lifetime must be calculated for each case. These rights take effect for a period equal to the period which elapsed between the date on which the basic patent application was made and the date of the first authorisation to place the product on the market in the Community, but reduced by five years[396]. However, the duration of the certificate may not exceed

---

[389] In case C-392/97 {1999}, the European Court of Justice ruled that where a product in the form referred to in the marketing authorisation is protected by a basic patent in force, the certificate can cover that product, as a medicinal product, in any of the forms enjoying the protection of the basic patent. To determine whether a product is protected by a basic patent, reference must be made to the rules which govern that patent.

[390] Article 9.

[391] Article 7.

[392] The applicant must provide a copy of the marketing authorisation. However, if the basic patent and the authorisation to place the product on the market as a medicinal product are held by different legal entities and the patent holder is unable to provide a copy of the authorisation, the application cannot be denied on that basis alone (see case C-181/95 {1997}).

[393] Article 6.

[394] Article 4.

[395] Article 5.

[396] Article 13. Note that the European Court of Justice in case C-110/95 {1997} found that the first authorisation to place the product on the market in the Community (Article 19, 1) is only necessary for the purposes of determining the duration of the certificate. The entitlement to the certificate is the authorisation to place the product on the market referred to in Article 3, b and not the first authorisation to place the product on the market in the Community (should they differ).

five years from the date on which it takes effect. The certificate will lapse prematurely if, among other things, the annual fees are not paid in time and if the authorisation to place the product on the market is withdrawn[397].

416.   A certificate becomes invalid if:

-        the basic patent lapses before its statutory duration expires; or
-        the basic patent is revoked or limited to such extent that the product for which the certificate was granted would no longer fall under the claims of the basic patent; or
-        after the basic patent has expired, grounds for revocation exist which would have justified its revocation or limitation[398].

417.   Unless national laws provide otherwise, the national law's procedural provisions for the corresponding basic patent apply to the certificate[399].

418.   The Regulation came into force on 2 January 1993 and applies to any medicinal product which on that date was protected by a valid basic patent and for which the first authorisation to place it on the market as a medicinal product in the Community, was obtained after 1 January 1985. However, a number of member States chose a different starting date. Some member States like Belgium and Italy chose an earlier date (i.e. 1 January 1982), while other countries like Greece, Portugal and Spain could only start granting certificates from 2 January 1998[400].

419.   We can expect the European Court of Justice to have to further clarify some of the criteria involved since:

-        the supplementary protection certificate is a rather new intellectual property right which only comes into play if the basic patents expires; and
-        practice shows that the competent authorities in a number of Member States widely differ in their application of the same criteria.

5.3. Trademark Law

5.3.1. Definition and Context

420.   Trademark law is designed to protect signs used to distinguish the products or services of one undertaking from those of other undertakings. The holder of a trademark is granted the right to basically prevent third parties from using the same trademark or a similar sign for identical and similar goods or services. Like in other industries, pharmaceutical companies extensively use trademarks to distinguish their medicinal products from those of competitors.

---

[397]   Article 14.
[398]   Article 15.
[399]   Articles 15, §2, 17 and 18.
[400]   Articles 19 and 21.

421. Trademarks must be distinguished from trade names of which the purpose is to identify the enterprise (apart from its products or services) in business, and from company names, which are names of the legal entities as such. In practice however, these signs often coincide. Names given to products are often called "trade names" but legally speaking "trademarks" is to be preferred.

5.3.2. Which Kinds of Signs may be Protected?

422. Signs able to constitute a trademark are any signs capable of being represented graphically, particularly words, including personal names, designs, letters, numerals, the shape of goods or their packaging, provided that those signs are capable of distinguishing the goods or services of one undertaking from those of other undertakings.

423. In the pharmaceutical industry, the most obvious sign which may constitute a trademark is the name of the medicinal product. Although not legally necessary, most companies prefer to file a specific name of their medicinal products as a trademark and therefore do not use the pharmaceutical substance's generic name (i.e. the International Nonproprietary Name or INN) as selected by the World Health Organisation. European Council Regulation 2309/93 created a centralised Community procedure for authorising certain medicinal products with a single application, single evaluation and single authorisation for the whole Community market. Under that Regulation, the applicant must submit a single trademark which must be used Community-wide.

424. The EMEA (European Agency for the Evaluation of Medicinal Products) established under Regulation 2309/93 must evaluate whether the proposed name could raise any identifiable public health risk. EMEA's Committee for proprietary products released its draft guidelines on the acceptability of trademarks[401]. These guidelines include the requirement that the trademark not cause confusion with the trademark of another medicinal product or with an established non-proprietary name. These grounds for refusal of the tradename/trademark are quite logical since otherwise medication errors may occur.

425. Among the other signs considered capable of constituting a trademark are three-dimensional signs, such as the shape of goods and their packaging. Therefore, the packaging of pharmaceutical products as well as the shape of the pharmaceutical product itself (tablets for instance) may enjoy trademark protection. However, most trademark laws do not protect shapes which are necessary for obtaining a technical result, nor shapes which result from the nature of the goods themselves, nor those which provide substantial marketing value to the goods.

426. It is generally accepted that colours, combinations of colours, or shades of colours are signs able to constitute a trademark. Of course, as case law shows,

---

[401] CPMP/328/98 (Draft, Rev. 1) of the Committee for proprietary medicinal products of the European Agency for the Evaluation of Medicinal Products (Human Medicines Evaluation Unit).

much depends on the goods and services and the commonness of the colour or shade for which protection is sought for the goods or services concerned.

427. Another more difficult question is whether smells can also form a sign capable of being registered as an (olfactory) trademark. Smells are not usually excluded as such, but the requirement that the sign must be capable of graphical representation seems to introduce substantial problems. Recently, in the first olfactory Community trademark case, the OHIM Board of Appeal decided that the trademark "the smell of freshly cut grass" for tennis balls complied with the graphical representation requirement[402].

428. Given the definition of a sign able to constitute a trademark, a sign which cannot be represented graphically and which is devoid of any distinctive character will be refused trademark protection absolutely. There are a number of other grounds for invalidation such as the purely descriptive character, the commonness in the current language, or being contrary to public policy or to morality. These elements have given rise to extensive case law.

429. For instance, the OHIM Board of Appeal has declared the following signs descriptive:

- the sign "Doublemint" for pharmaceutical, veterinary and sanitary preparations, including chewing gum for medical purposes; and
- the sign "Fast Prep" for surgical, medical, dental and veterinary apparatus and instruments[403].

430. However, it did not consider descriptive the sign "Bloodstream" for medical equipment for treating and recovering blood products[404].

5.3.3. How to get TM Protection?

431. The basic rule is that trademark rights are conferred on the (legal) person who first files the trademark for certain goods and services with the competent trademark office. In some countries, use alone is sufficient for acquiring the rights.

432. However, most laws contain exceptions for trademarks which are registered in bad faith, i.e. registration of a trademark knowing that another party has already used it. A trademark which is identical or similar if the goods and services applied for or registered, are identical or similar. For trademarks with a reputation, a trademark owner may also oppose subsequent registration for non-similar goods or services where the use of the later trademark would without due cause take unfair advantage of, or be detrimental to, the distinctive character or the repute of the earlier trademark.

---

402   Second Board of Appeal of 11 February 1999, case R 1 56/1998-2.
403   First Board of Appeal of 16 June 1999, case R 216/1998-1 en of 29 October 1998, case R 111/1998-1.
404   Second Board of Appeal of 22 September 1998, case R 33/1998-2.

433. The Trademark Directive has largely harmonised the national trademark laws of the Member States so that most basic requirements and protection rules, at least in theory, are the same at the European level as at the different national levels[405].

434. There are several routes one may take to obtain a trademark registration in Europe. The oldest route is the national route, i.e. to file the trademark in each of the countries where protection is desired, where possible taking advantage of the priority right for six months as provided for by Article 4 of the Paris Convention. Another option is to use the Madrid Agreement and Protocol. It basically allows, on the basis of valid registration or application in the country of origin, the filing of an international application with the International Bureau of Intellectual Property designating the contracting States in which protection is sought[406]. Lastly, if protection in all the Member States of the European Union is sought, an application for a Community trademark can be filed. If granted, it is a single title covering all Member States[407].

5.3.4. The Costs of Obtaining and Maintaining the Protection

435. If the national route is taken, a filing fee has to be paid in each country where trademark protection is sought. The fee will usually differ depending on the number of classes of goods and services for which the trademark is filed. If the rules of the Madrid Agreement and Protocol are followed, a flat fee is due which is supplemented depending on which countries are designated. For the filing of a Community trademark in less than 4 classes, the registration fee is currently around EUR 1,500.

436. For each subsequent renewal, a renewal fee must be paid.

5.3.5. Duration of Trademark Protection

437. A trademark registration usually grants the owner protection for ten years; however, the registration can be renewed an indefinite number of times. Therefore, theoretically, there is no time limit on trademark registration.

438. If a trademark however is not genuinely used without proper reason within five years of completing the registration procedure or within any uninterrupted period of five years, the trademark may, under certain circumstances, be declared invalid and revoked.

439. What constitutes non-use for proper reason? Non-use of a trademark could be with proper reason, if, for example:

---

[405] First Council Directive 89/104/EEC of 21 December 1988 to approximate the laws of the Member States relating to trademarks (amended).

[406] Madrid Agreement concerning the International Registration of Marks of April 14, 1891 (last revised in Stockholm, 1967) and the Protocol relating to the Madrid Agreement concerning the International Registration of Marks (signed in Madrid, 1989).

[407] Council Regulation 40/94 of 20 December 1993 on the Community trade mark.

- a pharmaceutical company is awaiting government approval to market its product, and the government has not observed the legal terms for granting that approval; and
- the pharmaceutical company can show it has done everything in its power to accelerate the approval process.

5.3.6. Infringement

440. A trademark confers exclusive rights on the trademark owner. A trademark owner is entitled first of all to prevent all third parties who do not have his consent, from using[408], in the course of trade:

- any sign which is identical to the trademark for goods or services which are identical to those for which the trademark is registered; and
- any sign where, because of its similarity to the trademark and the similarity of the goods or services covered by the trademark and the sign, there exists a likelihood of confusion on the part of the public, which includes the likelihood of association between the sign and the trademark.

441. Trademarks with a reputation generally enjoy a broader protection which extends to the use of these trademarks or similar signs for goods or services which are not similar to those for which these trademarks are registered, where such use would take unfair advantage of, or would be detrimental to, the distinctive character or the repute of these trademarks.

442. Most trademark laws also allow the trademark owner to oppose any use, without due cause and in the course of trade, of a trademark or similar sign other than for the purposes of distinguishing goods or services, where such use would take unfair advantage of, or would be detrimental to, the distinctive character or the repute of the trademark.

443. It is usually argued that a likelihood of confusion is more easily established if the medicinal products are distributed over-the-counter rather than by prescription only. The argument is that the latter are prescribed by physicians and distributed by pharmacists. As both the physician and the pharmacist are specialists, the likelihood of confusion is deemed less than for an over the counter product where the average consumer must be considered. This argument, however, is not convincing, since it limits the public concerned to the persons prescribing/buying the product. Even prescribed products will ultimately end up in the hands of the general public who may confuse products. Confusion may start when looking in a medicine cabinet which can typically be found in any household and where prescribed products may usually be found next to over-the-counter products.

444. The rights of the trademark owner are however limited. Besides the exhaustion of his rights discussed in Chapter 6 a trademark owner may not prevent a third party from using, in the course of trade, indications on the type, quality, intended purpose or other characteristics of goods or services as well as

---

[408] Using includes repackaging (see Chapter 6).

the trademark in question where it is necessary to indicate the intended purpose of a product of service, provided the third party uses them in accordance with the honest practices in industrial or commercial matters.

5.3.7. Remedies

445. The trademark owner may request the competent court to enjoin the infringer from further infringing the trademark, usually under penalty of a defined sum for each violation of the said court order. An injunction may be:

- temporary if it is granted after summary or *ex parte* proceedings; or
- permanent if it is ordered after proceedings on the merits.

446. In cases of bad faith the infringer is sometimes also subject to criminal penalties (fines or imprisonment or both).

447. Damages can be claimed for the actual damage caused by the trademark infringement. Under certain circumstances in cases of bad faith not only a claim for damages may be initiated but also a claim for the total profit which the infringer made as a result of the trademark infringement.

5.4. Copyright Law

5.4.1. Definition

448. Copyright law is designed to protect the rights of the author of an original work, i.e. a work bearing the personal hallmark of its creator.

5.4.2. What Works enjoy Copyright?

449. Works which can enjoy copyright protection are original works such as literary works (all sorts of writings, irrespective of their content, purpose or form), musical works, artistic works (drawings, paintings, etc), maps and technical drawings, photographic works, other works of applied art, etc. An exhaustive list of copyrightable works, does not exist.

450. The only requirement for a work to enjoy copyright protection is that it must be original, i.e. it must bear the personal hallmark of its creator or, in other words, it must contain the expression of a creation by a given person. Works will not be deemed original when they are considered banal or present only minor differences from a prior existing work. The technical, scientific or didactic nature of the work may limit the originality to only those aspects of the work which are not determined by the content itself. Therefore, a minimum of creativity is required although the work does not have to be novel nor attain a particular artistic standard.

451. Original drawings which are sometimes used on the packaging of pharmaceutical products may have copyright protection. It remains unclear whether writings such as the user package leaflet are copyrightable; however, this cannot be excluded since some user leaflets of other products have been held to be copyright protected. To that end, the leaflets must bear the personal hallmark of the author and may therefore not be totally dictated by regulatory requirements or by the scientific content.

5.4.3. Ownership

452. In principle, the physical person who created the work is the copyright owner. Most of these rights can be assigned however, and usually certain specific rules apply to works made for hire and works created by employees. Attention should be paid however to rules protecting authors, even in an employment relationship, vis-à-vis other contracting parties.

5.4.4. No Requirement to File or Register

453. To obtain copyright protection, there is no requirement to register, publish or deposit a work, nor to provide it with a copyright notice (the sign ©). The Berne Convention expressly provides that the enjoyment and exercise of copyright may not be subject to any formality[409]. The copyright notice may be used to facilitate production in some countries but it is not mandatory in most countries since the GATT-TRIPS agreement extended the geographical scope of the Berne Convention.

5.4.5. No Costs

454. As no formalities are required, there are no extra costs connected with obtaining copyright. The protection starts as soon as the work is created without any registration nor payment.

5.4.6. Duration

455. Most copyright laws provide protection for the lifetime of the creator plus 70 years. In some cases a 50-year limit applies instead of 70 years.

5.4.7. Rights and Infringement

456. Copyright offers protection against any unauthorised reproduction and any unauthorised communication to the public, of the original work in any manner or form, including distribution, performance, broadcast, translation or adaptation. In most copyright statutes, several minor exceptions to these rights exist, concerning such things as use for personal, informational, educational and freedom of expression purposes.

457. A court order may be obtained to enjoin infringers from further infringements. Such injunctions can be temporary if they are ordered after *ex parte* or summary proceedings (preliminary injunctions), or permanent if they

---

[409] Berne Convention for the Protection of Literary and Artistic Works. Other main principles are the national treatment principle (works originating in another contracting state enjoy the same protection as those granted to its own nationals) and the principle of independence (copyright protection is normally independent of the existence of protection in the country where the work originates).

are ordered after proceedings on the merits. Damages may be awarded for past infringements, usually only in proceedings on the merits.

5.5. Supplementary Measures for Protecting Patents, Trademarks and Copyright: the Border Control Measures

458. Under European Council Regulation 3295/94 of 22 December 1994, the customs authorities may now be requested by patent, trademark or copyright owners to inspect the goods which come under their control and to block those which correspond to the applicant's description of infringing or pirated goods. The customs authorities may also intervene on their own initiative and indeed they often do so. The IP right owner has to cooperate with the customs authorities and to make a deposit to secure possible (but in practice rather improbable) claims for compensation from the third party to whom the goods belong.

459. For the pharmaceutical industry, the introduction of Regulation 3295/95 to also cover patent infringement was very important. The request for intervention needs to be sufficiently detailed so that the customs authorities can more easily detect the infringed goods.

460. These border control measures are then followed by civil or criminal proceedings. They allow the origin of the infringing activities to be traced.

5.6. Other Possible Protection

461. Other possible protection derives from rules on unfair trade practices and protection of trade secrets.

462. The rules on unfair trade practices in the pharmaceutical industry do not differ much from those in other industries and cover such things as advertising, passing off and pricing. Statutory protection of trade secrets or know-how also sometimes offers the necessary legal basis for taking action against a competitor who tries to engage in unfair competition. However, proving the unfair behaviour which is at the origin of the competitor's use of the know-how may be very difficult. Injunctions as well as damages may be claimed while criminal prosecution is also often possible.

463. Contractual protection of know-how and secrets is another possibile form of protection.

464. A final word is deserved on controls by Health Authorities. Using their broad powers, they may intervene quickly against pirated products as they and the manufacturer of the genuine product have no control over the origin and quality of such products. These authorities may even block all suspected goods and have some samples analysed. This intervention usually results from a complaint from the authentic manufacturer who can later join the criminal proceedings which often follow such blocking measures.

6. PARALLEL IMPORT OF MEDICINAL PRODUCTS

6.1. Introduction

465. The pharmaceutical industry incurs very high research and development costs. In practice, it finances extensive research and development from its own resources and only occasionally resorts to borrowing. Thus, the research costs must be recovered in the price of the extremely small number of successful products. Given the very high research costs and the low product success rate, pharmaceutical manufacturers try to maximise their profits on their successful ("blockbuster") products.

466. One of the industry's main goals is to try to restrict the activities of parallel importers who are attracted by the sometimes significant price differences for the same pharmaceutical product in two or more Member States. This happens because, unlike other industries, pharmaceutical companies do not have much control over the price of their product in most Member States. The national authorities tend to set fixed prices in view of their own national health and budgetary policies so that considerable price discrepancies exist. Therefore, parallel importing is high from those Member States which apply lower prices toward those with higher prices. This not only disturbs the distribution of the pharmaceutical manufacturers, but also negatively affects their profits.

467. Among the legal means used to impede the activities of the parallel importers are: the enforcement of intellectual property rights (primarily patents and trademarks) protecting the pharmaceutical product in question and the application of national requirements for marketing authorisations, the purpose of which includes the protection of public health.

468. Of course, as we will see, parallel importers have challenged the legality of each of these impediments before the European Court of Justice ("the Court") on the basis of Articles 28 (ex Article 30) and 30 (ex Article 36) of the Treaty establishing the European Community ("the Treaty") regarding prohibition of quantitative restrictions between Member States ("free movement of goods"). Under Articles 28 and 29 of the Treaty, quantitative restrictions on imports and exports and all measures with the same effect are prohibited between Member States.

469. However, the provisions preclude prohibitions or restrictions on imports, exports or goods in transit on specific grounds, such as the protection of industrial (read "intellectual") property and public health, but such prohibitions or restrictions may not constitute arbitrary discrimination or a disguised restriction on trade between Member States (Article 30 of the Treaty).

470. In this chapter, we do not intend to discuss in detail the rules regarding free movement of goods, intellectual property rights or marketing authorisations. Rather, we will give an overview of the principles and legislation, and discuss the Court's most significant decisions, in so far as they are relevant to parallel importing of pharmaceutical products.

6.2. Intellectual Property Rights

6.2.1. The Principle of Exhaustion of Intellectual Property Rights

471. Intellectual property rights generally confer a certain monopoly on their owner, and, consequently, offer protection against competition. They are legal exceptions to the principle of the freedom of trade. Some of the rights are granted for a limited period (e.g. patent and copyright protection), where others are granted for a possibly indefinite period (e.g. trademarks). With only a few exceptions, these exclusive rights exist at the national level and are therefore territorially limited.

472. It is clear that the unrestricted application of these mainly national intellectual property rights would run contrary to the principles of the free internal market within the Community. To avoid this undesirable outcome, the Court has developed the principle of exhaustion of intellectual property rights. This means that, in certain specific circumstances, the intellectual property owner can no longer exercise his exclusive rights, and the rights are said to be "exhausted".

473. The Court found a legal basis for the principle of exhaustion by narrowing the scope of the exception for intellectual property rights in Article 30 of the Treaty. Only derogations that are justified to safeguard the rights that constitute the specific subject matter of the invoked intellectual property right fall within that exception. Therefore, the existence of an intellectual property right recognised by a Member State's legislation does not fall within the prohibitions of the Treaty. However, the exercise of that right may be prohibited when it is not justifiable for safeguarding the specific subject matter of the intellectual property right in question[410].

474. Below, we will focus on the way this principle has been applied in general by the Court and particularly for parallel importing of pharmaceutical products. Since to date, primarily patent and trademark rights have been at the forefront of the debate, we will not discuss the application of the same principle in copyright cases.

6.2.2. Patents

475. In the *Centrafarm* case[411], the Court ruled that the specific subject matter of a patent right consists of guaranteeing the patentee, to reward the inventor's creative effort, the exclusive right to use an invention with a view to manufacturing industrial products and putting them into circulation for the first time, either directly or by the grant of licences to third parties, as well as the right to oppose infringements.

---

[410] Case C-78/70, Deutsche Grammophon Gesellschaft v Metro-SB-Grossmärkte GmbH & Co. KG , *E.C.R.*, 1971, 487.

[411] Case C-15/74, Centrafarm BV and Adriaan de Peijper v Sterling Drug Inc., *E.C.R.*, 1974, I-1147.

476. Therefore, national provisions allowing a patentee to prevent the importing of patent protected products lawfully put on the market by him or with his consent in another Member State were deemed to constitute an unjustified obstacle to the free movement of goods. In those circumstances, the patentee would be able to partition off national markets, thereby unnecessarily restricting trade between Member States. As a result, the Court ruled that patent protection may only be invoked against a product coming from a Member State where:

(i)   the product is not patentable and has been manufactured by a third party without the patentee's consent; or

(ii)   a parallel patent for the product exists, but its original owner is legally and economically independent of the original owner of the patentee's patent.

477. Furthermore, the Court ruled that price differences due to government measures in the exporting country for controlling the price of the product are irrelevant in this respect. The Court accepted that these price differences could distort competition between Member States. However, it considered that the existence of such factors could not justify a measure considered incompatible with the rules on the free movement of goods. It stated that it is the Community authorities' task to eliminate these price differences by taking steps that include harmonising national measures for controlling prices.

478. In another case, to protect the substance of a patentee's exclusive patent rights, the Court allowed the patentee to prevent the importing and putting on the market of products manufactured under a compulsory licence (justified by the clear absence of the patentee's consent in such cases)[412].

479. According to the Court, the central issue is therefore whether the patentee consented, directly or indirectly, to putting the specific product on the market in the Community.

480. In the case of *Merck v Stephar*[413], referring to its judgment in the *Terrapin* case[414], the Court underlined once more the importance of the patentee's consent:

> "... it is for the proprietor of a patent to decide, in the light of all the circumstances, under what conditions he will market his product, including the possibility of marketing it in a Member State where the law does not provide patent protection for the product in question. If he decides to do so he must then accept the consequences of his choice as regards the free movement of the product within the common market, which is a fundamental principle forming part of the legal and economic circumstances which must be taken into account by the proprietor of the

---

[412]   Case C-19/84, Pharmon BV v Hoechst AG , *E.C.R.*, 1985, 2281.
[413]   Case C-187/80, Merck & Co. Inc. v Stephar BV and Petrus Stephanus Exler , *E.C.R.*, 1981; 2063.
[414]   Case C-119/75, Terrapin (Overseas) v Terranova Industrie C.A. Kapferer & Co., *E.C.R.*, 1976, 1039.

patent in determining the manner in which his exclusive right will be exercised."

481. Therefore, if the patent owner first puts a product on the market, directly or indirectly, in a Member State, he will exhaust his rights. This is so even if the product is not patentable in the Member State.

482. In *Merck v Primecrown*, Advocate General Fennelly recommended abandoning the rule in *Merck v Stephar*, as he considered that this rule fails to guarantee the subject matter of the patent. In his opinion, one undesirable effect of applying the exhaustion rule, even in cases where no parallel patent rights exist, would be to encourage a patentee to artificially partition the Common market, i.e. through refusing to put its product on the market in those Member States that do not offer any patent protection. The patentee would do this to avoid damaging the value of its national patent rights in those Member States which protect them.

483. Despite Advocate General Fennelly's recommendations, in *Merck v Primecrown*, the Court confirmed its former position[415]. It ruled that a patentee will exhaust his rights once he puts his products on a Member State's market, unless, under either national law or community law, he is required to market his products in that Member State. In that case, the patentee cannot be deemed to have consented. Only when such a genuine legal obligation to market the patented products exists in the exporting Member State may the patentee oppose importing and marketing of those products in the State where they enjoy patent protection. However, such derogation from the principle of free movement of goods cannot be justified by the patentee's mere ethical obligation to satisfy a demand for his products in the exporting Member State even though pharmaceutical products are not patentable there. According to the Court, such an ethical obligation may be difficult to appreciate and distinguish from commercial considerations.

484. In addition, the Court confirmed its previous opinion that the patentee's lack of freedom to decide on the marketing price of his products because of price controls imposed by the public authorities in the exporting Member State, is irrelevant. This fact cannot justify the derogation from the principle of free movement of goods:

> "... although the imposition of price controls is indeed a factor which may, in certain conditions, distort competition between Member States, that circumstance cannot justify a derogation from the principle of free movement of goods. It is well settled that distortions caused by different price legislation in a Member State must be remedied by measures taken by the Community authorities and not by the adoption by another Member State of measures incompatible with the rules on free movement of goods"[416].

---

[415] Joined cases C-267/95 and C-268/95, Merck & Co. Inc. v Primecrown Ltd., *E.C.R.*, 1996, I-6285.

[416] See paragraph 47 of joined cases C-267/95 and C-268/95.

485. However, considering the lack of Community price harmonisation measures at the moment, the Court's decisions seem to further distort the pharmaceutical products market by ignoring its specificity[417].

486. While it is true that the situations addressed by the *Merck* cases are becoming rare since all Member States now recognise the patentability of pharmaceutical products, the same problem could arise with the accession of new Member States as part of the enlargement of the European Union. The Court seems to suggest that the Member States should then deal with this problem by taking the necessary transitional measures.

487. As the Court based the principle of exhaustion on Articles 28 and 30 of the Treaty, a patentee of course remains entitled to block the import of a patented product into a Member State, if that product was marketed for the first time outside the Community and the patentee did not consent to the import[418]. In that case, the principle of exhaustion does not apply.

6.2.3. Trademarks

488. In *Centrafarm v Winthrop*[419], the Court first defined the specific subject matter of a trademark right as "the guarantee that the owner of the trademark has the exclusive right to use that trademark, for the purpose of putting products protected by the trademark into circulation for the first time, and is therefore intended to protect him against competitors wishing to take advantage of the status and reputation of the trademark by selling products illegally bearing that trademark".

489. The Court thereafter applied the same exhaustion rule and held that "the exercise, by the owner of a trademark, of the right which he enjoys under the legislation of a Member State to prohibit the sale, in that State, of a product which has been marketed under the trademark in another Member State by the trademark owner or with his consent, is incompatible with the rules of the EEC treaty concerning the free movement of goods within the common market"[420].

490. Similar to the application of the exhaustion rule in patent cases, the Court ruled that it does not matter that price differences exist between the exporting and importing Member States due to government measures in the exporting Member State for controlling prices.

491. In its *Sebago* ruling, the Court confirmed that the trademark proprietor's consent must relate to the individual items for which exhaustion of

---

[417] KON, S. and SCHAEFFER, F., "Parallel imports of pharmaceutical products: a new realism, or back to basics", *E.C.L.R.*, 1997, 139.

[418] An exception to this rule concerns products placed on the market by the patentee in a country that is not a Member State but which is part of the European Economic Area, since the Agreement on the European Economic Area contains similar provisions to Articles 28 and 30.

[419] Case C-16/74, Centrafarm and Adriaan de Peijper v Winthrop, *E.C.R.*, 1974, 1183.

[420] The exhaustion rule here also applies to the European Economic Area (see above).

rights was pleaded[421]. Consent to putting separate batches of identical goods on the market is not sufficient to exhaust the proprietor's rights over other batches of goods.

492. In its *Ideal Standard* case[422], the Court first stated that the exhaustion rule applies where the owners of the trademark in the exporting and importing Member States are economically linked so that the origin that the trademark is to guarantee is the same. This is so even if the two owners are separate persons or entities. The Court then ruled that there is no exhaustion when the trademark has been (voluntarily) assigned for one or several Member States where it was registered, to a third party who has no economic link with the assignor. The consent implicit in an assignment was held not to be the consent required for the doctrine of exhaustion. For the latter, the owner of the trademark in the importing Member State(s) must be able, directly or indirectly, to determine the products to which the trademark is affixed and to control their quality, which is not the case where an economic link no longer exists.

6.2.3.1. Directive 89/104/EEC: Community-wide or International Exhaustion?

493. On 21 December 1988, the Council adopted Directive 89/104/EEC on the approximation of the laws of the Member States relating to trademarks[423]. Article 7 of the Directive implemented the principle of Community-wide exhaustion of the rights conferred by a trademark.

494. According to the first paragraph of Article 7, the trademark does not entitle the owner to prohibit its use for goods that have been put on the market in the Community under that trademark by the owner or with his consent. It is obvious that Directive 89/104/EEC covers Community-wide exhaustion. Member States questioned whether their national law could nevertheless provide for world-wide exhaustion. In other words, could the national law of a Member State provide that a trademark owner may not prevent a third party from importing trademarked products into the Community, if they were put on the market by the trademark owner or with his consent outside the Community?

495. The Court answered this much debated question in *Silhouette v Hartlauer* (16 July 1998). It confirmed the principle of Community-wide exhaustion of trademark rights[424] and ruled that Member States may not provide for world-wide exhaustion. The Court stated that if some Member States provided for world-wide exhaustion while others provided for Community-wide exhaustion, this would inevitably create barriers to the free movement of goods and the freedom to provide services.

---

[421] Case C-173/98, Sebago Inc., Ancienne Maison Dubois et Fils sa v G-B Unic (1999) not yet reported, judgment of 1 July 1999.

[422] Case C-9/93, IHT Internationale Heiztechnik and Uwe Danzinger v Ideal Standard and Wabco Standard, *E.C.R.*, 1994, 2789.

[423] First Council Directive 89/104/EEC of 21 December 1988 to approximate the laws of the Member States relating to trademarks, *O.J.*, L 040, 11 February 1989, p. 1-7.

[424] Products put on the market in the European Economic Area; Agreement on the European Economic Area, *O.J.*, L 001, 3 January 1994, 0572-0605.

496. In addition, the Court held that a trademark owner may not obtain an order restraining a third party from using its trademark within the European Economic Area based on Article 7, 1 of Directive 89/104/EEC alone. He must also invoke Article 5 of the Directive, which defines the rights conferred by a trademark.

497. Recently, in a case in the UK, *Zino Davidoff SA v A & G Imports Ltd*[425], the English court challenged the *Silhouette* ruling. A & G acquired Davidoff goods in Singapore and imported them into the UK. Davidoff opposed the importation into the UK, but A & G argued that Davidoff had not put the goods on the market subject to an effective restriction of their sale. On the basis of that argument, the English court ruled that Davidoff had consented to the importation of the goods into the EEA, stating that "there are compelling reasons why the courts should not strain to give Article 7, 1 and the *Silhouette* decision any wider effect than absolutely necessary".

498. The English court also asked the Court for a ruling on whether:

(i)   the consent of the trademark owner can be given implicitly or indirectly; and

(ii)   a trademark owner who does not impose restrictions on resale (and is permitted to by the law of the non-EEA country in which the goods are distributed) is deemed to consent to marketing the goods in the EEA.

499. The Court has not yet answered these questions on the meaning of the trademark owner's "consent" and on where the burden of proof lies. A positive answer to these questions would significantly limit the effect of the *Silhouette* ruling.

500. In the meanwhile, however, most other national courts seem to place the burden of proving that the trademark rights are exhausted, i.e. that the trademark owner has given his consent, on the party who invokes this exception (the parallel importer)[426]. Moreover, decisions indicate that this exception should be construed narrowly, and that (even) failure to prevent importing does not amount to "consent"[427].

6.2.3.2. Repackaging

501. Due to great differences in the national rules and practices on marketing pharmaceutical products in the Member States, a parallel importer may have to repackage products to import them into other Member States. The question then

---

[425]   Zino Davidoff SA v A & G Imports Ltd., CH, 1998, *D*, NO 4517; Coppenholle, K. and Lawrence, R., "The relationship between EC law and IP rights", *Cahier du Juriste*, Bruylant, No 4/1999, 74-75.

[426]   Kipling v GB Unic, Benelux Court of Justice, 6 December 1999; Appellate Court of Paris, 24 September 1997, *PIBD*, 1998, III-180; Oberlandesgericht Kalsruhe, 26 August 1998, *GRUR*, 1999, 343; Appellate Court of Milan, 22 July 1994, *GADI*, 1995, 3250; Göta Court of Appeal, 22 December 1999.

[427]   Zino Davidoff SA v M & S Toiletries Ltd, Opinion of Lord Kingarth, Outer House, Court of Session (Scotland).

arises to what extent a trademark owner may enforce its intellectual property rights in the repackaged products.

6.2.3.2.1. Case Law before Directive 89/104/EEC

502. In *Hoffmann-La Roche v Centrafarm*[428] the Court confirmed that the essential function of the trademark is "to guarantee the identity of the origin of the trademarked product to the consumer or ultimate user, by enabling him without any possibility of confusion to distinguish that product from products which have another origin". The consumer or ultimate user can then be certain that at no previous marketing stage did a third party interfere with the product so as to affect its original condition, without the trademark owner's authorisation.

503. Here, for the first time, the Court held that the proprietor of a trademark, who enjoys protection in two Member States, may prevent a product, to which the trademark has lawfully been applied in one of those States, from being marketed in the other Member State after it has been repacked in new packaging, to which the trademark has been affixed by a third party.

504. However, at the same time, the Court ruled that such prevention of marketing is incompatible with the principle of free movement of goods if:

(i)   the use of the trademark by the owner will, in view of the marketing system he has adopted, contribute to artificially partitioning the markets between Member States;

(ii)   the repackaging cannot adversely affect the original condition of the product;

(iii)   the trademark owner receives prior notice of the marketing of the repackaged product; and

(iv)   the new packaging states who repackaged the product.

505. A similar decision was reached in *Centrafarm v American Home Products*[429]. There, the Court held that the owner of a trademark registered in one Member State may prevent a third party from marketing the product even if that product was lawfully put on the market in another Member State under another mark held by the same owner in that State. However, this rule no longer applies if it can be shown that the owner of different marks has used those marks to artificially partition the markets.

506. In *Pfizer v Eurim-Pharm*[430], an importer repackaged the products of a trademark owner. He replaced the external wrapping without touching the internal packaging; he made visible the trademark affixed by the manufacturer to the internal packaging through the new external wrapping; he clearly indicated on the external wrapping that the product was manufactured by (the subsidiary of) the owner and that the product was repackaged by the importer.

---

[428]   Case C-102/77, Hoffmann-La Roche & Co. AG v Centrafarm Vertriebsgesellschaft Pharmazeutischer Erzeugnisse GmbH, *E.C.R.*, 1978, 1139.

[429]   Case C-3/78, *Centrafarm BV v American Home Products Corporation, E.C.R.*, 1978, 1823.

[430]   Case C-1/81, *Pfizer Inc. v Eurim-Pharm GmbH*, *E.C.R.*, 1981, 2913.

The Court ruled that the trademark owner could not prevent the importer from marketing those products.

6.2.3.2.2. Directive 89/104/EEC

507. Since those cases were decided, the Council has adopted Directive 89/104/EEC on the approximation of the laws of the Member States relating to trademarks[431]. Article 7 implements the principle of exhaustion of the rights conferred by a trademark. However, the second paragraph of that article states that the principle of exhaustion "shall not apply where there exist legitimate reasons for the proprietor to oppose further commercialisation of the goods, especially where the condition of the goods is changed or impaired after they have been put on the market".

508. Recently, the Court restricted the trademark owner's ability to block the activities of parallel importers by refining former decisions. In separate cases *Bristol-Myers Squibb v Paranova*[432], *MPA Pharma v Rhône Poulenc*[433] and *Eurim-Pharm v Beiersdorf*[434], the Court had to rule on this paragraph of Article 7.

509. The Court held that Article 7, 2 must be interpreted to mean that the trademark owner may legitimately oppose the further marketing of a pharmaceutical product if the importer has repackaged the product and re-affixed the trademark to it without the owner's authorisation unless:

–   the owner's reliance on trademark rights to oppose the marketing of repackaged products under that trademark would contribute to artificially partitioning the markets between Member States; this is particularly so where the owner has placed an identical pharmaceutical product on the market in several Member States in various forms of packaging, and the importer must repackage the product to market it in the importing Member State, and the repackaging does not alter the product's original condition; that condition does not imply, however, that the trademark owner must be shown to have deliberately sought to partition the markets between Member States;

–   the repackaging cannot affect the original condition of the product inside the packaging; this is particularly so where the importer has incurred no risk of affecting the product, such as: removing blister packs, flasks, phials, ampoules or inhalers from their original external packaging and replacing them in new external packaging, affixing self-stick labels to the product's

---

[431]   First Council Directive 89/104/EEC of 21 December 1988 to approximate the laws of the Member States relating to trademarks, *O.J.*, L 040, 11 February 1989, p. 1-7.

[432]   Joined cases C-427/93, C-429/93 and C-436/93, *Bristol Myers Squibb v Paranova A/S and C.H. Boehringer Sohn, Boehringer Ingelheim KG and Boehringer Ingelheim A/S v Paranova A/S and Bayer Aktiengesellschaft and Bayer Danmark A/S v Paranova A/S* (1996), *E.C.R.*, I-3457.

[433]   Case C-232/94, *MPA Pharma GmbH v Rhône-Poulenc Pharma GmbH* (1996), *E.C.R.*, I-3671.

[434]   Joined cases C-71/94, C-72/94 and C-73/94, *Eurim-Pharm Arzneimittel GmbH v Beiersdorf AG, Boehringer Ingelheim KG and Farmitalia Carlo Erba GmbH* (1996), *E.C.R.*, I-3603.

inner packaging, adding new user instructions or information to the packaging, or inserting an extra article; the national court must verify that the product's original condition inside the packaging is not indirectly affected, for example, by the fact that the external or inner packaging of the repackaged product or new user instructions or information omits certain important information or gives inaccurate information, or the fact that an extra article inserted in the packaging by the importer and designed for the product's ingestion and dosage does not comply with the method of use and the doses envisaged by the manufacturer;

–   the new packaging clearly states who repackaged the product and the name of the manufacturer in print such that a person with normal eyesight, exercising a normal degree of attentiveness, would be able to understand; similarly, the origin of an extra article from a source other than the trademark owner must be indicated so as to dispel any impression that the trademark owner is responsible for it; however, it is not necessary to indicate that the trademark owner did not consent to the repackaging;

–   the presentation of the repackaged product could not damage the reputation of the trademark and of its owner; thus, the packaging must not be defective, untidy or of poor quality; and

–   the importer gives notice to the trademark owner before the repackaged product is offered for sale, and, on demand, supplies him with a specimen of the repackaged product.

510.   It follows from the Court's decisions that in practice a trademark owner may only object to repackaging if:

–   it alters the original condition of the product,
–   it is liable to damage the reputation of the trademark or its owner,
–   the importer does not give notice to the trademark owner or does not supply a specimen of the repackaged products on demand, or
–   it does not mention who repackaged the product and the manufacturer's name.

511.   Most pharmaceutical manufacturers are not happy with this position, restricting their ability to oppose parallel imports and thus creating unequal market conditions. It has been suggested to the European Commission that patented products should be protected from parallel trade and competition encouraged in products no longer having patent protection[435].

512.   In *Pharmacia & Upjohn v Paranova* the Court ruled that Article 7 of Directive 89/104/EEC only applies where, after repackaging the product, the original trademark is reaffixed[436]. It does not apply where the parallel importer replaces the original trademark with a different one, e.g. with the trademark used

---

[435]   CALLENS, S. and VAN DER VLIES, R., "Protection of innovation in the pharmaceutical industry", *B.S.L.R.*, 1998, 10.
[436]   Case C-379/97, Pharmacia & Upjohn sa (formerly Upjohn sa) and Paranova A/S (1999) not yet reported.

by the trademark owner in the importing Member State. In that case, the respective rights of the trademark owner and the parallel importer are determined by Articles 28 and 30 of the Treaty.

513. The Court considered whether national law allows a trademark owner to prevent a parallel importer of medicinal products from replacing the trademark used in the exporting Member State with that which the trademark owner uses in the importing Member State. The Court ruled that the circumstances prevailing at the time of marketing in the importing Member State must be assessed to see whether such replacement is objectively necessary for the parallel importer to market those products in that Member State.

514. This condition of necessity will be satisfied if, in a specific case, the prohibition imposed on the importer against replacing the trademark would hinder effective access to the markets of the importing Member State, e.g. because the marketing of the products in that State under the trademark used in the exporting Member State is forbidden through specific consumer protection rules. There is no need to establish that the trademark owner deliberately sought (subjective intent) to partition the markets between Member States.

515. In contrast, the Court held that the condition of necessity will not be satisfied if the only explanation for replacing the trademark is the parallel importer's attempt to secure commercial advantage.

516. However, it has been argued that it is *never* objectively necessary to replace the trademark since the product could always be sold using only its unique generic name, i.e. its international non-proprietary name[437].

6.3. Marketing Authorisation

6.3.1. Directive 65/65/EEC: The Principle

517. As explained in Chapter 3, Article 3 of Council Directive 65/65/EEC of 26 January 1965 on the approximation of provisions laid down by law, regulation or administrative action relating to medicinal products states that a medicinal product may only be placed on the market of a Member State if:

– the competent authority of that Member State granted a (national) marketing authorisation in accordance with the Directive; or
– a Community marketing authorisation was granted in accordance with Council Regulation 2309/93 of 22 July 1993.

518. The need for a national or Community marketing authorisation before a medicinal product is placed on the market is to safeguard public health by keeping products which that are potentially hazardous to human health and life out of the market. Therefore, before a marketing authorisation is granted the applicant must file an application containing a lot of very detailed information

---

[437] MUTIMEAR, J., "Parallel wars rage on in Europe", *Managing Intellectual Property*, December 1999/January 2000, 15.

on the product, its content and its effects. The Directive harmonised these requirements.

519. Problems about parallel importing arise where national marketing authorisations for the same product have been granted in different Member States. A parallel importer cannot submit such a full application because most of the information required is not normally in his possession and would be impossible or very costly to obtain. As a result, these regulatory requirements may impede parallel imports. In a number of cases, the Court examined the extent to which provisions on marketing authorisations are compatible with the principle of free movement of goods and consequently, the extent to which they apply to parallel imports.

6.3.2. Directive 65/65/EEC: Procedures and Case Law

520. Directive 65/65/EEC places very burdensome requirements on the applicant for a marketing authorisation (see also Chapter 2 and Chapter 3). These stringent requirements (which include presenting the results of extensive tests and trials conducted on humans and animals) are fully justified for a new medicinal product (innovative product) whose safety and efficacy is not yet clear.

521. However, these requirements are no longer justifiable for:

–   parallel imports, i.e., imported products which have been put on the market in the exporting Member State (under a national marketing authorisation) by the marketing authorisation holder in the importing Member State or with his consent, or
–   generic products, i.e., products essentially similar to already authorised products put on the market by a third party, usually after expiry of the patent protection.

6.3.2.1. The Abridged Procedure

522. Article 4, 8 of Directive 65/65/EEC introduced an abridged and simplified procedure for obtaining marketing authorisations (see also Chapter 3). This procedure applies mainly to applications for (secondary) marketing authorisations for generic versions of proprietary products, but does not apply to parallel imports.

523. Under Article 4, 8, the applicant for a marketing authorisation need not provide the results of pharmacological and toxicological tests or the results of clinical trials if he can demonstrate that:

(i)   the medicinal product is essentially similar to a product authorised in the country concerned by the application, and the holder of the marketing authorisation for the original proprietary medicinal product consents to the use of the data contained in the file of the original product for examining the application; or

(ii)   the constituents of the medicinal product have a well-established medicinal use with recognised efficacy and an acceptable level of safety, by detailed reference to published scientific literature[438]; or

(iii)   the medicinal product is essentially similar to a product that has been authorised within the Community for at least six years (ten years for certain products and in certain Member States) and is marketed in the Member State for which the application is made.

524.   However, where the medicinal product is intended for a different therapeutic use from that of the other medicinal products marketed or is to be administered differently or in different doses, the results of appropriate pharmacological and toxicological tests or clinical trials must be provided.

525.   Recently, the Court defined the term "essentially similar", within the meaning of Article 4, 8 of Directive 65/65/EEC:

"... a medicinal product is essentially similar to an original medicinal product where it satisfies the criteria of having the same qualitative and quantitative composition in terms of active principles, of having the same pharmaceutical form and of being bio-equivalent, unless it is apparent in the light of scientific knowledge that it differs significantly from the original product as regards safety or efficacy"[439].

526.   A Member State's competent authority must consider these criteria when required to determine whether a particular medicinal product is "essentially similar" to an original, medicinal product.

527.   Finally, the Court ruled that a medicinal product that is essentially similar to a product that has been authorised for at least six (or ten) years and is marketed in the Member State for which the application is made, may be authorised under the abridged procedure for those therapeutic indications and dosage forms, doses and dosage schedules already authorised for that product, including those indications authorised for less than six or ten years.

6.3.2.2. Parallel Import

528.   Directive 65/65/EEC does not contain an express exception to the requirement of a marketing authorisation for parallel imported medicinal products.

---

[438]   Once these conditions are satisfied, the national authorities authorised to issue a national marketing organisation must issue the authorisation under the abridged procedure: Case C-440/93, The Queen v Licensing Authority of the Department of Health and Norgine Ltd., ex parte Scotia Pharmaceuticals Ltd., *E.C.R.*, 1995, I-2851.

[439]   Case C-368/96, The Queen v the Licensing Authority established by the Medicines Act 1968 (acting by The Medicines Control Agency), ex parte Generics (UK) Ltd, The Wellcome Foundation Ltd. and Glaxo Operations UK Ltd and Others, *E.C.R.*, 1998, I-7967.

529. In the *de Peijper* case[440], the Court ruled that only if the manufacturer shows that there are several variants of the medicinal preparation that have a therapeutic effect, would their treatment as different medicinal preparations for the purpose of authorising them to be placed on the market be justified. The public health authorities of the importing Member State must verify this. These national authorities have legislative and administrative powers to compel the manufacturer to supply certain particulars. Those particulars enable the authorities to ascertain that the medicinal preparation, which is the subject of parallel importation, is "identical"[441] to the medicinal preparation of which they have already been informed (doctrine of common origin of the products). In those cases, the parallel importer will not need to file a separate application, but will fall under the marketing authorisation already granted and will be granted a parallel import licence.

530. National authorities may check:

(i)   whether the products imported in parallel are "identical" to those that have already been registered: or

(ii)   where variants of the same medicinal product are placed on the market, whether the differences between those variants have a therapeutic effect[442].

531. However, the national authorities may only check the products' conformity. The Member State in question must have required the manufacturer or authorised importer to provide full information on the different forms in which the medicinal products are manufactured or marketed in the various Member States by either the manufacturer itself, its subsidiary or related undertakings, or undertakings manufacturing such products under licence.

532. More recently, the Court refined its definition of "identical" from the *de Peijper* case. In the *Smith & Nephew* case[443], the Court decided that a Member State's competent authority must treat the imported proprietary medicinal product as being covered by the original marketing authorisation if:

–   a proprietary medicinal product covered by a marketing authorisation in another Member State and the proprietary medicinal product for which it has already issued a marketing authorisation are manufactured by independent companies under agreements with the same licensor;

–   although not "identical" in all respects, those two products have been manufactured according to the same formulation and using the same active ingredient and also have the same therapeutic effects; and

–   there are no countervailing considerations relating to the effective protection of the life and health of humans.

---

[440]   Case C-104/75, Adriaan de Peijper, Managing Director of Centrafarm BV, *E.C.R.,* 1976, 613.

[441]   Case C-104/75, Adriaan de Peijper, *o.c.*, 613.

[442]   Case C-32/80, Criminal proceedings against J.A.W.M.J. Kortmann, *E.C.R.,* 1981, 251.

[443]   Case C-201/94, The Queen v The Medicines Control Agency, ex parte Smith & Nephew Pharmaceuticals Ltd. and Primecrown Ltd. v The Medicine Control Agency, *E.C.R.,* 1996, I-5819.

533. For the Court, it is irrelevant that the grantor of the licences for the two proprietary medicinal products in question is situated inside or outside the Community. In the latter case, the Court seems to somewhat blur the distinction between the "essential similarity test" of Directive 65/65/EEC and the more restrictive "identicality test" of the *de Peijper* case. Indeed, if the products are "sufficiently similar", the competent authority should issue a parallel import licence based on the information it already possesses.

534. However, if the competent authority concludes that the proprietary medicinal products to be imported do not satisfy these criteria, a new marketing authorisation is required. It may only issue such an authorisation in accordance with the conditions in Directive 65/65/EEC.

535. The Court further ruled that the holder of an original, properly issued marketing authorisation may challenge the validity of an authorisation issued to a competitor for a proprietary medicinal product with the same name. To do so, it the Court may rely on Article 5 of that Directive in proceedings before a national court. On that point, the Court recently decided that Community law, including Directive 65/65/EEC, does not require a Member State to establish a procedure for reviewing a national decision to revoke a marketing authorisation for a proprietary medicinal product, empowering the national court or tribunal to substitute its own assessment of the facts, particularly the scientific evidence relied on to support the decision to revoke, for the national authority's assessment of the facts[444].

536. In *Rhône-Poulenc v Licensing Authority*, one of the issues in dispute was whether or not the Community provisions on parallel importing apply only while the product concerned is covered by marketing authorisations, which are simultaneously in force[445]. The Court ruled that where a parallel importer seeks to import medicinal product X from Member State A into Member State B, he may obtain a parallel import licence from the competent authority in Member State B if:

(i)   medicinal product X is the subject of a marketing authorisation granted in Member State A and was the subject of a marketing authorisation or which has ceased to have effect in Member State B;

(ii)   medicinal product Y is the subject of a marketing authorisation granted in Member State B, but is not the subject of a marketing authorisation granted in Member State A;

(iii)   medicinal product X has the same active ingredients and therapeutic effect as medicinal product Y, but does not use the same excipients and is manufactured by a different manufacturing process, where the competent authority in Member State B is in a position to verify that medicinal product X complies with the requirements relating to quality,

---

[444]   Case C-120/97, Upjohn v The Licensing Authority established by the Medicines Act 1968 and Others , *E.C.R.*, 1999, I-223.

[445]   Case C-94/98, Rhône Poulenc Rorer v The Licensing Authority established by the Medicines Act 1968 and Others (1999).

efficacy and safety in normal conditions of use and can also ensure normal pharmacovigilance;

(iv) the marketing authorisations referred to above were granted to different members of the same group of companies and the manufacturers of medicinal products X and Y are also members of that group; and

(v) companies within the same group as the holder of the marketing authorisation for product X which has been withdrawn in Member State B continue to manufacture and market product X in Member States other than Member State B.

537. In the situations described above, the competent authority is not required to take into account that:

–   medicinal product Y was developed and introduced to provide a particular benefit to public health which that medicinal product X does not provide; or
–   that particular benefit to public health would not be achieved if product X and Y were both on the market in Member State B at the same time.

538. In this case, the Court seems to further depart from the "identicality test" of the *de Peijper* case. Unlike the *Smith & Nephew* case, the products in question even had a different formulation.

539. Finally, the Court recently confirmed that at the international level, outside the European Economic Area, there is no harmonisation or general principle of free movement of goods. Therefore goods which that are imported from outside this European Economic Area may only be authorised if all the stringent Community marketing requirements are fulfilled[446].

---

[446]   Case 100/96, The Queen and Ministry of Agriculture, Fisheries and Food, *E.C.R.*, 1999, I-1499.

7. PATIENT INFORMATION LEAFLETS AND LABELLING REQUIREMENTS

7.1. The Importance of Patient Information

540. Medicinal products are very often defined as "undesirably unsafe products"[447]. Indeed, they are in principle aimed at treating illnesses, but may nevertheless react adversely on the basis of external circumstances. A patient taking a medicinal product for the flu, may, depending on what he is eating, drinking or doing meanwhile, be confronted with side effects of the product. Often the term "adverse drug reactions" (ADR's), is used in this context which covers adverse effects, side effects, adverse events and intoxications[448].

541. Once the advantages of medicinal products are considered to be more important than its dangers, although its dangers have become unavoidable and a safe alternative does not exist, the medicinal product is considered to be an unavoidably unsafe product[449]. The patient, being the consumer of the medicinal product, may be a vulnerable victim of desinformation. It is therefore of main importance that he is duly informed on all the aspects of the product (e.g. its origin, its method of administration...) and in particular on these ADR's.

542. In this Chapter, we start with an overview of the prevailing legislation on patient information leaflets and labelling requirements. Thereupon, the aspects of product liability for medicinal products in which the requirements for the packaging leaflets or the labelling are not fulfilled will be analysed. Finally we will examine some practical and concrete implications in connection with this subject.

7.2. European Regulatory Framework

7.2.1. From a Variety of Rules to a Harmonisation

7.2.1.1. A Variety of Different Rules

543. Already Directive 65/65/EEC[450] was aimed at reaching a harmonisation between the Member States of the rules concerning the production and distribution of medicinal products and contained some stipulations on their

---

[447] BROEKHUIJSEN – MOLENAAR, A., en STOLKER, C., *Geneesmiddelen en Aansprakelijkheid, Deventer*, Kluwer, 1986, p. 30; DOMMERING – VAN RONGEN, L., "Aansprakelijkheid voor ongewenste schadelijke effecten van geneesmiddelen", *Nederlands Juristenblad*, 1989, p. 653; See also: DIAMOND, A., LAURENCE, R., "Product Liability in respect of drugs", *British Medical Journal*, 1985, vol. 290, p. 366.

[448] Cf. the scheme in VANHAECHT, C., *Onderzoek naar de impact van patiëntgerichte geneesmiddelenbijsluiters*, Universiteit Gent, J.F. & C. Heymans Instituut voor farmacodynamie en therapie, 1992, p. 62.

[449] GIESEN, D., *International Medical Malpractice Law*, Dordrecht, Martinus Nijhoff Publishers, 1988, No 1264.

[450] Directive 65/65/EEC of the Council of 26 January 1965 on the approximation of provisions laid down by law, regulating or administrative action relating to medicinal products, *O.J.*, L 369/65, 9 February 1965.

labelling requirements. Chapter IV provided for a list of elements to be mentioned on the inner and outer packaging of the medicinal product.

544. Directive 75/319/EEC[451] must be seen as a successor of the premises of Directive 65/65/EEC. This Directive contains rules on the information obligation of the packaging leaflet included with the medicinal product[452] and offers the possibility to the Member States to require other labelling obligations essential for the safety and the protection of human health[453].

545. In 1989, the scope of both these Directives has been extended to immunological medicinal products consisting of vaccines, toxins or serums and allergens[454], to radiopharmaceuticals for human use[455] and to medicinal products derived from human blood or human plasma[456]and in 1992 to homeopathic medicinal products[457]. Next to the application of the labelling provisions of Directives 65/65/EEC and 75/319/EEC, these four Directives also create some additional requirements for the labelling and package leaflets of these specific categories of medicinal products.

7.2.1.2. To a Harmonisation

546. From the concern to guarantee the well-being of the patient, i.e. to protect human health in general and to guarantee the consumer's safety, who takes the medicinal product and being aware of the possible adverse effects of desinformation, the European legislator created a specific and very well detailed harmonisation directive concerning the labelling of medicinal products. On 31 March, 1992 the Council adopted Directive 92/27 on the labelling of medicinal products for human use and on package leaflets[458].

547. It is mainly inspired by the idea that complete and understandable information on the package leaflet and/or on the labelling of the medicinal

---

[451] Directive 75/319/EEC of the Council of 20 May 1975 on the approximation of provisions laid down by law, regulation or administrative action relating to medicinal products, *O.J.*, L 147, 6 June 1975.

[452] Article 6 of Directive 75/319.

[453] Article 7 of Directive 75/319.

[454] Directive 89/342/EEC of the Council of 3 May 1989 extending the scope of Directives 65/65/EEC and 75/319/EEC and laying down additional provisions for immunological medicinal products consisting of vaccines, toxins or serums and allergens, *O.J.*, L 142, 25 May 1989.

[455] Directive 89/343/EEC of the Council of 3 May 1989 extending the scope of Directives 65/65/EEC and 75/319/EEC and laying down additional provisions for radiopharmaceuticals, *O.J.*, L 142, 25 May 1989.

[456] Directive 89/381/EEC of the Council of 14 June 1989 extending the scope of Directives 65/65/EEC and 75/319/EEC on the approximation of provisions laid down by law, regulation or administrative action relating to proprietary medicinal products and laying down special provisions for medicinal products derived fromhuman blood or human plasma, *O.J.*, L 181, 28 June 1989.

[457] Directive 92/73/EEC of 22 September 1992 widening the scope of Directives 65/65/EEC and 75/319/EEC on the approximation of provisions laid down by law, regulation or administrative action relating to medicinal products and laying down additional provisions on homeopathic medicinal products, *O.J.*, L 297, 13 October 1992.

[458] Directive 92/27/EEC of 31 March 1992 on the labelling of medicinal products for human use and on package leaflets, *O.J.*, L 113, 30 April 1992.

product is essential for the patient to allow him to use the medicinal product correctly and safely and to protect him from ADR's[459]. Therefore, the patient must be informed about how the medicinal product should be taken and, if necessary, be prevented from a potential incorrect use.

548. Moreover the use of certain medicinal products may contain an inherent risk. A warning on the labelling or package leaflet offers the possibility to the patient to make an informed decision not to expose himself to this risk[460]. Finally, a good labelling or package leaflet may play a considerable role in the selection process of the consumer while buying a specific medicinal product.

549. This European Directive has created a general framework harmonising all rules making sure that the patient, the "consumer" of the medicinal product, is completely and understandably informed on e.g. the method of administration, the composition, the side effects and the origin of the medicinal product. This Directive, repealing the articles on labelling requirements of Directives 65/65/EEC and 75/319/EEC, co-ordinates and completes the existing labelling requirements for medicinal products[461]. The Directive contains provisions on the labelling and on the package leaflet of the medicinal product.

7.2.2. Labelling and Package Leaflet Requirements

7.2.2.1. Labelling Requirements

550. This subdivision deals with the labelling requirements on the packaging of the medicinal product.

551. The Directive distinguishes the outer packaging of a medicinal product from its immediate packaging. The outer packaging is the packaging in which the immediate packaging is placed; the immediate packaging is the container or other form of packaging immediately in contact with the medicinal product[462].

552. The labelling on the medicinal product itself and on its outer packaging must facilitate a correct use of the medicinal product on the basis of complete and understandable information[463].

553. From this point of view, Article 2, 1 lists what must appear on the outer or, where there is no outer packaging, on the immediate packaging of the medicinal product:

---

[459] STRAETMANS, G., "Reclamebeperkingen voor geneesmiddelen: grenzen aan informatie?", *Het Geneesmiddel juridisch bekeken*, Mys & Breesch, 1998, Gent, p. 135-136.

[460] BALTHAZAR, T., VAN HECKE, S., "Productenaansprakelijkheid voor gebrekkige geneesmiddelen: de invloed van de informatie in de bijlsuiter op de aansprakelijkheid van de geneesmiddelenproducent", *Het Geneesmiddel, juridisch bekeken*, Mys & Breesch, 1998, Gent, p. 224; JONES, M., *Medical Negligence*, London, Sweet & Maxwell, 1996, 8-031.

[461] The specific labelling and package leaflet requirements stipulated in Directives 89/342/EEC, 89/343/EEC, 89/381/EEC and 92/73/EEC are not repealed by this Directive.

[462] Article 1,2 of Directive 92/27/EEC.

[463] Recital No 5 of Directive 92/27/EEC.

1. the name of the medicinal product, followed by the common name, where the product contains only one active ingredient and if its name is an invented name (...);

2. a statement of the active ingredients expressed qualitatively and quantitatively per dosage, unit or according to the form of administration for a given volume or weight, using their common names;

3. the pharmaceutical form and the contents by weight, by volume or by number of doses of the product;

4. a list of those excipients known to have a recognised action or effect (...);

5. the method and, if necessary, the route of administration;

6. a special warning that the medicinal product must be stored out of reach of children;

7. a special warning, if this is necessary, for the medicinal product concerned;

8. the expiry date in clear terms (month/year);

9. special storage precautions, if any;

10. special precautions for disposal of unused medicinal products or waste materials derived from such products, if appropriate;

11. the name and address of the holder of the authorisation for placing the medicinal product on the market;

12. the number of the authorisation for placing the medicinal product on the market;

13. the manufacturer's batch number;

14. in the case of self-medication, instructions on the use of medicinal products.

554. Despite this detailed enumeration of Article 2, the manufacturer[464] maintains a certain margin of freedom: the opportunity of mentioning certain particulars on the packaging may be interpreted or appreciated differently from Member State to Member State. Moreover, Member States may not prohibit or impede the placing on the market by the manufacturer of medicinal products on the grounds connected with labelling where such labelling complies with the above mentioned requirements.

555. Article 5, 2 provides, however, that Member States may require the use of certain forms of labelling making it possible to indicate the price of the medicinal product, the reimbursement conditions, the legal status for supply to the patient and the identification and authenticity (see below). In case of doubt, it is therefore recommended to be cautious that all litigious particulars appear on the packaging in order to avoid any discussion with the national authorities[465].

556. All those particulars must, in principle, appear on the outer packaging of the medicinal product or on the immediate packaging. If there is no outer packaging, there is no choice and the particulars must appear on the immediate packaging.

---

[464] Numbers 5, 7, 9 and 10 and 14, the term of 'self-medication' not being defined by the Directive.

[465] HENIN, C., *Le médicament en droit communautaire*, p. 250.

557.   There are, however, two exceptions:

-   on the one hand, the labelling requirements for the immediate packaging taking the form of blister packs (Article 3, 2) are more severe: in the case that the products are put inside an outer packaging on which all the particulars required by Article 2, 1 are already labelled they must at least contain the following essential indications:

    -   the name of the medicinal product;
    -   the name of the holder of the authorisation for placing the product on the market;
    -   the expiry date;
    -   the batch number;

-   on the other hand small immediate packaging units, on which the particulars laid down in Article 2 cannot be displayed, must only mention:

    -   the name of the medicinal product and, if necessary, the strength and the route of administration;
    -   the method of administration;
    -   the expiry date;
    -   the batch numbers;
    -   the contents by weight, by volume or by unit (Article 3, §3).

7.2.2.2. Package Leaflets

558.   The inclusion of a package leaflet in the packaging of the medicinal product clearly has a supplementary function. Article 6 states nevertheless that it is obligatory, unless all the information required to appear on the package leaflet (see below) is directly conveyed on the outer packaging or on the immediate packaging.

559.   The package leaflet must include seven categories of product characteristics[466]. It can be noticed that, as it is the case for the labelling requirements, some of the package leaflet particulars are subject to interpretation by the manufacturer. The required particulars are:

1.   information on the identification of the medicinal product. This concerns the name of the medicinal product, its qualitative and quantitative composition, its form and weight, the name and address of the holder of the authorisation for placing the medicinal product on the market and of the manufacturer, and, what is new and different from the information required to figure on the outer or immediate packaging: the pharmaco-therapeutic group or type of activity;
2.   the therapeutic indications;
3.   information necessary before taking the medicinal product, in particular: the contra-indications, appropriate precautions for use,

---

[466]   Article 7, §1 of Directive 92/27/EEC.

interactions with other medicinal products and other forms of interaction which may affect the action of the medicinal product and special warnings (...);

4.   the necessary and usual instructions for proper use (...);

5.   a description of the undesirable effects which can occur under normal use of the medicinal product and, if necessary, the action to be taken in such a case. Moreover, the patient must expressly be invited to communicate any undesirable effect not mentioned in the package leaflet to his doctor or pharmacist;

6.   a reference to the expiry date indicated on the label (...);

7.   the date on which the package leaflet was last revised.

7.2.2.3. Common Requirements

560.   Some labelling requirements are identical to some package leaflet requirements; they concern the prohibition of marketing and the readability and understandability.

561.   Article 2, 2 and Article 7, 3 provide for the inclusion on, respectively, the outer packaging and the package leaflet of "symbols or pictograms designed to clarify certain information" required by, respectively, Article 2, 1 and Article 7, 1, "and other information compatible with the summary of the product characteristics which is useful for health education, *to the exclusion of any element of a promotional nature.*"

562.   It is thus forbidden to include any element promoting the medicinal products. But on the other hand, the labelling information should be very detailed and clear, which supposes the inclusion of clarifying symbols.

563.   This illustrates the ambiguity in the distinction between labelling and marketing. The latter contains labelling whereas the opposite is not true[467].

b. Formal Requirements

564.   Article 4 stresses the importance of the particulars being "easily legible, clearly comprehensible and indelible" and following Article 8, "the package leaflet must be written in clear and understandable terms for the patient and be clearly legible...". Indeed, the particulars on the labelling being aimed at informing the patient must be clear and readable. The terms "legible", "comprehensible", and "indelible" are however subject to a large freedom of interpretation. In this view, Article 12 of Directive 92/27/EEC foresees guidelines being published, as necessary, by the Commission concerning, *inter alia*, the legibility of particulars on the labelling and package leaflet. This has improved the Readability Guideline of 24 September 1998 (see below).

---

[467]   In this respect, it is also important to mention that the Belgian Law of 25 May 1999 modifying the Law of 14 July 1991 on commercial practices and the information and protection of the consumer *(Belgian Official Gazette*, 23 June 1999) allowing, under certain conditions, comparative publicity, does however still prohibit publicity in comparative package leaflets.

565. Moreover, the particulars must appear in the official language(s) of the Member State where the product is placed on the market[468]. This means that in a country with two or even three official languages, much more information must be placed on the packaging than in a country with only one official language. Consequently, by lack of space on the packaging, the particulars in these countries will be typed in a smaller letter-type. This may enter into conflict with the "easily legible" requirement.

566. Finally, Article 4, 2 in fine and Article 8 in fine of the Directive and Section A, 3 of the Guideline on the packaging information of medicinal products for human use authorised by the community applicable since 1 September 1997 state also that, if more than one language is used, then all of the text must be in each language. The language(s) used on the label must be the same as the language(s) used in the leaflet.

567. The particulars may be indicated in several languages, provided the same particulars appear in all the languages used. It is thus required that the content of all language versions is identical. This may cause some problems of identicalness of the content: is the particular "Do not breast-feed during treatment with product X" identical to "When you are treated with product X, you must not breast-feed", to "Women treated with product X must not breast-feed" and to "Product X must not be administered during lactation"? In essence, they all mean the same, but the approach of saying it is each time different. Their identicalness can be questioned.

568. But it may even be worse: a small but important word may be dropped while translating particulars:
- "Adverse reaction X may occur *especially* in patients with condition A or following high-dose therapy" is often changed into "Adverse reaction X may occur in patients with condition A or following high-dose therapy".
- "Gastrointestinal reactions (*e.g.* nausea, diarrhoea) may occur" is often translated into "Gastrointestinal reactions (nausea, diarrhoea) may occur".

569. Or, even real translation errors may occur:
- "Otherwise, you may *experience more* side effects" translates into "Otherwise, you may *suffer increasingly* from side effects".
- "Men who could potentially father a child must use condoms *during sex when being treated with product X*" translates into "Men who could potentially father a child must use condoms *while taking product X*"!

7.2.3. Useful Recommendations for Obtaining a Marketing Authorisation

570. Under Directive 92/27/EEC[469] three Guidelines have been adopted. Whereas these Guidelines do not have any binding force, they do however

---

[468]   Article 4, 2 and Article 8 of Directive 92/27/EEC and Article 13, 1 of the Law of 14 July 1991 on commercial practices and information and protection of the consumer, as modified by the Law of 25 May 1999, *Belgian Official Gazette*, 23 June 1999.

[469]   More in particular under Article 12 of the Directive, which states: "As necessary, the Commission shall publish guidelines concerning in particular:

contain important practical recommendations for the Member States. These Guidelines are mainly for use by applicants for a marketing authorisations: one or more specimens or *"mock-ups"*[470] of the sales presentation and the package leaflet are required by Article 4, 9 of Directive 65/65/EEC and Article 10, 1 of Directive 92/27/EEC to accompany marketing authorisation applications. Applicants for a marketing authorisation should use these guidelines when preparing these *"mock-ups"*.

571. Once the Community marketing authorisation has then been issued, samples of the finalised outer and immediate packaging and of the package leaflet, should be submitted to the Commission and to the EMEA, before the actual commercialisation of the product. This mechanism ensures that any changes introduced during the decision making process have been incorporated and that the information on the label required by some Member States under Article 5, 2 of Directive 92/27/EEC and the additional information included in the label pursuant to Article 2, 2 are in conformity with the legislative provisions and are correctly presented.

572. Prior to Directive 92/27/EEC, the labels and leaflets of medicinal products were rarely a reason not to grant a Marketing Authorisation for the product, since the adoption of this Directive, the approval of leaflet and labelling has become a condition for granting a Marketing Authorisation[471]. From 1 January 1994, Member States are even bound to refuse an application for a Marketing Authorisation or for a renewal of an existing authorisation, where the labelling and package leaflet do not comply with the requirement of the Directive[472]. It is thus of considerable importance to respect the recommendations outlined in these Guidelines.

7.2.3.1. Guideline on the Excipients in the Label and Package Leaflets of Medicinal Products for Human Use

a. History and Purpose

573. This Guideline has been approved by the Pharmaceutical Committee on 12 June 1997 and applies to all applications for a marketing authorisation and to all renewals of a marketing authorisation made after 1 September 1997.

574. Samples of the finalised outer and immediate packaging and of the package leaflet must be submitted to the competent authority for approval, before commercialisation of the product.

-     the formulation of certain special warnings for certain categories of medicinal products
-     the particular information needs relating to self-medication
-     the legibility of particulars on the labelling and package leaflet
-     methods for the identification and authentication of medicinal products
-     the list of excipients which must feature on the labelling of medicinal products and the way these excipients must be indicated."

[470] A mock-up is a flat artwork design in full colour, presented so that, (following cutting and folding, where necessary), it provides a replica of both the outer and immediate packaging so that the three dimensional presentation of the label text is clear.

[471] Cf. Article 10 and 11 Directive 92/27/EEC.

[472] Article 14 Directive 92/27/EEC.

b. Excipients on the Label

575. For parenteral (or injectable) products, topical products and ophthalmic products all excipients need to be declared on the label[473]. Topical products can be taken to include all inhaled products. For all other medicinal products, only those excipients known to have a recognised action or effect must appear on the label[474].

576. The excipients listed in the Annex of the Guideline have such a recognised action or effect. Therefore, when a medicinal product contains any of these, it must be stated on the label, together with a statement such as: "*see leaflet for further information*". The label statement of these excipients should be phrased so that it does not imply that these are the only excipients present in the product; therefore, "*includes*" would be preferable to "*contains...* ".

577. However, certain excipients in the Annex only need to be declared on the label in certain circumstances related to the dose form and/or the quantity[475].

c. Excipients in the Leaflet

578. Article 7, 1 a) second indent of Directive 92/27/EEC states that all of the excipients must be declared on the package leaflet by name. Thus even those excipients which are present in very small amounts should be stated in the leaflet. Article 7, 1 c states that the package leaflet must include a list of information which is necessary before taking the product and more specifically:

- information on those excipients knowledge of which is important for the safe and effective use of the product and included in the guidelines[476]
- special warnings[477]. Therefore the fourth column in the Annex provides information corresponding to each excipient.

7.2.3.2. Guideline on the Packaging Information of Medicinal Products for Human Use authorised by the Community

a. History and Purpose

579. Council Regulation EEC/No 2309/93[478] has laid down a centralised community procedure for the authorisation of medicinal products, for which there is a single application, a single evaluation and a single authorisation allowing direct access to the EU market of a medicinal product bearing a single set of information. Following this Regulation, the legal status of medicinal

---

473   Article 2, 1, a of Directive 92/27/EEC.
474   Article 2, 1, d of Directive 92/27/EEC.
475   As specified in the third column in the Annex.
476   Article 7, 1, c, seventh indent.
477   Article 7,1 c, fourth indent.
478   Regulation No 2309/93/EEC of the Council of 22 July 1993 laying down Community procedures for the authorisation and supervision of medicinal products for human use and veterinary use and establishing a European Agency for the Evaluation of medicinal products, *O.J.*, L 214, 24 August 1993.

products for human use to be authorised by the community should be fixed in accordance with the criteria laid down in Directive 92/26/EEC[479] and the text of the label and of the labelling or package leaflet should be presented in accordance with Directive 92/27/EEC. As already indicated above Article 5(2) of Directive 92/27/EEC provides that, notwithstanding the requirement of Article 5, 1, Member States may require the use of certain forms of labelling making it possible to indicate the price of the medicinal product, the reimbursement conditions, the legal status and the identification. Furthermore Article 2, 2 of Directive 92/27/EEC provides that the labelling may include symbols or pictograms and other information compatible with the summary of the product characteristics which is useful for health education, to the exclusion of any element of a promotional nature.

580. In this respect, the Guideline on the packaging information of medicinal products for human use authorised by the community, which has been declared applicable to all market authorisation applications made after 1 September 1997, describes how the provisions in Article 2, 2 and 5, 2 apply in the case of an authorisation to be granted by the community.

581. Hereinafter, an overview is given of the most important packaging information requirements developed by this Guideline.

b. Label

582. The label text must be in accordance with the summary of product characteristics (SPC). For products authorised by the community there is a single SPC agreed at community level, which forms part of the community decision. Moreover, this text must be identical for all packs of the medicinal product throughout the community, with exception of country specific information and it must be easily legible, clearly comprehensible and indelible (see below). Some Member States require, in accordance with Article 5, 2 of Directive 92/27/EEC, some additional information, i.e. the use of certain forms of labelling making it possible to indicate the price of the medicinal product, the reimbursement conditions, the legal status for supply to the patient, the identification and authenticity: such information specific to a Member State should be accommodated on the label in a boxed area (the so-called "blue-box") to appear on one side of the pack. Each "blue-box" should only be presented in the official language(s) of the Member State concerned and should state the name of that Member State. The location of the "blue-box" on the package should be the same for all language versions. When one pack is intended for marketing in several Member States, it is preferable to have only one "blue box" on the pack. This box will contain different information in each Member State. This could be achieved in practice, for instance by printing a blank "blue box" on this pack into which a sticker with the appropriate Member State information can be securely affixed. When in exceptional circumstances, this can not be achieved, each "blue box" should have the same dimensions and appear, whenever possible, on the same side of the pack.

---

[479]   Directive 92/26/EEC of the Council of 31 March 1992 concerning the classification for the supply of medicinal products for human use, *O.J.*, L 113, 30 April 1992.

583. According to Article 2, 2 of Directive 92/27/EEC Member States may also require the inclusion of some additional optional information. In this way certain expressions, including symbols and pictograms, have become established in some Member States for expressing certain items of information. As these particulars are only known or relevant in some Member States, they should also appear in the "blue-box".

c. Package Leaflet

584. The label text requirements concerning the SPC conformity, the language and the additional information (here, according to Article 7, 3 of Directive 92/27/EEC), apply also on the text of the package leaflet.

585. Some holders of community marketing authorisations have requested that there be also a contact point identified in the package leaflet and on the label. This would normally be the holder of the Community marketing authorisation. However where the marketing authorisation holder wishes to add the name of another (local) contact point, the 'local representative' may be indicated in the leaflet by name, address and telephone number and in the "blue box" on the label.

586. "Local Representative" shall be taken to mean: any private *or* legal person established in the Community charged, through a civil contract with the marketing authorisation holder, with representing him in a defined (geographical) area; this contract excluding any transfer of any responsibility imposed on the marketing authorisation holder.

587. Designation of a local representative can not be a requirement but, when the holder of a Community marketing authorisation wishes to identify a local representative, in the leaflet, all of the Community must be covered so that the consumer in each Member State has equivalent access to a local representative.

d. Presentation of the Medicinal Product

588. When presenting a range of pack sizes for a medicinal product, the principles of rational use of medicinal products should be taken into consideration. This means that the appropriate range of pack sizes should be chosen in accordance with the duration of treatment and the posology in the SPC and not in accordance with local traditions or prescription habits.

589. For practical and linguistic reasons holders of Community marketing authorisations are likely to present the medicinal product packaging in several linguistic and/or "national" versions (i.e. with the relevant boxed areas). In such case the logo, format, layout, style, colour scheme and pack dimensions must be identical for all the versions throughout the Community.

7.2.3.3. Guideline on the Readability of the Label and Package Leaflet of Medicinal Products for Human Use

a. History and Purpose

590. This Readability Guideline has been adopted by the Pharmaceutical Committee on 24 September 1998 and has come into effect in January 1999. It provides guidance, for use by applicants for a marketing authorisation, on the factors which influence readability.

b. Readability of the Label and Package Leaflet

591. In this section of the Guideline it is outlined how the readability of the label and the package leaflet can be reached by providing recommendations on the print size and type, the print colour, the syntax (i.e. the use of short sentences, different fonts, upper and lower case, the length of the words, the number of clauses per sentence, punctuation, the use of bullet points) and the paper size and weight and encouraging – but not obliging – the use of braille.

592. It should however be noted that the primary objective of this Guideline is ensuring that the label and package leaflet are readable It may, therefore, be acceptable for a package leaflet, which achieves an acceptable level of performance in a readability test, to deviate from the guidance in this section.

c. Label Format

593. This section gives guidance on how each item listed in Article 2, 1 of Directive 92/27/EEC, which must appear on the label (outer packaging) of the medicinal product, should be expressed.

d. Leaflet Format

594. In this section, guidance is given on the content of the package leaflet, its headings, its style, the order of the items, the product ranges and on the package leaflets for products not for self-administration. Further information compatible with the SPC and useful for health education may also be included provided it is not of a promotional nature. Annex 1,a provides, then, an example of a model leaflet together with further guidance on its content in Annex 1 b. In Annex 2 there is an example of a method for use by applicants for a marketing authorisation to test readability before finalising a package leaflet.

7.2.4. Conclusion

595. The patient information leaflets and labelling requirements are thus subject to a harmonised European regimentation. Following to Article 14 of Directive 92/27/EEC national authorities were bound to adapt their national legislation to this Directive before 1 January 1993[480].

---

[480] In Belgium, Directive 92/27/EEC has been implemented into Belgian Law trough a modification of 2 Royal Decrees and a publication of a third one:

596. Anyway, it remains important to know what requirements are foreseen by the different Member States, whereas in the light of the Dassonville jurisprudence[481] a national provision on labelling may have direct effect in the sense of Article 28 of the Treaty of Amsterdam[482] (old Article 30 EC Treaty).

597. Moreover, although Article 5, 1 of Directive 92/27/EEC states that Member States may not prohibit or impede the placing on the market of medicinal products within their territory on grounds connected with labelling where such labelling complies with the requirements of the Directive, Article 5(2) of the Directive provides however for the possibility for the Member States to require the use of certain forms of labelling making it possible to indicate:

- the price of the medicinal product;
- its reimbursement conditions;
- its legal status for supply to the patient;
- its identification and authenticity[483].

7.3. Practical Implications

598. In this section, some practical problems resulting from the application of the labelling and package leaflet requirements will be analysed. First of all it will be examined under which circumstances the manufacturers of medicinal products might be held responsible for not duly informing the patient of undesirable effects which can occur under normal use of the medicinal product.

7.3.1. Liability for not Warning the Patient?

599. In general, the consumer of a product may expect this product to be in conformity with the applicable legislation. For medicinal products, this means that the patient may expect that the legislation on labelling requirements and package leaflets is respected; he may thus expect that the undesirable effects, contra-indications and special warnings are mentioned on the packaging of the medicinal product and/or on its package leaflet. As it has already been explained above, Directive 92/27/EEC requires mentioning several special warnings on the packaging of the medicinal product, whereas the contra-

---

- the Royal Decree on the registration of medicinal products of 3 July 1969, *Belgian Official Gazette*, 10 July 1969.
- the Royal Decree on the manufacturing and distribution of medicinal products of 6 June 1960, *Belgian Official Gazette*, 22 June 1960.
- the Royal Decree determining the conditions whereby medicinal products for human use may be given in the form of samples of 11 January 1993, *Belgian Official Gazette*, 30 January 1993.

[481] E.C.J., Case 8-74 Dassonville, 11 July 1974, , *E.C.R.*, 1974, 837.

[482] Treaty of Amsterdam of 2 October 1997 amending the Treaty on the European Union, the Treaties on the creation of the European Communities and some other acts, signed at Amsterdam, *O.J.*, C 340, 10 November 1997.

[483] Annex 1 to Directive 92/27/EEC: Label information which may be required by Member States (under Article 5, 2 of Directive 92/27/EEC) gives an overview of the label information required by the different Member States concerning the labelling of those four elements.

indications, appropriate precautions, interactions with other medicinal products, special warnings and undesirable effects must be mentioned on the package leaflet.

600. Not warning the patient for undesirable side effects, or not informing him on one of the above mentioned special warnings or precautions, might result in the liability of the manufacturer of the medicinal product. The legal basis for this liability can be found in the legislation on product liability[484]. Following this legislation, the manufacturer of a medicinal product might be held responsible for not warning the patient adequately on the packaging or the package leaflet of the medicinal product for the risks inherent in the product, provided these risks caused damage to the patient.

601. The patient will, however, have to prove that the damages effectively result from the inadequate information. Moreover, the "development risk" theory can safeguard the liability of the manufacturer. This development risk means that the manufacturer of medicinal products is not held responsible if he can prove that at the moment he commercialised the product, it was not possible for him to be aware of the defect on the basis of scientific and technical knowledge. The European Directive on product liability[485] itself does not offer this possibility of defence for the manufacturer of medicinal products, but it foresees that member states can exclude manufacturers from liability on the basis of this "development risk"[486].

602. Although this means of defense for the manufacturer should be interpreted very strictly: the impossibility for the manufacturer to be aware of the defect must be absolute; no manufacturer should have been able to develop the defect. Moreover, the manufacturer of medicinal products has the continuing duty to adapt the package leaflet following the evolution of the knowledge of the risks; once a risk becomes clear and known, the manufacturer has the obligation to put the necessary warnings on the package leaflet or even to stop the commercialisation of the product[487].

7.3.2. Exception on the Information Obligation for Therapeutic Reasons

603. The question is, however, whether the package leaflet should really mention all known risks. The doctrine is divided on this point: some authors are of the opinion that the manufacturer has a large information obligation, following from which he must inform the patient "even about relatively rare and

---

[484] See discussion of the *Halcion*-case, Hof Arnhem (NL), 7 July 1987 and Hoge Raad, 30 June 1989, in BALTHAZAR, T. and VAN HECKE, S., "Productenaansprakelijkheid voor gebrekkige geneesmiddelen: de invloed van de informatie in de bijsluiter op de aansprakelijkheid van de geneesmiddelenproducent", in *Het Geneesmiddel, juridisch bekeken*, 1998, Gent, p. 232-233.

[485] Directive 85/577/EEC of the Council of 25 July 1985 on the approximation of the laws and regulations of the Member States on Product Liability, *O.J.,L.*, 210/29, 7 August 1985.

[486] Besides many other Member States, the Belgian Law on Product Liability used this possibility in its Article 8, e).

[487] See BALTHAZAR, T., VAN HECKE, S., *l.c.*, p. 238.

unpredictable known side effects"[488]. Others warn against overwhelming the patient with information on side effects in such a way that the package leaflet becomes a horror list of side effects which heavily affects consumers' compliance[489].

604. Following the informed consent theory the physician is, in exceptional circumstances, allowed not to inform the patient on certain side effects or even, on the diagnosis. The "informed consent" theory determining what information on the medicinal product a physician has to provide to the patient, is, however, only useful for the communication of the indications of the medicinal product, but not of its risks.

605. Also with regard to the indications, Article 7, 2 has created an important but controversial exception to the list of particulars to mention on the package leaflet: "The competent authorities may decide that certain therapeutic indications shall not be mentioned in the package leaflet, where the dissemination of such information might have serious disadvantages for the patient". This clause was introduced in Directive 92/27/EEC to avoid circumstances where a patient might not have been informed of the diagnosis (cancer, for instance) and would learn about it when reading the leaflet of the medicinal product which has been prescribed. Such a fundamental departure from the principle that the package leaflet should be in accordance with the SPC and from the principle that patients should be fully and correctly informed about the medicinal products they are using should obviously only occur in exceptional circumstances.

606. For the risks or side effects, however, the Directive does not make any distinction on grounds of their frequency, seriousness or possible impact on the patient. Article 7, 1, e even stipulates that the package leaflet must contain a "description of the undesirable effects which *can* occur under normal use of the medicinal product ..." This means: all reported effects must be mentioned unless it can be shown they are not produced by the medicinal product. Not informing the patient on risks or undesirable effects of the medicinal product, even for therapeutic reasons, might thus very often lead to the responsibility of the manufacturer of medicinal products. Some[490] deplore, therefore, that the exception on the information obligation for therapeutic reasons only concerns certain therapeutic indications, but not certain undesirable effects. One can also demand if it is really necessary to inform the patient on all the possible undesirable effects, as this might create adverse reaction with some patients.

---

[488] See BALTHAZAR, T. and VAN HECKE, S., *l.c.*, p. 234, where they refer to MEDAWAR, C., *Patient package inserts, drug information and liability issues: a consumer view*, in *Patient package insert as a sort of drug information*, BOGAERT, M., VANDER STICHELE, R., KAUFMAN, J. and LEFEBVRE, R. (ed.), Amsterdam, Excerpta medica, 1989, 84.

[489] See BALTHAZAR, T. and VAN HECKE, S., *l.c.*, p. 234, where they refer to KAHLSTORF, J., "Liability issues: an industry viewpoint", in *Patient package insert as a sort of drug information*, BOGAERT, M., VANDER STICHELE, R., KAUFMAN, J. and LEFEBVRE, R. (ed.), Amsterdam, Excerpta medica, 1989, 90.

[490] BALTHAZAR, T. VAN HECKE, S, *l.c.*, p. 236.

7.3.3. Prescription or Marketing of a Medicinal Product Based on an Indication not Mentioned on the Packaging

607.   The indications for which the medicinal product have been registered must be mentioned on the package leaflet. In what way should the persons prescribing (see 7.3.3.1.) or marketing (see 7.3.3.2.) medicinal products take into account these indications? Is it allowed to prescribe or market a medicinal product for an indication not mentioned on the package leaflet?

7.3.3.1. Prescription of Medicinal Products

608.   In principle physicians are competent to prescribe all medicinal products: magisterial medicinal products, officinal medicinal products and industrial preparations. Moreover, they are not bound by the indications for which the medicinal product is registered. This means that, whereas under normal circumstances they indeed prescribe the medicinal product for the indication for which it has been registered, the physician also has the possibility to prescribe the medicinal product for a non-registered indication, for example on the basis of scientific information.

609.   Finally, the physician may even be obliged to prescribe a medicinal product for a non-registered indication, *i.e.* when the optimal treatment of the patient requires it. The physician must offer his patients the best possible treatment and is not allowed to refuse this under the pretext that the registration holder has not asked for the registration of his medicinal product for such treatment.

610.   Prescribing a medicinal product for a non-registered indication does, however, put some extra obligations on the physician, such as informing the patient, being sure of the applicability of the medicinal product, etc. The applicable medicinal professional standard as touchstone for the evaluation of his medical action becomes thus more exigent in this case[491].

7.3.3.2. Marketing of Medicinal Products

611.   As opposed to the prescription of a medicinal product its marketing may refer exclusively to the indication for which it has been registered[492]. In this respect, it will be important for the marketing of the medicinal product to follow securely the evolution of the medicinal product and more particularly the

---

[491]   Cfr. LISMAN, J.A., "Mag een geneesmiddel worden voorgeschreven buiten de geregistreerde indicatie?", *Nl. T. Gez.*, 1999, No 5.

[492]   Cfr. LISMAN, J.A., *l.c.*, No 4; cfr. also Article 9 of the Belgian Law on Medicinal Products of 25 March 1964, *Belgian Official Gazette*, 17 April 1964, which stipulates that every marketing for a non-registered medicinal product is forbidden. Article 4, §1 of the Belgian Royal Decree of 7 April 1995 stipulates the same and §2 of this Article states that all elements of the marketing of a medicinal product must be in conformity with the information mentioned on the scientific package leaflet and with the elements of the file accepted at the moment the medicinal product was registered.

changes made to the labelling or package leaflet. Each time the marketing authorisation holder makes an amendment to the contents of documents such as they existed at the moment of the decision on the marketing authorisation of the medicinal product or to the documentation proposed by the marketing authorisation holder of the medicinal product, such variations must be approved by the competent authority.

612. Changes to an aspect of the labelling or the package leaflet covered by Directive 92/27/EEC on the labelling of medicinal products for human use and on package leaflet and not connected with the summary of product characteristics are examined in accordance with Article 10, §3 of that Directive, *i.e.* the proposed changes are submitted to the authority competent for marketing authorisation. If the competent authority has not opposed a proposed change within 90 days following the introduction of the request, the applicant may put the change into effect.

613. Changes to an aspect of the labelling or package leaflets of medicinal products for human use connected with the summary of product characteristics follow two different procedures foreseen for variations. These procedures for approval of the variations are set out in two different Commission Regulations of 10 March 1995: Commission Regulation (EEC) No 541/95 concerning mutual recognition variations and Commission Regulation (EEC) No 542/95 for centralised variations.

614. These procedures are very complex and may take a long time. Consequently, it may not always be clear from which moment the new registration will hencefrom have effect and will allow to refer to the new characteristics of the medicinal product in its marketing. For example, in the case of a mutual recognition procedure, Article 7, 4 of the Regulation 541/95/EEC states that each competent national authority concerned by the variation application takes a decision in conformity with the proposed decision. These national decisions will then take effect on the date agreed by the competent national authority of the reference Member State and the marketing authorisation holder in consultation with the other national authorities concerned.

7.3.4. Reuse of Medical Devices

615. As the scope of this book is limited to medicinal products, medical devices do not really come up for consideration. It is nevertheless worth mentioning that the label of the medical devices plays an important role as it frequently leads to problems in hospitals. The term "medical device" concerns irradiation apparatus, computer and measurement equipment, catheters, bandages, plasters and needles.

616. Following the annexes of the European Directives 93/42/EEC concerning medical devices[493], 90/385/EEC on active implantable medical devices[494] and 98/79/EC on in vitro diagnostic medical devices[495], the manufacturer of medical devices must mention on the label and in the instructions for use of the medical devices the information needed to use the devices safely and to identify the manufacturer. One of the particulars the label must bear is, where appropriate, the indication that the device is for single use.

617. It should, however, be said that many hospitals, by lack of financial means, do reuse medical devices, even if they are for single use[496]. In order to determine who will be held liable on the basis of the Product Liability Legislation for damages caused to a patient by a treatment with reused medical devices, it will be important to know if the hospital reusing the medical devices is to be considered as a 'manufacturer' of the medical devices or not. At first sight the hospital sterilising and reusing medical devices is not to be considered as 'manufacturer' under the Directive concerning medical devices. The term 'manufacturer' means:

> *"the natural or legal person with responsibility for the design, manufacture, packaging and labelling of a device before it is placed on the market under his own name, regardless of whether these operations are carried out by that person himself or on his behalf by a third party."*[497]

Directive 93/42/EEC continues by saying that

> *"the obligations of this Directive to be met by a manufacturer also apply to the natural or legal person who assembles, packages, processes, fully refurbishes and/or labels one or more ready-made products and/or assigns to them their intended purpose as a device with a view to their being placed on the market under his own name. This subparagraph does not apply to the person who, while not a manufacturer within the meaning of the first subparagraph, assembles or adapts devices already on the market to their intended purpose for an individual patient."*

618. There is no doubt that the sterilisation of medical devices for single use falls within the meaning of the term "fully refurbishing". Moreover, it will be difficult to defend that the reuse of medical devices *for single use* can be

---

[493]   Directive 93/42/EEC of the Council of 14 June 1993 concerning medical devices, *O.J.*, L 169, 12 July 1993, p. 1: Article 13 of Annex I.

[494]   Directive 90/385/EEC of the Council of 20 June 1990 on the approximation of the laws of the Member States relating to active implantable medical devices, *O.J.*, L 189, 20 July 1990, p. 17: Article 15 of Annex I.

[495]   Directive 98/79/EC of 27 October 1998 on in vitro diagnostic medical devices, *O.J.*, L 331, 7 December 1998, p. 1: Article 8 of Annex I.

[496]   LIERMAN, S., "De Richtlijnen en het Koninklijk Besluit medische hulpmiddelen en de gevolgen van technische voorschriften op de aansprakelijkheid van de fabrikant en het ziekenhuis", *T. Gez./Rev. Dr. Santé*, 1998 – 1999, p. 367.

[497]   Article 1, f of Directive 93/42/EEC concerning medical devices.

considered as assembling or adapting the devices *to their intended purpose*. Finally the hospital reusing medical devices will put them at the disposition of patients or physicians. This is an action which can be considered as placing the devices on the market under its own name.

619. Although there is no certainty about it, it can be said that, on the basis of the above mentioned arguments, the hospital sterilising medical devices for single use will have to respect the obligations resulting from the Directive concerning medical devices. This is the *ratio legis* of the Directive, i.e. only devices that do not compromise the safety and health of patients, users and other persons when properly installed, maintained and used in accordance with their intended purpose, may be placed on the market. If a medical device is sterilised in contrast with the manufacturers' indications, the safety is not longer guaranteed. The device need to follow the CE-labelling procedures before it can be used by patients or physicians[498].

---

[498]   LIERMAN, S., "European Product Liability in a medical context and single use devices", *Proceedings of the World Medical Law Congress I,* 13th World Congress on Medical Law, Helsinki, 6-13 August 2000, p. 669.

8. LEGAL ISSUES RELATING TO ECOMMERCE IN THE EUROPEAN HEALTH-CARE SECTOR

8.1. Introduction

620. In the *United States* (US), the health-care sector was quick to respond to a growing demand by providing health-related information on-line as well as directly advertising and selling medicines on the Internet.

621. In Europe, the health-care sector has well understood the opportunities associated with ecommerce at business-to-business level[499]. By contrast, it is more hesitant to engage in business-to-consumer electronic transactions and there are currently a number of regulatory restrictions in this respect. The situation is, however, rapidly changing and a growing number of operators in the European health-care sector (including pharmacists, drug wholesalers and pharmaceutical companies) are currently exploring the issues associated with providing health-related information to, and electronic contracting with, consumers (*i.e.*, doctors and patients).

622. This Chapter examines the most important legal issues for the European health-care sector when considering introducing ecommerce solutions at the retail level, namely: (1) the applicable law; (2) the establishment of providers of Information Society services; (3) free movement of Information Society services; (4) provision of health-related information on-line; (5) advertising of medicinal products; (6) distribution of medicinal products; (7) electronic contracts; and (8) jurisdiction of courts. There are, of course, other important legal issues which should be considered before starting ecommerce operations in Europe which are not covered by the present article.

623. The article is largely exploratory. It is based on the fundamental assumption that the "real world" will run ahead of European legislation. It is submitted that the situation in third countries such as the US, the dramatic growth of the Internet and the strong desire of consumers to receive health-related information on-line will create irresistible pressures for a liberalisation of the European regulatory environment applicable to ecommerce in the health-care sector. This pressure for reform will also come from the fact that clear limits exist to the jurisdiction of, and the technical means which are available to, the enforcement authorities when taking an aggressive jurisdictional line on Internet websites which are based outside their national territories but available to national Internet users. Even those operators who are currently the most hesitant to use the Internet as a commercial tool in Europe (*e.g.*, the drug wholesalers and the pharmacists) are likely to gradually find that there are several advantages associated with providing health-related information on-line and generally developing ecommerce solutions at the retail level.

---

[499] Such opportunities include lower purchasing costs, reductions in inventories, lower cycle times, more efficient and effective customer service, lower sales and marketing costs and new sales opportunities.

8.2. Applicable Law

624. The first legal issue to consider when developing ecommerce solutions at the retail level is the law applicable. As illustrated below, the examination of this issue leads to the conclusion that it is relatively easy for consumers using the Internet to rely on the laws of the country where in they reside.

625. As far as *contractual obligations* are concerned, the issue of the applicable law is governed by the rules of the 1980 *Rome Convention*[500] which has been or will be adopted by all Member States as an instrument of international law. In the absence of choice of law, the contract will be governed by the law of the country with which it is most closely connected. This usually means that on-line contracts are governed by the law of the country of the consumer's habitual *residence*. Moreover, the *Rome Convention* contains special rules for consumer contracts[501]. Accordingly, any choice of law cannot deprive the consumer of the protection afforded to him by mandatory rules such as consumer protection laws. This right is subject to certain conditions[502], which are almost always fulfilled in the case of Internet communications. Finally, the *Rome Convention* allows for additional protection by the so-called "*lois de police*".

626. The law applicable to *non-contractual* issues has not been extensively harmonised by private international law conventions[503] and will generally be determined by national conflict rules which follow the *lex loci delicti* principle (*i.e.*, the law of the place where the crime or wrong doing took place). In *criminal matters*, this principle is complemented by the rule that the offence is presumed to have taken place on a particular national territory when any of the factors that constitute the offense have taken place on that territory. For instance, the mere reception in a Member State of an Internet message which constitutes a criminal offence, usually suffices to render the criminal laws of that State applicable. Similarly, in *civil matters*, the application of this principle most often means that the non-contractual issues associated with Internet websites are governed by the laws of the country where the consumer resides.

627. The impracticalities for industry regarding compliance with the *lex loci delicti* principle (or the "country of reception" principle) has led the European

---

[500] Convention on the Law Applicable to Contractual Obligations, see *O.J.*, C 27/34, 1998.

[501] A consumer contract is defined under the *Rome Convention* as a contract the object of which is the supply of goods or services to a person (the consumer) for a purpose which can be regarded as being outside his trade or profession.

[502] Such conditions are: (1) the conclusion of the contract was preceded by specific invitation or advertising in the country of habitual residence of the consumer and the consumer has taken in that country the steps necessary on his part for the conclusion of the contract; or (2) the other party or his agent received the consumer's order in that country; or (3) the contract is for the sale of goods and the consumer travelled from that country to another country and there gave his order, provided that the consumer's journey was arranged by the seller for the purpose of inducing the consumer to buy.

[503] For instance, only *France, Finland, Luxembourg, The Netherlands* and *Spain* have ratified the 1973 Hague Convention of 2 October 1973 on the Law Applicable to Products Liability,

Commission to propose[504] the principle that the law of the country where an Information Society service provider (*e.g.*, the website of a pharmaceutical company) is established, controls the legality of its activities. Despite this principle, it is far from certain that the *Ecommerce Directive* will later substantially reduce the industry's burden of having to comply with different legal regimes for their websites. Indeed, the "country of origin" principle of the *Ecommerce Directive* is not applicable in the following areas which are particularly important for the European health-care sector: (1) copyrights, neighbouring rights, and industrial property rights; (2) the freedom of the parties to choose the law applicable to their contracts; (3) the permissibility of unsolicited commercial communications by electronic mail; and (4) contractual obligations concerning consumer contracts[505]. This later exception is particularly relevant for the on-line trade of medicines which necessarily involves a contractual relationship between the seller and the patient.

628. The *Ecommerce Directive* also does not aim to establish additional rules of private international law relating to conflicts of law. In other words, it does not aim to change the above-mentioned rules of the *Rome Convention* or of other private international conventions. The *Ecommerce Directive* and is not a substitute for such rules.

629. Industry has very little chance of escaping from the obligation of having to comply with the "country of reception" principle under the so-called draft *Rome II Convention*, which aims to regulate the law applicable to non-contractual obligations at the Community level[506]. Indeed, the current text of the draft *Rome II Convention* mandates the applicability of the law of the country where the harmful conduct occurred in all cases where parties do not have their habitual residence in the same country. This typically means the country where the action or omission that caused the damage has its effect. Transposed to the world of Internet communications, this often means that the law of the country where the Internet user resides will be applicable since this place often coincides with the place where the damage has its effect. If the obligation arises from unfair practices and the parties do not have their habitual residence in the same country, the law of the country where the unfair practices affect collective consumer interests would apply. It would, however, be possible for the parties to choose the law applicable to non-contractual obligations, although the issue of how this freedom of choice should be exercised in an on-line environment is not addressed by the draft *Rome II Convention* and is not entirely clear yet.

---

[504]   *Directive Regarding Certain Legal Aspects of Information Society Services in Particular, Electronic Commerce, in the Internet Market*, see Council of the European Union, Brussels, 28 February 2000, 98/0325 (COD), 14263/1/99 REV 1 (not yet published). Since the European Parliament has recommended approving the above Council's Common Position unchanged, it is likely that the Ecommerce Directive will be adopted soon and that the final text will be very similar to the Council's Common Position.

[505]   See Article 3(3) and Annex 1 of the Ecommerce Directive.

[506]   Draft Convention on the Law Applicable to Non-contractual Obligations, Brussels, 9 November 1998, 12356/98.

8.3. Establishment of Providers of Information Society Services

630. The second legal issue to consider when developing ecommerce solutions in the European health-care sector is the establishment of providers of Information Society services. This issue is covered by the *Ecommerce Directive* which is applicable to all Information Society services. This includes any service normally provided for remuneration, at a distance, by electronic means and at the individual request of a recipient of such services. Accordingly, the on-line sale of medicines and other consumer products is an Information Society service within the meaning of the *Ecommerce Directive*. By contrast, the *Ecommerce Directive* does not apply to the direct marketing of medicines by telefax/telephone or to the sale of medicines *via* radio and television broadcasting services. It is also arguable that the *Ecommerce Directive* does not apply to the on-line sale of medicines by "push" technologies such as Internet webcasting since such services are not provided at individual request. Clearly, the provision of services by doctors and other health-care professionals off-line is excluded from the scope of the *Ecommerce Directive,* even if such services involve the use of electronic devices and/or electronic mail. Finally, the *Ecommerce Directive* does not apply to providers of Information Society services who are established in third countries (*i.e.*, non-EU Member States) and its provisions are without prejudice to other Community acts that are generally applicable to Information Society services[507].

631. The *Ecommerce Directive* sets out that each Member State must ensure that the Information Society services provided established on its territory comply with the relevant national provisions applicable in the Member State in question. It also prohibits Member States from requiring Information Society service providers to seek authorisation to provide services, with respect to which they would not require authorisation if the services were provided off-line. This is, however, without prejudice to the rules of the *Licensing Directive*[508] which enables the Member States to subject providers to general authorisation requirements, in certain circumstances.

632. Once a provider of Information Society services is established, it should disclose certain basic information concerning its operations[509]. According to the *Ecommerce Directive*, the information in question must be easily, directly and

---

[507] In particular, the Electronic Signatures Directive (Directive 1999/93/EC); the Unfair Contracts Terms Directive (Directive 93/13/EEC); the Distance Selling Directive (Directive 97/7/EC); the Misleading and Comparative Advertising Directive (Directive 84/450/EEC, as amended); the Sale of Consumer Good Directive (Directive 1999/44/EC); the Consumer Credit Directive (Directive 87/102/EEC); the General Product Safety Directive (Directive 92/59/EEC), the Product Liability Directive (Directive 85/374/EEC, as amended); the Data Protection Directive (Directive 95/46/EC); and the Directive on the Processing of Personal Data and the Protection of Privacy in the Telecommunications Sector (Directive 97/66/EC).

[508] Directive 97/13/EC of the European Parliament and of the Council of 10 April 1997 on a common framework for general authorisations and individual licences in the field of telecommunications services, *O.J.*, L 117/15, 1997.

[509] Such as: (1) its name and geographic address; (2) the details of the service provider, including its electronic mail address; (3) the trade register in which the service provider is entered and its registration, if applicable; (4) the particulars of the relevant supervisory authority, if applicable; and (5) the VAT identification number, if applicable.

permanently accessible whilst the service is being provided. Prices are to be indicated clearly and, in particular, it must be indicated whether they are inclusive of tax and delivery costs.

633. Finally, under the *Ecommerce Directive*, commercial communications and advertisers must be clearly identifiable. Service providers must ensure that unsolicited commercial communications are clearly identifiable as such and must consult regularly and respect available "opt-out registers" for such commercial communications[510]. That does not prevent Member States with an "opt-in system"[511] for unsolicited commercial communications from keeping it at national level.

8.4. Free Movement of Information Society Services

634. If a provider is properly established, its services should be able to freely circulate within the Community. The *Ecommerce Directive* clearly sets out in this respect that a Member State may not restrict the freedom to provide Information Society services from another Member State. Member States are, nevertheless, entitled and empowered to take measures to derogate from the "free movement" principle (after notifying the Commission and the other Member States involved) for a certain number of reasons, including public policy, the protection of public health and the protection of consumers. It is clear that a large number of measures and restrictions which are applicable in the European health-care sector are justified by the need to protect public health and patients.

8.5. The Provision of Health-Related Information On-line

635. Health-related information is amongst the most frequently accessed information on the Internet. In the US, Internet users have access to information concerning medicinal products, including indications and counter-indications, medical effectiveness, dosage, side effects and sometimes even price[512]. The Drug Marketing, Advertising and Communications (DDMAC) Division of the US Food and Drug Administration (FDA) monitors the Internet, routinely "surfing" the web, receiving company submissions and following up complaints from companies, health-care professionals and consumers. Companies are required to submit information regarding the web sites to the FDA at the time such information is posted on the Internet.

636. The provision of health-related information in Europe is currently not as developed as in the US. However, the pace of change in the medical environment is accelerating and European manufacturers are often obliged to warn consumers about the risks associated with their products. It is remarkable in this respect that the March 2000 European Commission Proposal for a

---

[510]   Some Member States have opted for the minimum solution of banning commercial communications when the consumer expressly states that he does not want to receive commercial communication ("opt-out").

[511]   Other Member States require prior consent of the consumer before a commercial communication can be sent to him ("opt-in system").

[512]   See Impact of Electronic Commerce on the European Pharmaceutical Sector, Ashurts, Norris, Crisp, November 1998, p. 10.

General Product Safety Directive[513] requires all producers, including pharmaceutical companies, to provide consumers with relevant information to enable them to assess the risks inherent in a product throughout the normal or reasonably foreseeable period of its use[514]. Member States must lay down rules on penalties applicable to infringements of this requirement.

637. In view of the above, it is likely that it will become increasingly unacceptable for a patient to be denied access to information that could help him assess and discuss with health-care professionals alternatives to his prescribed treatment. It is therefore essential when considering introducing ecommerce in the European health-care sector to determine clearly whether, and which sort of, health-related information could be provided on-line.

638. Currently, this issue is essentially not regulated at Community level. In particular, the *Advertising Directive*[515] mentions that its scope does not extend to the factual, informative announcements and reference materials relating notably to adverse reaction warnings as part of general drug precautions, trade catalogues and price lists, provided that they include no product claims and statements relating to human health and diseases.

639. The *Ecommerce Directive* will not introduce major changes to the current situation. Indeed, since it is only applicable to Information Society services which are provided for remuneration, it does not, in principle, apply to the mere on-line offering by pharmaceutical companies and other operators of health-related information, except arguably if the websites concerned are also used to provide services against, or for, remuneration. The *Ecommerce Directive* will, nevertheless, remove certain barriers to the development of cross-border services and to commercial communications which doctors and other health-care professionals might provide or offer on the Internet.

640. The competitive pressures arising from the situation applicable in the US have led the European pharmaceutical industry to ask for a more liberal approach towards the provision of health-related information on the Internet. The first step in this direction is the acknowledgement, by the Pharmaceutical Committee in April 1999, that a distinction between "legal information" and possibly "illegal advertising" should be drawn[516]. Accordingly, the Pharmaceutical Committee suggests that the "*unmodified and unabridged publication on the Internet of* (certain) *information on medicinal products which has been authorised by competent authorities*[517] *should normally not be considered as advertising*". This position could tentatively be interpreted as meaning that the provision of information on medicines over the Internet does

---

[513] Proposal for a Directive of the European Parliament and of the Council on general product safety, COM(2000) 139 final.

[514] See Article 5 of the Proposal for a Directive of the European Parliament and of the Council on general product safety, *o.c.*

[515] Council Directive 92/28/EEC of 31 March 1992 on the advertising of medicinal products for human use, *O.J.*, L 113/13, 1992.

[516] Pharmaceutical Committee - Information on the outcome of the 47th meeting, 15-16 April 1999 at http:\\dg3.eudra.org.

[517] E.g., the Summaries of Product Characteristics, the Patient Information Leaflets of medicinal products and Public Assessment Reports of medicinal products.

not constitute direct-to-consumer advertising, but rather indirect communications and should, therefore, not be regulated by the provisions of the *Advertising Directive* but instead by those of the *Labelling Directive*[518]. Under this interpretation, appropriate information about prescription-only medicinal products could be provided over the Internet.

641. The European Commission initiative entitled "*eEurope an Information Society for All*"[519] arguably marks a turning point for provision of health-related information on-line in Europe. The Commission focuses on ten priority areas, one of them being to maximise the use of networking and smart technologies for health monitoring, information access and health-care. As a follow-up to this initiative, the Commission will soon adopt an *eEurope 2002 Action Plan*[520]. The draft *eEurope 2002 Action Plan* proposes ambitious targets to bring the benefits of the Information Society within reach of all Europeans. It sets out the deadline of end-2001 to establish a set of criteria for health-related websites and of end-2002 to ensure that all health-care providers have health telematics infrastructure in place. The Commission will also draft a Communication which will be entitled "*Legal Aspects of eHealth*" and which will review current legislation which has a bearing on the area and seek to build industry confidence to enter the market[521].

8.6. Advertising of Medicinal Products

642. In the US, direct-to-consumer advertising of prescription drugs is allowed, although the content of such advertisements is strictly controlled. In that country, the use by wholesalers and chains of pharmacists of ecommerce solutions is already at an advanced stage. This contrasts with the situation in the Community where the advertising of medicinal products is subject to the following regulatory restrictions:

643. The *Classification Directive*[522] which lays down general criteria to differentiate between prescription-only and non-prescription products but leaves the door open to divergences between Member States as to whether products must be used under prescription.

644. The *Labelling Directive* which requires the labelling of medicinal products and leaflets to comply with a set of criteria and that all such information must be easily legible, indelible and labelled in all the official language(s) of the Member States where the products are placed on the market[523].

---

[518] Council Directive 92/27/EEC of 31 March 1992 on the labelling of medicinal products for human use and on package leaflets, *O.J.*, L 113/8, 1992.

[519] eEurope 2002 - An Information Society for All - Communication on a Commission Initiative for the Special European Council of Lisboa, 23 and 24 March 2000 at http:\\\www.ispo.cec.be.

[520] See eEurope - An Information Society for All - Draft Action Plan at http:\\\www.ispo.cec.be.

[521] See eEurope 2002 - An Information Society for All - Draft Action Plan, op. cit.

[522] Council Directive 92/26/EEC of 31 March 1992 concerning the classification for the supply of medicinal products for human use, *O.J.*, L 113/5.

[523] Member States could only exempt this requirement if the products are not intended to be delivered to the patient for self-administration.

645. The *Television Without Frontiers Directive*[524] which strictly prohibits the television advertising for prescription-only medicinal products and medical treatments in the Member State within whose jurisdiction the broadcaster falls and the teleshopping of any medicinal product and medical treatment[525].

646. The *Advertising Directive* which extends this prohibition to the advertising of non-registered medicinal products and the direct-to-consumer advertising of all prescription-only products by any other means, including on-line communications.

647. The *Comparative Advertising Directive*[526] which prohibits any misleading advertisements and allows on-line comparative advertising under certain strict conditions.

648. The advertising of medicinal products is covered by a plethora of international resolutions[527] and Codes of Practice relating to the marketing of medicinal products in general[528], or the advertising of medicinal products in particular[529].

649. The *Distance Selling Directive*[530] which allows the Member States to prohibit any distance selling of medicinal products on their territory[531].

650. A large number of Member States have seized the opportunity created by the *Distance Selling Directive* and, more generally, by the EC Treaty and have adopted stricter requirements relating to the advertising of medicinal products. For instance, in *Germany*, certain indications specified in the *Advertising Directive* cannot be advertised to the general public. It is only in countries such as *The Netherlands* and the *United Kingdom* that there are generally no prohibitions on the distance selling (including on-line sales) of non-

---

[524]   Council Directive 89/552/EEC of 3 October 1989 on the coordination of certain provisions laid down by law, regulation or administrative action in Member States concerning the pursuit of television broadcasting activities, *O.J.*, L 298/23, 1989. This Directive was amended by Directive 97/36/EC, *O.J.*, L 202/60, 1997.

[525]   Pharmaceutical companies may, however, sponsor television programmes and promote the name or the image of the company but not of specific prescription-only medicinal products or medical treatments.

[526]   Council Directive 84/450/EEC of 10 September 1984 relating to the approximation of the laws, regulations and administrative provisions of the Member States concerning misleading advertising, *O.J.*, L 250/17, 1984. This Directive was amended by Directive 97/55/EC, *O.J.*, L 290/18, 1997.

[527]   E.g., the WHO Resolution on cross-border advertising, promotion and sale of medicinal products using the Internet of 11-16 May 1998, WHA51.9.

[528]   E.g., the IFPMA Code of Pharmaceutical Marketing Practices and the EFPIA Code of Practice for the Promotion of Medicines.

[529]   E.g., the European Code of Standards for the Advertising of Medicines.

[530]   Directive 97/7/EC of the European Parliament and of the Council of 20 May 1997 on the protection of consumers in respect of distance contracts, *O.J.*, L 144/19, 1997.

[531]   Such restrictions include the reservation of the supply of certain (or all) categories of medicinal products to authorised retailers (e.g., pharmacists), prohibitions to advertise certain medicines remedying certain diseases as identified by the national health authorities, the prohibition to advertise licensed medicines by certain means (e.g., software) and the obligation to use the national language in all communications relating to goods and services.

prescription medicines. In *The Netherlands*, advertising of non-prescription medicinal products, including reimbursed medicines, is allowed in all media. However, only indications which are suitable for self-medication and which are included on a list annexed to the Code of Public Advertising of Medicines are allowed[532]. In the *United Kingdom*, sales of non-prescription medicines through pharmacies only account for about 73% of all purchases of such medicines[533].

651. In view of the current situation prevailing in the US, the European pharmaceutical industry has urged the European Commission to permit the advertising of non-prescription medicines. As mentioned above, the Pharmaceutical Committee considers that certain health-related information could be provided on-line. The Committee, however, takes the view that the provision of such information would be prohibited if there is a "*hidden inducement*" *to promote the (...) product*". The existence of a "hidden inducement" must be verified on a case-by-case basis, taking into account the overall presentation of the information. Similarly, the exchange of electronic messages needed to answer a specific question about a particular medicinal product must not be considered as advertising, unless this constitutes unsolicited correspondence, which may in turn constitute "illegal advertising".

652. It is particularly difficult for pharmaceutical companies and other operators in the European health-care sector to put the opinion of the Pharmaceutical Committee into practice. It is very easy to determine that information on a medicinal product which is contained on a web page constitutes "illegal advertising". For instance, it follows from the *Television Without Frontiers Directive* that advertising may include any form of announcement for self-promotional purposes by a public or private undertaking. As a result, even if the information on a web page is not designed to promote a particular medicinal product, is could easily be determined that it is designed to promote the pharmaceutical company which controls the website. In this case, the entire content of the web page would be considered as advertising, subject to the above-mentioned specific restrictions applicable to the advertising of medicinal products. An electronic message sent to a particular recipient is generally considered as a private communication and not as advertising. It can even be argued that an e-mail message sent to a particular recipient which contains some form of advertisement does not constitute advertising. On the other hand, any electronic message which is not specifically targeted to a particular recipient could easily be considered as advertising.

653. Following the above position of the Pharmaceutical Committee, a series of discussions and meetings between the officials of the European Commission, the Member States and the professionals of the health-care sector have taken place[534]. As a result of such meetings, the Pharmaceutical Committee has agreed that the Commission services will circulate a questionnaire on advertising and ecommerce requesting comment before 15 July 2000.

---

[532] See Economic and Legal Framework for Non-prescription Medicines in Europe, AESGP, June 1997.

[533] Ibidem.

[534] See Brainstorming on advertising and electronic commerce for medicinal products, *o.c.* See also information on the outcome of the 49th meeting of the Pharmaceutical Committee, 22-23 March 2000 at http://dg3.eudra.org.

8.7. Distribution of Medicinal Products

654. The distribution of medical products in the Community and in third countries is largely driven by the restrictive regulatory regime in which it currently operates.

655. First, Community law on medicinal products prohibits placement of medicinal products on the market of a Member State without a marketing authorisation. This obligation extends to the partial manufacture of medicinal products and packaging operations. By contrast, under Community law, there is no prohibition to export medicinal products to third countries which have not received a marketing authorisation. In those circumstances, it is up to the Member States to determine the conditions for the export of medicinal products to third countries[535].

656. Second, the *Wholesale Distribution Directive* subjects the wholesale distribution of medicinal products to the holding of a licence[536]. Whereas the holder of a manufacturing authorisation has, in principle, the right to distribute by wholesale the products covered by that authorisation, certain Member States require it to obtain a separate authorisation in order to do so.

657. Third, the price of medicinal products is heavily regulated and there are currently important variations in the levels of price of medicinal products across the Member States.

658. Finally, the pharmacist's monopoly is still prevalent in a number of Member States such as *Austria, France, Germany, Italy* and *Spain.* In these countries, only qualified pharmacists are entitled to sell medicines (including most often all non-prescription products, herbal, with certain exceptions, and homeopathic medicines). This prohibition is reinforced in a number of Member States by prohibitions of chains of pharmacies and prohibitions to advertise and promote pharmacies (*e.g.,* in *Germany* and *Italy*).

659. This restrictive situation is unlikely to change as a result of the *Ecommerce Directive,* as it is not applicable to the legal requirements relating to the delivery and the transport of goods, including the distribution of medicinal products[537].

660. There is also currently much less pressure in Europe towards the creation and the encouragement of Internet pharmacies. In fact, a number of professionals are concerned about the availability of products on the Internet. This is probably due to the fact that the increase brought by the Internet in the ability of patients to acquire medicines from abroad might have an impact on parallel prices. There is, however, a general consensus on the need to develop a realistic legislative framework which takes clear account of the global nature of

---

[535] Fore more developments, see Overview of the Export of Pharmaceuticals from the European Union, Alexandre Mencik, New World Health, June 1997.

[536] See Article 3, 1 of Council Directive 92/25/EEC of 31 March 1992 on the wholesale distribution of medicinal products for human use, *O.J.,* L 113/1, 1992.

[537] See Recital 21 of the Ecommerce Directive.

recent changes in technology. There is also a recognition that the trend for pharmacies to come together as a purchasing group and acquire their products needs directly from manufacturers and for wholesalers to acquire chains of pharmacies is growing[538]. This trend is likely to encourage manufacturers to engage in significant wholesale and retail distribution of their products.

8.8. Electronic Contracts

661. A number of important regulatory issues related to electronic contracts in the European health-care sector are already covered by existing pieces of Community legislation.

662. First, the *Distance Selling Directive* requires the provision of specific information prior to the conclusion of the contract such as the price of the goods, including all taxes, any delivery costs, the cost of using distance communication and the period for which the offer or the price remains valid. It also grants to consumers a general right to withdraw from a contract during seven working days and to request cancellation and refund of a payment where fraudulent use has been made of their payment cards.

663. Second, the *Sales of Good Directive*[539] establishes the basis of a uniform set of fair rules governing the sale of medicines and consumer products and the non-conformity to contractual specifications.

664. Third, the *Electronic Signatures Directive*[540] establishes an enhanced legal status for electronic signatures[541] and certification services[542]. It provides that a signature cannot be legally discriminated against solely on the grounds that it is in electronic form. If a certificate and the service provider that issues the certificate meet certain essential requirements, electronic signatures must be legally recognised in the same manner as hand-written signatures.

665. The *Ecommerce Directive* does not harmonise the issue of contract formation and leaves it to the Member States to individually regulate this issue. Instead, it requires Member States to take the necessary action to enable electronic contracts to be used. Member States must carry out a systematic review of existing national rules and identify all possible impediments that, in

---

538	See Impact of Electronic Commerce on the European Pharmaceutical Sector, *o. c.*, at 4.
539	Directive 1999/44/EC of the European Parliament and of the Council of 25 May 1999 on certain aspects of the sale of consumer goods and associated guarantees, *O.J.*, L 171/12, 1999.
540	Directive 1999/93/EC of the European Parliament and of the Council of 13 December 1999 on a Community framework for electronic signatures, *O.J.*, L 13/12, 1999.
541	An electronic signature is a signature in digital form that is attached to, or logically associated with, data. It is used by a signatory to indicate his approval of the content of the data. Electronic signatures based on "public key cryptography" are called digital signatures. The Electronic Signatures Directive does not cover electronic signatures within closed groups.
542	The recipient of an electronic message often wants to know the identity of the electronic signatory. Such information can be given by the signatory himself or it can be provided by a third party, such as a certification authority. Such providers authenticate the signature using a public key and are responsible for issuing a certificate. They can be described as mutually trusted third parties who certify that the key belongs to the party which is using it.

practice, may create obstacles for the use of electronic contracts, with certain exceptions, or result in such contracts being deprived of legal effectiveness or validity.

666. Under the *Ecommerce Directive*, except when otherwise agreed between professionals or for contracts concluded exclusively by exchange of electronic mail, a service provider must furnish specific information prior to the conclusion of the contract[543] and must promptly send an acknowledgement that an order has been received; the order and the acknowledgement of receipt are deemed to be received when the parties to whom they are addressed are able to access them. In addition, the provider must make available to the recipient of the service effective and accessible technical means to identify and correct input errors before the placing of the order. In all cases, contract terms and general conditions must be made available to the recipient in a way that allows him/her to store and reproduce them.

8.9. Jurisdiction of Courts

667. The last legal issue to consider when developing business-to-consumer ecommerce solutions in Europe is the jurisdiction of courts.

668. Currently, this issue is essentially governed by the 1968 *Brussels Convention*[544].

669. Under the *Brussels Convention*, in civil and commercial matters relating to a contract for sale of goods, including the on-line sale of medicines, the court of the area where the delivery of the goods was, or should have been, carried out has jurisdiction. In matters relating to tort, delict or quasi-delict (*e.g.*, copyright infringement), the *Brussels Convention* sets out that the court of the area where the event giving rise to the damage occurred (usually the business seat of the wrong doer) or the court of the area where the damage was sustained (usually the habitual residence of the victim) has jurisdiction. Thus, the victim often has choice of jurisdiction and may proceed to "forum shopping".

670. In July 1999, the European Commission proposed the replacement and update of the *Brussels Convention* by a Council Regulation with a view to taking account, *inter alia*, of new forms of commerce[545]. This Proposal is currently under review by the European Parliament and the Council.

671. The proposed Council Regulation makes it clear that, in the case of the sale of goods, the court of the area where, under the contract, the goods were, or

---

[543]   In particular, the different technical steps to follow to conclude the contract; whether or not the concluded contract will be filed by the service provider; whether the contract will be accessible; the technical means for identifying and correcting input errors; and the languages offered for the conclusion of the contract.

[544]   *Convention on Jurisdiction and Enforcement of Judgements in Civil and Commercial Matters*. The consolidated version of the *Brussels Convention* was published in *O.J.*, C 27/1, 1998. The *Brussels Convention* served as a model for the drafting of a similar Convention between the Member States and the States belonging to the European Free Trade Area (the *Lugano Convention*), see *O.J.*, L 319/9, 1998.

[545]   Proposal for a Council Regulation (EC) on jurisdiction and the recognition and enforcement of judgements in civil and commercial matters, COM(1999)348 final.

should have been, delivered has jurisdiction, unless the parties to the contract have explicitly agreed on the area of performance. It also removes an ambiguity in the interpretation of the *Brussels Convention* and makes clear that, in matters relating to tort, delict or quasi-delict, the court of the area where the harmful event occurred or there is a risk of it occurring has jurisdiction. Transposed to the Internet environment, this often grants victims the possibility of suing in another country than the one where the owner of the website is established. The proposed Council Regulation also establishes the principle that the courts of the Member States in which intellectual property rights (*e.g.,* patents and trade marks) are deposited or registered, have exclusive jurisdiction.

672. Finally, the proposed Council Regulation reinforces the protection granted to consumers. In particular, in the case of any consumer contract[546], including a contract for the sale of medecines, the consumer could sue in the courts of the State of his domicile, provided that the contract has been concluded with a person who pursues commercial or professional activities in such State and directs such activities towards that State, and the contract falls within the scope of such activities. Thus, if a pharmaceutical company sells medicines *via* an interactive website which is accessible in the State of the consumer's domicile, such company could be sued by the consumer in that State. By contrast, if the consumer simply has knowledge of the possibility to buy medicines *via* a passive website accessible in his country of domicile, this will not, in principle, trigger the protective jurisdiction.

673. Despite the fact that industry is generally opposed to the above protective jurisdiction and has strongly argued that it could be exposed to the risk of being sued before the courts of each country where its website can be consulted, it is very likely that the protective jurisdiction will remain in the Council Regulation. Industry is therefore currently trying to amend the proposed Council Regulation to specify clearly the conditions under which service providers would be considered as directing their web sites to the State of the domicile of the consumer and to be able to freely determine by contracts with customers the choice of jurisdiction[547].

8.10. Conclusion

674. The industry has probably lost the battle to introduce the "country of origin" principle regarding the applicable law and the jurisdiction of courts for ecommerce solutions in the European health-care sector. This has essentially two consequences for the actors of the European health-care sector. First, they must ensure that their websites comply with at least all the relevant laws of all the countries specifically targeted by such sites (and it may be necessary to ensure compliance with the laws of all the countries from which such sites are accessible). Second, pharmaceutical companies and other actors must contend with potential litigation in every country where relevant Internet users reside.

---

[546] The proposed Council Regulation defines a consumer contract differently than under the *Brussels Convention* as a contract concluded by a person, the consumer, for a purpose which can be regarded as outside his trade or profession.

[547] See revision of the *Brussels Convention*, Position on the European Parliament reading, Brussels, 17 February 2000 (unpublished).

675. The fact that the "country of reception" principle is likely to reign in the on-line environment may not be much of a concern for the European health-care sector as opposed to other industry sectors. Indeed, under the current and future regulatory framework, Member States are entitled to adopt and have indeed adopted a large number of regulatory restrictions on the "free movement" of health-related on-line services. As a result, operators must often ensure in all cases that their websites comply with the strict national rules related to a number of issues such as the advertising of medicines in the countries targeted by such advertising.

676. What is of much more concern for the European health-sector is to succeed in developing an "industry-friendly" regulatory framework for ecommerce activities at the retail level. One of the most crucial challenges in this respect is to succeed in dismantling the regulatory barriers that currently inhibit the development of: (1) the provision of health-related information on-line; (2) the advertising of; and (3) the on-line distribution of medicines.

677. It is submitted that there exists an appropriate intermediate approach between doing business as usual without changing the current regulatory barriers and introducing major changes which could indeed have certain negative consequences for public health and patients.

678. The opinion of the Pharmaceutical Committee is an illustration of this intermediate approach. This opinion should, nevertheless, be complemented by additional regulatory measures designed to ensure the necessary degree of legal certainty. In this respect, it seems appropriate to consider that pharmaceutical companies and other actors should be allowed to present on their websites all information for the patients which constitutes labelling of medicinal products within the meaning of the *Labelling Directive* and which has been authorised by the competent health authorities. In return for complying with the strict regulations on the labelling of medicinal products, such companies and actors should be granted a clear authorisation to provide this information, including price, on the Internet and it should be clear that this activity does not constitute, in any case, a "hidden inducement" to promote medicines. Similarly, there should be a recognition that on-line messages and sale offers relating to medicines can reach consumers in other Member States where the product is not registered or available on medical prescription only as long as there is no evidence that this is the real purpose of the activity considered (*i.e.*, the website is not clearly targeting consumers in that country). Finally, the purchase of non-prescription medicines by Internet users by way of websites should be allowed and the purchased products should be authorised under the regime applicable to the private import of pharmaceutical products[548].

---

[548]   In this respect, the European Court of Justice has ruled that the importation of medicinal products (which are authorised in the Member State of importation and are available in that State without or without prescription) that were purchased in a pharmacy in another Member State by a private individual for his personal needs cannot be prohibited by national provisions, such provisions being incompatible with ex-Article 36 of the EC Treaty, see Case C-215/87, Schumacher v. Hauptzollant Frankfurt am Main-Ost, *E.C.R.*, 1990, 317; Case C-62/90, Commission v. Federal Republic of Germany, *E.C.R.* 1992, I-2575.

679. When changing the current regulatory restrictions, it would be appropriate to adopt a constructive approach to the introduction of ecommerce solutions in the European health-care sector. This requires focusing on adopting enabling legislation and remaining confident in the ability of the European health-care sector to adopt appropriate self regulatory responses and voluntarily approaches to regulatory concerns. For instance, appropriate statements and warnings on websites and/or "click wrap" procedures might be appropriate means to address a number of legitimate regulatory concerns. There are also certain technology tools (*e.g.*, cookies) which could be used to comply with the current price disparities across Member States and to ensure that the prices of medicinal products vary depending on the location of the customer who has accessed the website concerned. Possible sanctions on misleading information and advertising practices under existing general rules on unfair trade practices should also not be overlooked.

680. It is submitted that the European health-care sector will only succeed in developing the appropriate regulatory framework for ecommerce if it proposes innovative technical and regulatory solutions that satisfy the traditions of such sector as well as the legitimate concerns of the health enforcement authorities.

9. PRICING AND REIMBURSEMENT ISSUES OF MEDICINAL PRODUCTS

9.1. Introduction

681. The market of medicinal products has specific characteristics, which distinguish it from other consumption products. The consumer of medicinal products, for example, has little or no influence on the choice of a medicinal product on prescription. Rather, it is the physician who has that therapeutic freedom[549]. Because only specific medicinal products are efficient for particular diseases, the products are not always interchangeable. Further, the social security organisms bear the medical costs (or a substantial part of it) instead of the patient. It is, thus, understandable that the Member States try to restrict those costs by declaring measures relating to the price and the reimbursement of medicinal products. These social security measures aim at allowing physicians to provide the best possible treatment without resulting in excessive costs. Because of the competency of the Member states for social security measures, the national markets can be rather disparate, thus delaying the integration of the national markets into one community market.

9.2. Control of Prices and the Free Movement of Medicinal Products

682. Member States have the capability to regulate the price control of medicinal products. Essentially, those measures are compatible with community law, if their regulating result does not burden the free common market excessively[550]. Article 3 of the Directive 65/65/EEC stipulates:

> *"No medicinal product may be placed on the market of a Member State unless a marketing authorisation has been issued by the competent authorities of that Member State in accordance with this Directive or an authorisation has been granted in accordance with Regulation (EEC) No 2309/93 of 22 July 1993 laying down Community procedures for the authorisation and supervision of medicinal products for human and veterinary use and establishing a European Agency for the Evaluation of Medicinal Products (1). The provisions of this Directive shall not affect the powers of the Member States' authorities either as regards the setting of prices for medicinal products or their inclusion in the scope of national health insurance schemes, on the basis of health, economic and social conditions".*

683. Article 28 (old Article 30) of the EEC-Treaty forbids every measure of equal action as a quantitative restriction, which can obstruct, direct or indirect,

---

[549] DEBOYSER, P., "Le marché unique des produits pharmaceutiques", *Rev. Marché Un. Eur.* 1991, p. 148, No 43.

[550] In the same sense: CASSIA, P. and SAULNIER, E., "L'autorisation de mise sur le marché des médicaments à usage humain dans l'union européenne", *Rev. Marché Commun et de l'Union européenne* 1996, 754; DEBOYSER, P., "Le marché unique des produits pharmaceutiques", *Rev. Marché Un. Eur.* 1991, p. 150, No 44.

actual or potential, the free market between Member States[551]. It is important that such measures do not contain an unequal treatment of products imported from other Member States. Further, measures may not make the distribution of imported products more difficult than the distribution of national products[552]. Therefore, price regulations, applicable without any distinction on internal and imported products, are as such not a measure of equal action as a quantitative restriction, but they can become one when the distribution of imported products becomes more difficult than that of the internal products[553]. Regulations with different price setting rules, which obstruct the distribution of imported products, are also forbidden. Also forbidden are measures that impose only for imported products minimum or maximum prices or special requirements, which can obstruct importation, or measures that give less profitable prices than for internal products, or measures that renders the possible increase of the price of the imported product impossible, or measure that put the prices, on the basis of the cost price or quality, at such a level that an import obstruction arises[554].

684.   The Court of Justice has emphasised important principles regarding the price and the reimbursement of medicinal products in two-mile stone decisions: i.e. the *Roussel*-case[555] and the *Duphar*-case[556] . In the *Roussel-case* regarding the price setting of medicinal productsthe Court condemned the regulation that imposes different price systems for domestic and imported medicinal products as a measure having an effect equivalent to a quantitative restriction, forbidden by Article 28 (old Article 30) of the Treaty.   In the *Duphar*-case regarding the reimbursement of medicinal products the Court stated that that in view of the special nature of *"the trade in pharmaceutical products, namely the fact that social security institutions are substituted for consumers as regards responsibility for the payment of medical expenses, legislation of the type in question cannot in itself be regarded as constituting a restriction on the freedom*

---

[551]   See E.C.J., 11 July 1974, Dassonville, case No8/74, *E.C.R..,*1974, p. 813-874. See also Commission v. Germany, case No 62/90, *E.C.R.* 1992, 2611; Schumacher-case No 215/87, *E.C.R.* 1989, 617; cases Kohl and Decker, Court of Justcie 28 April 1998, *T. Gez. / Rev. Dr. Santé* 1998-99, 56 (note CALLENS, S.).

[552]   See for example: Commission v. Belgium, case No 249/88. Although the Court of Justice did, not condemn Belgium for its low prices as a result of a series of price freezes, it did condemn various contracts concluded between the Belgian Minister of Economic affairs and producers and importers that allowed the latter to obtain higher prices in return for a commitment to engage in investment, employment and exportation. See also Commission v. Italy, case No 56/87, *E.C.R.* 1988, 2919. ANDERSEN, R., "La réglementation des prix des médicaments. Heurts et malheurs d'une réglementation", p. 14 .

[553]   E.C.J., 6 November 1979, Danis, case No 16/79 to 20/79, *E.C.R.*, 1979, p. 3327-3342.

[554]   "Although a maximum price applicable without distinction to domestic and imported products does not in itself constitute a measure having an effect equivalent to a quantitative restriction, it may have such an effect, however, when it is fixed at a level such that the sale of imported products becomes, if not impossible, more difficult than that of domestic products. A maximum price, in any event in so far as it applies to imported products, therefore constitutes a measure having an effect equivalent to a quantitative restriction, especially when it is fixed at such a low level that, having regard to the general situation of imported products compared to that of domestic products, dealers wishing to import the product in question into the Member State concerned can do so only at a loss" (E.C.J., Tasca, case No 65/75, *E.C.R.*, 1976, 291).

[555]   E.C.J., 29 November 1983, case No 181/82, *E.C.R.,* 1983, p. 3849-3871.

[556]   E.C.J., 7 February 1984, case No 238/82, *E.C.R.*, 1984, p. 523-545.

to import guaranteed by Article 30 of the Treaty if certain conditions are satisfied[557].

685. When Member States adopt economic measures on the marketing of medicinal products they want to control public health expenditure. These measures may, however, also promote efficiency in the production of medicinal products and public health by ensuring the availability of adequate supplies of medicinal products at a reasonable cost. Such measures may encourage research and development into new medicinal products, on which the maintenance of a high level of public health within the European Community ultimately depends. However, those measures can control direct and indirect the prices of medicinal products because of the inadequacy or absence of competition in the medicinal products market and the limitations on the range of products covered by national health insurance systems. Disparities in such measures can hinder or distort intra-Community trade and directly affect the functioning of the common market on medicinal products[558]. Therefore, there was a need of an European Directive that allows Member States to have a price and reimbursement system for medicinal products without hindering the free movement of medicinal products These are the aims of the Directive 89/105/EEC of 21 December 1988 relating to the transparency of measures relating the pricing of medicinal products for human use and their inclusion in the scope of national health insurance systems[559].

9.3. Directive 89/105/EEC and the Price of a Medicinal Product

686. Directive 89/105/EEC requires a certain transparency in the way competent authorities make reasoned decisions in pricing and reimbursement. Thus, the Directive provides all concerned a tool to verify that the decision is in accordance with community regulation[560].

687. The transparency of the price is essential. Every medicinal product must have his own price, calculated on the real costs and a transparent calculation procedure[561]. Normally, the manufacturers or the importers fix a price for every medicinal product. The competent authorities will evaluate this price in the light of the measures of controlling the prices. Several elements will be taken into consideration: costs of research and development, raw materials, publicity, transport, importation costs, etc. However, it is clear, that only reasons of public health can be grounds for refusal or withdrawal of the authorisation to market a medicinal product. A Member State cannot refuse an authorisation because the price of the medicinal product seems too high[562].

---

557   E.C.J., 7 February 1984, case No 238/82, *E.C.R.*, . 1984, p. 523-545.
558   See also Commission Communication on the Single Market in Pharmaceuticals, 25 November 1998, COM (98) 588.
559   Directive 89/105, *O.J,.* L 40/8, 1989.
560   HANCHER, L., "Pricing of medicinal products parallel imports and competition", p. 5.
561   Announcement of the European Commission regarding the compatibility with Article 30 (new Article 28) of the EEC-Treaty of measures by the Member States concerning price control and reimbursement of medicinal products 86/C 310/08, *O.J.*, 4 December 1986, No C310/7.
562   E.C.J., 26 January 1984, Clin Midy, case No 301/82, *E.C.R.*, 1984, p. 251-260.

688. Before a manufacturer or a distributor can market a medicinal product, he must obtain a price for his product. For this, the holder of a marketing authorisation must submit an application with a proposed price, in accordance with certain national requirements. He must furnish the appropriate authorities with adequate information. If the given information is inadequate, the competent authorities must notify the applicant of what detailed, additional information is required. The appropriate authorities must make a decision on the price for the medicinal products that may be charged, within 90 days of the receipt of the application submitted or, within 90 days of receipt of the additional information (Article 2, 1). In the absence of a decision within the mentioned period – a maximum duration of 180 days, the applicant is entitled to market the product at the price proposed.

689. If the appropriate authorities decide not to permit the marketing of the medicinal product at the price proposed by the applicant, their decision must be motivated by reasons based on objective and verifiable criteria. Further, the applicant must be informed of the remedies available under the law in force and the time limits allowed for applying for such remedies (Article 2, 2).

690. Once a year, at least, the appropriate authorities must publish a list with the price of the medicinal products, fixed for a certain period, together with the prices that may be charged for these products. This list must also be communicated to the European Commission.

691. A holder of a marketing authorisation can submit an application for an increase of price. He must furnish the competent authorities with adequate information, including details of those events intervening since the price setting of the medicinal product, which in his opinion justifies the price increase requested. The competent authorities must adopt a decision and communicate it to the applicant within 90 days of its receipt (Article 3, 1). They have an additional 90 days when the given information is inadequate and when they have notified the applicant of what detailed additional information is required. In case of an exceptional number of applications for an increase of price, the period can be extended to a period of 60 days (Article 3, 1, second alinea). In that case, the appropriate authorities must notify the applicant(s) of such extension before the expiring of the period. In the absence of a decision regarding the price increase, the applicant is entitled to apply for the full the price increase requested (Article 3, 1 *in fine*).

692. If the competent authorities decide not to permit the whole or a part of the price increase requested, they must motivate their decision with objective and verifiable reasons (Article 3, 2). Again, the applicant must be informed of the remedies, available under the law in force and the time limits allowed for applying for such remedies.

693. Normally, a price increase is excluded if a price freeze is imposed on all medicinal products or certain categories of medicinal products by the competent authorities of a Member State. Once a year, however, the Member State must review this price freeze to ascertain that the macro-economic conditions, which justify the freeze, are still unchanged (Article 4, 1).

694. But, the holder of a marketing authorisation can ask for derogation in exceptional cases and for particular reasons with a motivated application.[563] The Member States have 90 days, augmented with an additional 90 days in the case that they need more detailed additional information, to grant or refuse such a derogation (Article 4, 2). In the case of an exceptional number of applications, the period can be extended for a further 60 days (Article 4, 2 *in fine*).

9.4. Directive 89/105/EEC and Reimbursement of a Medicinal Product

695. A Member State can decide to cover a medicinal product by the national health insurance system by putting it on a positive list, or can decide to exclude it from reimbursement through a negative list. The decision to exclude or to reimburse medicinal products must be based on objective criteria, independent of whether it is an internal or imported product (Article 66, 2). The decision also has to be motivated. Decisions refusing approval for reimbursement that do not contain an adequate statement of the reasons on which they are based, lack transparency[564].

696. Objective criteria can be, for instance:

- the availability of other, less expensive medicinal products with the same therapeutic action;
- medicinal products not on prescription;
- pharmacotherapeutic and public health arguments.

697. In the *Duphar* case the Court stated *"for such legislation to be in conformity with the Treaty the choice of the medicinal preparations to be excluded must be free of any discrimination to the detriment of imported medicinal preparations. To that end, the exclusionary lists must be drawn up in accordance with objective criteria, without reference to the origin of the products, and must be verifiable by any importer"*[565].

698. It is discriminatory when domestic products continue to be eligible for reimbursement even if the increase in price no longer satisfy the requirements for reimbursement and the prices of imported products continue to be frozen[566].

699. The indication of groups or categories of medicinal products, which can or cannot be reimbursed, must be grounded on objective and general therapeutic criteria. Therapeutic groups do not consist of only one product or one active substance. If this were the case, such a system could easily lead to the reimbursement of one specific medicinal product and the exclusion of another with the same therapeutic action. It is not because a specific category of medicinal products is reimbursed, that all products of this category must be

---

[563]   Court of Justice 24 November 1998, E-2/98.
[564]   E.C.J., 19 March 1999, case No C 249/88, *E.C.R.*, 1991, p. I-1275.
[565]   E.C.J., 7 February 1984, case No 238/82, *E.C.R.*, 1984, p. 523-545.
[566]   E.C.J., 19 March 1999, case No C 249/88, *E.C.R.*, 1991, p. I-1275.

reimbursed. Exclusion of one or more individual products of this category is possible as long as it is based on objective criteria[567].

700. The refusal of reimbursement of specific medicinal products must be based on an evaluation of the (economic) costs and the (therapeutic) action of the treatment, regarding other treatments. Medicinal products that do not have a proven therapeutic action or that have exceptionally high costs can, thus, be excluded from reimbursement. The same way, refusal of reimbursement is possible for certain indications that lead to unjustified costs for the national health security.

701. The only economic criteria, accepted by the European Commission, are the treatment costs[568]. A medicinal product can be excluded from reimbursement if there exists on the market one or more medicinal products with a comparable action and when the indications and side effects are taken into consideration. Further, the doses and the approximately duration of the treatment are also important for the evaluation of the treatment costs.

702. The competent authorities must decide whether an applicant must include along with the medicinal product, a positive list of medicinal products covered by the national health insurance system within 90 days of the receipt (Article 6, 1). If the competent authorities decide not to include the medicinal product on the list of products covered by the national health insurance system, they must ground their decision on objective and verifiable criteria and include, if possible, any experts opinions or recommendations on which the decision is based (Article 6, 2). Again, the applicant must be informed of the remedies, available under the law in force and the time limits, allowed for applying for such remedies (Article 6, 2 *in fine*).

703. If the holder of a marketing authorisation can apply for reimbursement before the competent authorities have agreed the price to be charged for the product concerned or where a decision on the price and the reimbursement of the medicinal product are taken after a single administrative procedure, the limit will be extended for a further 90 days. If the applicant must first obtain a price setting of his medicinal product before he can apply for reimbursement, the competent authorities must ensure that the overall period of time taken by the two procedures does not exceed 180 days (Article 6, 1).

704. Any decision to exclude a product from the list of reimbursable products must contain a statement of reasons based on objective and verifiable criteria. This statement must be communicated to the applicant, and he must be informed of the available remedies and the time limits. The same exigencies apply for the exclusion of a category of medicinal products (Article 6, 5 and Article 6, 6).

---

[567] Announcement of the European Commission regarding the compatibility with Article 30 of the EEC-Treaty of measures by the Member States concerning price control and reimbursement of medicinal products 86/C 310/08, *O.J.*, 4 December 1986, No C 310/10.

[568] Announcement of the European Commission regarding the compatibility with Article 30 of the EEC-Treaty of measures by the Member States concerning price control and reimbursement of medicinal products 86/C 310/08, *O.J.*, 4 December 1986, No C 310/10.

10. THE PROCESSING OF PERSONAL DATA IN THE PHARMACEUTICAL INDUSTRY

10.1. Introduction

705. The use of personal data for several purposes has been influenced by the rapid evolutions in the fields of informatics and telematics[569]. The exercising of these techniques has increased the amount of personal information that can be stored[570] and also the efficiency and ease with which the information can be searched, retrieved, rearranged, copied and transmitted to users. Analysis of complex data, which formerly required months or years to complete may now be executed rapidly and repeatedly. Investigations that previously would have been impractical because of their scale are now possible[571]. In general, the *telestroika*[572] made the transfer of personal data from one Member State to another Member State easier.

706. In the light of Article 100 A of the Treaty establishing the European Community, a Directive has been proposed in order to create equivalent protection resulting from the approximation of national laws. This has given rise to the Directive of the European Parliament and of the Council of 24 October 1995 on the protection of individuals with regard to the processing of personal data and on the free movement of such data[573]. This Directive became effective on 25 October 1998.

707. This chapter mainly explains the definitions used in the Directive as well as requirements imposed by the Directive on the processing of personal data in the pharmaceutical industry. This chapter gives also practical guidance for the processing of data in this area.

---

[569] CALLENS, S., *Goed Geregeld? Het gebruik van medische gegevens voor medisch onderzoek*, Antwerpen, Maklu, 1995, p. 148-159; CALLENS, S., "The Privacy Directive and the Use of Medical Data for Research Purposes", *Eur. J. Health Law*, 1995, p. 309-340.

[570] BLÜME, P., "An EEC policy for data protection", *Computer/Law Journal 400*, 1992; KLÜGE, E.-H.W., "Health Information, the Fair Information Principles and Ethics", *Meth. Inform. Med.*, 1994, p. 337.

[571] Medical Research Council, "Responsibility in the use of personal medical information for research: principles and guide to practice", *B.M.J.*, 1985, p. 1120-1121; KLÜGE, E.-H.W., "Health Information, the Fair Information Principles and Ethics", *Meth. Inform. Med.*, 1994, p. 337; GOSTIN, L.O., a.o., "Privacy and Security of Personal Information in a New Health Care System, *JAMA*, 1993, 270, p. 2488; Newcombe, H.B., "Cohorts and privacy", *Cancer Causes and Control*, 1994, p. 287.

[572] DE MOOR, G.J.E., "Telestroika in Health Care Informatics: a challenge for standardization", *Cards, databases and medical communication*, KÖHLER, C.O.K. & WAEGEMANN, C.P. (eds.), Heidelberg, Medical Records Institute Europe, 1992, p. 86.1-86.6.

[573] Directive 95/46/EC of the European Parliament and the Council of 24 October 1995 on the protection of individuals with regard to the processing of personal data and on the free movement of such data, *O.J.*, L 281, 23 November 1995, p. 0031-0050.

10.2. Why a Privacy Directive?

708. The Data Protection Directive of 24 October 1995 creates for Europe a harmonised framework for data protection. The Directive aims to guarantee a high level of protection of privacy. At the same time, the Directive wants to promote the free flow of personal data in the European Union. Until this Directive, the legal protection in many EU Member States has not been the same. These differences in protection could prevent the pursuit of several economic activities at Community level. They could distort competition and impede authorities in exercising their duties under Community law. To remove the obstacles to flows of personal data, the Data Protection Directive aims to provide equivalent protection of privacy on processing personal data in all member states.

709. Under the Directive, divergence in national data protection legislation will be limited but not excluded. The national Member States may enact different rules on for example the processing of health data for research purposes. The processing of health data for research purposes is not regulated in detail. The Directive only provides that this type of processing is permitted if mutual safeguards are provided.

10.3. Field of Application of the Privacy Directive

710. Now, we will list the field of application of the Privacy Directive and explain some terms used in the Directive. According to the Directive, the Data protection legislation of the Member State where the activities of the controller of the processing of personal data are based, must be complied with. If the controller is based on the territory of several Member States he must ensure that each of these establishments complies with the applicable national law.

711. If the processing is carried out under the responsibility of a controller who is based in a third country, the Member State in which the means (such as computers, telecommunication equipment, etc), of processing the data are located will determine the applicable legislation.

712. In these circumstances the controller who is not based in an EU member state, must appoint a person who will be responsible for the processing, and who is based in the Member State concerned.

713. The processing of personal data is covered by the Directive, if the data is processed wholly or partly by automatic means or if the data processed is contained or intended to be contained in a filing system structured according to specific criteria relating to individuals, so as to permit easy access to the personal data in question[574].

714. Article 2, a of the Directive defines 'personal data' as any information relating to an identified or identifiable natural person ("data subject"); an

---

[574] See in detail CALLENS, S., The Privacy Directive and the Use of Medical Data for Research Purposes, *Eur. J. Health Law*, 1995, p. 309-340.

identifiable person is one who can be identified directly or indirectly, in particular, by reference to an identification number or to one or more factors specific to his physical, physiological, mental, economic, cultural or social identity. Consequently, the Directive does not apply to information on legal entities.

715. The definition of the term 'personal data' is however very broad. It is also obvious that as soon as information is not longer related to an identified or identifiable natural person, there will no longer be talk of personal data. The question that arises, however, is which criterion can be used to make a distinction between personal and non-personal data. One might think of an absolute criterion, as is applied by the French *Commission Nationale de l'Informatique et des Libertés*[575]. According to this criterion, data are considered to be personal data even if they allow identification only in a theoretical way. A physician, for instance, who is communicating encoded medical data to a researcher is communicating personal data under French law[576], though the researcher does not possess the key for decoding the data. It is not clear whether this interpretation is in conformity with the Directive. In the explanation to the Directive it is stated that one should take into account all the means reasonably likely to be used by the controller or by any other person to identify the data subject. The Directive shall not apply to data rendered anonymous in such a way that the data subject is no longer identifiable[577]. At first glance, it seems that the Directive is favouring, instead of an absolute criterion, a criterion of reasonableness[578]. According to this criterion, an individual shall not be regarded as 'identifiable' if identification requires an unreasonable amount of time and manpower[579]. Factors that should be taken into account besides time and manpower are the information, the knowledge which one has already[580], the structure of the data set, the available techniques,

---

[575] CALLENS, S., *Goed geregeld? Het gebruik van medische gegevens voor onderzoek*, Antwerpen, Maklu, 1995, p. 381-384.

[576] See e.g. CNIL, *Rapport au Président de la République et au Parlement*, Paris, La documentation Française, 1983, p. 143; CNIL, *Rapport au Président de la République et au Parlement*, Paris, La documentation Française, 1985, p. 247-248; CNIL, *9ᵉ Rapport d'activité 1988*, Paris, La documentation Française, 1989, p. 141-149; CNIL, *10ᵉ Rapport d'activité 1989*, Paris, La documentation Française, 1989, p. 195; see also Article 40.3 of the French Law of 6 January 1978 modified by the Law No 94.54 of 1 July 1994.

[577] Recital 26 of the Directive. Codes of conduct may be a useful instrument in providing guidance as to the way in which data may be rendered anonymous and retained in a form in which identification of the data subject is no longer possible (Recital 26 of the Directive).

[578] See also Article 2, a) of the amended proposal for a Council Directive submitted by the Commission.

[579] See also Article 1 of Recommendation N° R (97) 5 on the protection of medical data; see in detail Callens, S. *Goed geregeld? Het gebruik van medische gegevens voor onderzoek*, Antwerpen, Maklu, 1995, p. 66-70 and p. 370-378.

[580] This is called in German *das Zusatzwissen*. Cfr. BRENNECKE, R., "Kriterien zur Operationalisierung der faktischen Anonymisierung", *Datenzugang und Datenschutz, Konsequenzen für die Forschung*, KAASE, M., KRUPP, H.-J., PLANZ, M., SCHEUCH, E.K. & SIMITIS, S. (eds.), Königstein, Athenäum, 1980, p. 162; BURKERT, H., "Das Problem des Zusatzwissens", *Datenzugang und Datenschutz, Konsequenzen für die Forschung*, KAASE, M., KRUPP, H.-J., PLANZ, M., SCHEUCH, E.K. & SIMITIS, S. (eds.), Königstein, Athenäum, 1980, p. 143; DITTRICH, K. & SCHLÖRER, J., "Anonymisierung von Forschungsdaten und Identifikation anonymer Datensätze", *Datenschutz und Datensicherung*, 1987, p. 31.

the nature of the data, the number of characteristics that are processed, etc. So-called factual anonymous data is considered to be non-personal data according to a majority of German and Dutch authors. The Data Protection Legislation should not apply to these data[581], which does not mean that one should not be careful while processing them. If medical data is encoded and communicated to a researcher who has no access to the code so as to identify the person whose data he received, these data can be considered as non-personal data. Contrary to absolute anonymous data, these coded data allow identification as long as the key is not destroyed. Therefore, these data is called factual anonymous data. Unfortunately, the Directive leaves room for discussion. It is indeed possible that encoded data will be considered as personal data. According to the Directive[582], one should take – in order to determine whether a person is identifiable – into account all the means likely reasonably to be used either by the controller or *by any other person* to identify a data subject.

716. The Directive defines the 'controller' as the natural or legal person, public authority, agency or any other body that alone or jointly with others determines the means of processing personal data and the purposes for doing so. The controller is the person who has the power or responsibility to decide what processing is carried out and how it is carried out.

717. Several persons may be considered the controller. In order to be the controller a person does not need to actually possess the data. The processor is a natural or legal person, public authority or agency or any body that processes personal data on behalf of the controller.

718. According to the Directive, processing means any operation or set of operations performed on personal data, whether or not by automatic means, including collection, recording, organisation, storage, adaptation or alteration, retrieval, consultation, use, disclosure by transmission, dissemination or otherwise making available, alignment or combination, blocking, erasure or destruction. Under the Directive even collecting personal data is considered processing of personal data and may fall under the Data Protection Directive.

719. The principles of the Data Protection Directive do not apply to the processing of personal data by a natural person pursuing of a personal activity. Thus, the processing of the personal data in an electronic agenda that is never used for business, does not fall under the Directive

---

[581]   BIZER, J., "Forschungsfreiheit und Informationelle Selbstbestimmung", Baden-Baden, Nomos Verlagsgesellschaft, 1992, p. 152; OLSTHOORN-HEIM, E.T.M., "Gebruik van medische gegevens verenigbaar met privacy?", *Medisch Contact*, 1993, p. 816; see als Gezondheidsraad, *Privacy bij post-marketing surveillance*, Den Haag, SDU, 1993, p. 13; Nationale Raad voor de Volksgezondheid, *Advies privacy en gegevensverstrekking*, Zoetermeer, 1992, p. 27; Foundation Federation of Medical Scientific Organisations, *Good conduct. Code of good conduct Health Research*, explanatory memorandum, 1995, p. 9. However, the Dutch Privacy Commission has recently stated that coded data are personal data (*Staatscourant*, 1995, p. 140).

[582]   Recital 26 of the Privacy Directive

10.4. Data Quality and the Need for Legitimate Processing

720. The Directive specifies the principles relating to data quality and to the reasons for making data processing legitimate. According to Article 6,1 Member States shall provide that personal data be

- processed fairly and lawfully;
- collected for specified, explicit and legitimate purposes and not further processed in a way incompatible with those purposes.

721. Personal data must be adequate, relevant and not excessive in relation to the purposes for which the data is collected and/or for which they are further processed. They must also be accurate and, where necessary, kept up to date. Every reasonable step must be taken to ensure that data that is inaccurate or incomplete, with regard to the purposes for which they were collected or for that they are further processed, are erased or rectified. Personal data must be kept in a form that permits identification of data subjects for no longer than is necessary for the purposes for which the data were collected or for which they are further processed.

722. To verify that the processing is compatible with the original purpose, the expectation of the data subject must be met. Personal health data used for commercial purposes without first informing the patient would probably be incompatible with the purpose of treating the patient. Other examples of the use of data for purposes other than the original purpose are health data collected for treatment purposes and used for medical research, or purchases billed for consumer products that are later directly marketed.

723. Such secondary use of data is, as we wrote above, only allowed if this use is compatible with the original purpose. The Directive has taken into account the notion of processing for research purposes. It is stipulated in Article 6, 1, b that the further processing of data for historical, statistical or scientific purposes shall not be considered as incompatible provided that Member States provide appropriate safeguards.

724. This viewpoint was already expressed in the past by the Dutch legislature with regard to the processing of medical data by the treating physician for scientific purposes carried out by himself[583]. The Directive has also taken into consideration the need for identification with regard to scientific use of personal data. Member States shall lay down appropriate safeguards for personal data stored for longer periods for historical, statistical or scientific use[584].

725. The controller must always verify the legal basis for all data processed. Following Article 7 of the Directive, processing of data is only legitimate under one of the following conditions:

---

[583]   This does not mean that the data subject should not be informed about this use of medical data and the he does not have a right to object (cfr. infra).

[584]   Article 6.1, e) Directive.

1°   the data subject has given unambiguous consent;

2°   the processing is necessary to perform a contract;

3°   the processing is necessary for the controller to comply with a legal obligation[585];

4°   the processing is necessary to protect vital interests of the data subject;

5°   the processing is necessary to perform a task in the public interest or in the exercise of official authority;

6°   the processing is necessary for legitimate interests pursued by the controller or a third party to whom the data are disclosed, except where those interests are overridden by the fundamental rights and freedoms of the data subject.

726.   Under the principle of legitimate processing, the controller of the file must verify the legal basis for each processing.

10.5. Informing the Data Subject and Informed Consent

727.   Whether the data is collected directly from the data subject or a third party, the data subject whose data is processed must be informed of:

-     the identity of the controller;
-     the purposes of the processing for which the data is intended.

Any further information such as:

-     the (categories of) recipients,
-     the existence of the right of access to and
-     the right to rectify the data concerning him,

could also be given to the data subject in so far as that further information is necessary to guarantee fair processing towards the data subject in the specific circumstances in which the data is collected.

728.   This information obligation applies to the processing of data in Europe. According to Article 11, 2 of the Directive this obligation does not apply where, in particular for processing for statistical purposes or for purposes of historical or scientific research, the provision of such information proves impossible or would induce a disproportionate effort or if recording or disclosure is expressly laid down by law[586].

729.   The information must be given to the data subject as soon as possible. If the data is obtained from a third party, the information must be given when the data is recorded or if disclosure to a third party is envisaged, and not later than the time when the data is disclosed for the first time.

---

[585]   The use of health data for pharmacovigilance is an example of this ground. Another example is the processing of data for paying wages and fringe benefits.

[586]   In this case, Member States must provide appropriate safeguards.

10.6. Right of Access, Right to Correct and Right to Object

730.   A data subject can require the data controller to confirm whether or not data concerning him or her is being processed. He has the right to obtain from the controller information at least as to the purposes of the processing, the categories of data concerned, and the recipients or categories of recipients to whom the data is disclosed. The data subject has also the right to obtain from the controller communication to him in an intelligible form of the data undergoing processing and of any available information as to their source and knowledge of the logic involved in any automatic processing of data concerning him at least in the case of an automated decision referred to in Article 15, 1 of the Directive.

731.   The right of access does not necessarily give an individual a right to copy the accessible data. The Directive only requires to our opinion that the data subject be informed what data is being processed. Article 13 of the Directive lists exceptions and restrictions to the right of access or the right to be informed. Member States may adopt legislative measures to restrict the scope of the right of access when such restriction constitutes a necessary measure to *safeguard the protection of the data subject or of the rights and freedoms of others.* According to recital 42 of the Directive, Member States may specify that access to medical data may be obtained only through a health professional. Subject to adequate legal safeguards, Member States may, where there is clearly no risk of breaching the privacy of the data subject, restrict by a legislative measure the right of access to data and the right to correct, erase or block data when data is processed solely for purposes of scientific research or are kept in personal form for a period that does not exceed the period necessary for the sole purpose of creating statistics[587].

732.   A data subject can require the controller to correct, erase or block data which, when processed, does not comply with the law, especially if the data is incomplete or inaccurate.

733.   A data subject can object to data being processed if there are compelling grounds for this.

734.   The data subject can object freely to data being processed for direct marketing purposes. The controller must not charge the data subject for making the objection.

10.7. Specific Rules on Processing Health and Other Sensitive Data in the Pharmaceutical Industry

735.   Article 8, 1 of the Privacy Directive prohibits the processing of sensitive data such as personal data revealing racial or ethnic origin, political opinion, religious or philosophical beliefs, trade union membership, as well as data concerning health or sexual activity.

---

587   Article 14, 2 of the Directive.

736. However, sensitive data may be processed if[588]:

- the individual expressly consents to the processing of the data,
- the processing is necessary for the controller to comply with its obligations under employment law; or
- the processing is necessary to protect the vital interests of the data subject or of another person where the data subject is physically or legally incapable of giving his consent; or
- the processing relates to data which are manifestly made public by the data subject; or
- the processing is necessary for the establishment, exercise or defence of legal claims; or
- the processing of health data is required for the purposes of preventive medicine, medical diagnoses, the provision of care or treatment, or the management of health care services, or if the health professional or other person is subject to a secrecy obligation.

737. Sensitive data, including health data used for scientific purposes, may only be processed if local legislation or regulations provide suitable safeguards[589].

10.8. Examples of Common Processing in the Pharmaceutical Industry

Below we describe briefly several types of processing that are common in the Pharmaceutical Industry. We analyse what the legal basis of the processing may be and which basic principles have to be followed by the controller of the file.

10.8.1. Personnel/Employee Administration and data on investigators

738. Processing data for personnel or employee administration includes administering prospective, current and past employees. It includes, where applicable, self-employed or contract staff, temporary staff or voluntary workers. It includes recruitment, recording of working time, administration and payment of wages, salaries, as well as career planning and evaluation.

739. In most cases consent will not be required. The controller will be able to rely on the second or third criteria of article 7 of the Directive (cf. supra). If one must rely on the consent form, the purpose must be clearly mentioned in the labour contract and, if required, in the labour convention applicable to the company. Some countries do oblige the employees to negotiate the introduction of video cameras before a delegation of employees. The use of image data is prohibited if the delegation of employees has not consented to the use of video cameras, and if the use is not mentioned in the Labour Convention. In the labour contract, a clause informing the employee on the processing must be inserted.

740. A similar clause could be used in each contract the pharmaceutical company has with other natural persons such as investigators or physicians,

---

[588]   These exceptions are provided in Article 8, 2 and Article 8, 3 of the Privacy Directive.
[589]   Article 8, 4 of the Directive.

whose data will be processed by the pharmaceutical company. By signing the agreement that contains this clause, and which mentions that one agrees with the processing as described, the data subject agrees to the processing of his personal data.

741. The obligation to inform the data subject about the processing will be verified for each type of processing. The information to be given may vary depending on whether the data subject is an employee of the pharmaceutical company, an investigator, a monitor, a visitor of the company, a client participating in a clinical or cosmetic trial, a consumer, etc.

10.8.2. Administration of Visitors

742. A pharmaceutical company can process a visitor's relevant data to allow people to visit the company's personnel without violating secrecy. This type of processing is necessary to fulfil a legitimate interest of pharmaceutical company. However, only data that is relevant for the processing can be processed. The storage time should be rather short, such as e.g. 1 month and the data subject must be informed of the processing.

10.8.3. Direct Marketing by a Pharmaceutical Company and Data of Prescribing Physicians

743. In our opinion, the processing of personal data on consumer products for direct marketing purposes may be permitted if the processing is necessary for legitimate interests or if those interests are not overridden by the fundamental rights and freedoms of the data subject[590]. In order to verify whether the privacy of the data subject does not prevail, the controller of the file must apply a case by case approach. The judgement depends on the type of information that is processed, the category of recipients, the duration of storage, the way the data subject is informed, the fact that data are encoded or not, etc. To avoid subjects being sent marketing materials without their knowledge, the Directive gives an individual the right to object to this. The individual must be informed before his or her data is disclosed to a third party for the first time or used by third parties for direct marketing. The individual must be expressly offered the right to object.

10.8.4. Processing for Research Purposes

744. The benefit of research for our society should not be underestimated[591]. Nearly all advances in medicine and technology are the results of scientific research, in one way or another[592]. Further, there is an enormous need for information and persons that will analyse, evaluate and steer our complex

---

[590] On the relation between the processing of anonymised prescribing data and the Directive, see Court of Appeal, London, *Source Informatics Ltd*, 21 December 1999.

[591] See in detail on the use of data for research purposes, LOWRANCE, W.W., *Privacy and Health Research. A report to the U.S. Secretary of Health and Human Services*, 1991, p. 21.

[592] VUIJSJE, H., *Mens, erger je niet. Privacybescherming en wetenschappelijk onderzoek*, Den Haag, SDU, 1992, p. 9; The Danish Council of Ethics, *Ethics and mapping of the human genome*, 1993, p. 14.

society. A society that strives to move forward and improve the health of its constituents needs scientific research; hence the attention devoted to the freedom of research and the freedom of information is well directed[593]. The possibilities unfolded by the development of informatics and telematics will make scientific research (including post marketing surveillance) also more interesting. If physicians, hospitals, pharmacists etc. will work in a standardised environment, it increases sciences' ability to collect significant data for several patients over a period of time. We predict that the use of medical data for research purposes will increase as the health sector becomes standardised[594]. Member States are advised to enact specific rules on the use of health data, taking into account appropriate safeguards.

745. Epidemiology is the study of the distribution and determination of disease in populations. Pharmacoepidemiology is the application of medicines to the diseases and populations in need of treatment, while attempting to ensure that medicines are developed to meet health needs and are used safely and optimally.

746. It is difficult to set forth in the law information should be given to a patient and how the information must be given. The French legislator, for example, tried to do this. However, whether the information should be general or specific will depend on the knowledge we have about the research at the moment of the collection of the data for treatment by the physician. In the case of an existing research project, we should give specific information at the time of the collection of the data. If the research project as such is not known, but it is sure that data will be used for research, rather general information might suffice. If the research project is not yet designed, the data subject should be informed, as much as possible, about the research purpose.

747. We view it as necessary that a data subject should also be informed of the possibility, if any, of important findings should such findings be of direct clinical importance to him[595]. In view of the openness and carefulness of the treating physician vis-à-vis the patient, it should also be pointed out to the data subject that findings with positive clinical importance would be communicated to him. The care that should be displayed by the researcher and the treating physician compel them to inform the subject if the research should show that he is suffering from an illness that can be treated or for which prevention is possible[596]. Findings that might be "embarrassing" for the data subject should

---

[593] KERSTEN, S., "Datenschutz in der Medizin", *Computer und Recht*, 1989, p. 1025; LILIE, B., *Medizinische Datenverarbeitung, Schweigepflicht und Persönlichkeitsrecht im Deutschen und Amerikanischen Recht*, Göttingen, Verlag Otto Schwartz, 1980, p. 103.

[594] KLUGE, E.H.W., "Health Information, the Fair Information Principles and Ethics", *Meth. Inform. Med.*, 1994, p. 337; GOSTIN, L.O. a.o., "Privacy and Security of Personal Information in a New Health Care system", *JAMA*, 270, 1993, p. 2488; Council for international organisations of medical sciences, *International guidelines for ethical review of epidemiological studies*, Geneva, 1991, p. 9.

[595] Principle 8,4 of the Recommandation N° R (97) 5 on the protection of medical data; Explanatory Memorandum to the Recommandation, No 160.

[596] See also Council for International Organisations of Medical Sciences, *International guidelines for ethical review of epidemiological studies*, Geneva, 1991, p. 14; THAR, W.E., "The epidemiologist's responsibilities to research subjects in the occupational setting", *J. Clin. Epidemiol.*, 44, Suppl. I, 1991, p. 93-94; FEINLEIB, M., "The

not automatically be communicated or without discretion. In the discussion preceding the communication of medical data for research purposes, it is advisable to attempt to agree whether and how the data subject will be informed should harmful and/or embarrassing information arise. By doing so, naturally, one avoids difficult and painful situations in the future.

748. Another issue with regard to the information that should be given specific attention is the problem of informing a patient of a new, second research project. If a new research project arises that is different from the research purpose or the research project for which the data subject was informed, from our viewpoint this does not imply, necessarily, that information should be given about this second research project. As a matter of fact, this would not only be detrimental for medical research, it would also be annoying for the data subject if he is again and again confronted with his diagnosis and/or treatment. Therefore, one should always question whether the new research project is of the same nature as the original project. If the information originally given is connected to one of the new projects, it will not be necessary to contact once again the data subject.

749. The use of personal data is also essential in different stages in the development of new medicines and in the safe, effective use of existing medicines. There are further points to be made about this type of research and the processing of data.

750. The development of new medicines requires indeed the collection, verification, analysis and interpretation of enormous amounts of data derived from carefully designed clinical studies in patients and healthy volunteers to develop new medicines, a new indication of medicines, medical devices, cosmetics. A clinical research program for a new medicine may involve studies of tens of thousands of patients in many countries carried out over several years. The data are assembled and submitted to regulatory authorities for evaluation and approval for medical use. According to the data protection directive, volunteers must be informed in one way or another of this type of processing of data (see below). Moreover, we believe that the patient or volunteer must consent to processing the personal (health) data for clinical or cosmetic trials.

751. In our view, the information sheet for a clinical trial should contain the following information concerning the processing of health data:

1   the identity of the controller of the file;
2   the purpose of the processing activity;

---

epidemiologist's responsibilities to research subjects", *J. Clin. Epidemiol.*, 44, Suppl. I, 1991, p. 74-77; SPIVEY, G.H., "Health Risk Communication – A view from within industry", *J. Clin. Epidemiol.*, 44, Suppl. I, 1991, p. 63-64; HIGGINSON, J. & CHU, F., "Ethical considerdations and responsibilities in communicating health risk information", *J. Clin. Epidemiol.*, 44, Suppl. I, 1991, p. 53; LAST, J.M., "Obligations and responsibilities of epidemiologists to research subjects", *J. Clin. Epidemiol.*, 44, Suppl. I, 1991, p. 98; GORDIS, L., "Ethical and professional issues in the changing practice of epidemiology", *J. Clin. Epidemiol.*, 44, Suppl. I, 1991, p. 11; see also LEENEN, H.J.J., *Handboek gezondheidsrecht*, Alphen aan den Rijn, Samsom, 1994, p. 227.

3   a general description of the categories of recipients (e.g., affiliates, contract research organisations or regulatory authorities) to whom data could be disclosed;

4   the fact that if personal data are disclosed to a third party, all appropriate measures will be taken to protect such data;

5   the existence of the right to access and rectify personal data concerning him/her when possible;

6   the obligation of confidentiality regarding all company personnel involved in personal data processing who could either directly or indirectly identify the data subject;

7   the assurance that if the results of the research project are published, the personal data elements which could identify the data subject will remain confidential.

10.8.5. Processing for Post Marketing Research, Drug Safety, Pharmacoviligance, Drug Utilisation Review and Pharmacoeconomics

Below we describe several types of processing that is common in the pharmaceutical company, for which a Member State may or may not provide for specific rules. If a company cannot rely on a rule or regulation allowing the processing of health data on the basis of Article 8,4 of the Directive, the controller of the file will often need a consent of the data subject to process the health data.

752. Processing for post marketing research involves clinical research after a medicine, a medical device or a cosmetic has been put on the market. It is used to broaden knowledge of the medicine's safety and efficacy in a larger and more varied group of clients and in more varied circumstances than was possible during development.

753. *Drug safety surveillance or pharmacovigilance* is a fundamental responsibility of all research based pharmaceutical companies. It requires the pharmaceutical company to:

- enquire promptly into reports from all sources,
- maintain a comprehensive data set on each base and all related cases,
- compile the information so as to permit summary and analysis and
- establish a response system to ensure that action is taken to protect the public health.

754. Companies routinely collect safety data during clinical trials. Also, physicians report unexpected or unusual problems encountered during routine medical practice and reports are received from other health care practitioners and from patients. These reports are sent to the company and to regulatory authorities. A global pharmaceutical company must be able to exchange information with its subsidiaries and with regulatory agencies world-wide, quickly and effectively.

755. *Drug utilisation review* is the systematic analysis of the actual use of medicine, which aims to improve the effectiveness and cost efficiency of treatment. It may take place prospectively, concurrently or retrosspectively, with the dispensing of the medicine.

756. *Pharmacoeconomics* is the science of evaluating the benefits and costs of medicines and can help to determine the value of medicines.

757. For each kind of processing, the pharmaceutical company must analyse whether or not the processing is compatible with the original processing. It must analyse whether, e.g. the data subject would be likely to oppose the processing or whether the data is kept in a form that permits identification of the data subject for longer than is necessary for the purpose for which the data is further processed. The pharmaceutical company must also verify the legal basis on which the processing is allowed (consent, law, legitimate interest etc.).

10.9. Confidentiality and Security Measures

758. A controller of a file who is processing (sensitive) personal data should provide that the only persons who process data are those who are allowed to do so. These persons should sign a confidentiality agreement, in particular if they process sensitive data. The most relevant clauses of such agreements are given below.

759. The controller must implement appropriate technical and organisational measures to protect personal data against accidental or unlawful destruction or accidental loss, alteration, unauthorised disclosure or access, and against all other unlawful forms of processing. The security must be tighter when the processed data are sensitive, such as with health data.

760. The technical and organisational measures must be taken both when the processing system is designed and at the time of the processing itself.

761. Data may only be kept for as long as is necessary to fulfil the purpose for which the data was collected. A controller must encrypt data or take other appropriate action, to preserve the security of the data. The controller must strike the right balance of security between the nature of the data to be protected, the costs involved, and the leading edge technology.

762. A natural or legal person may process personal data on behalf of the controller. That processing must be governed by a written contract between the processor and the controller. The contract must stipulate that the processor will act only on instructions from the controller, and that he will comply with the applicable legislation.

763. The same is true for contracts entered between the company and the investigator or the CRO concerning clinical trials. These persons should be obliged to adhere to the rules and legislation on processing of personal data.

764. It is important to be insured against breaches in security, as the Data Protection Directive and, possibly, local national law, applies a risk liability. Any person who has suffered damage as a result of an unlawful processing operation or of any act incompatible with the national provisions is entitled to compensation from the controller for the damage suffered. The controller may be exempted from this liability, in whole or in part, if he proves that he is not responsible for the event giving rise to the damage.

765. Some industry sectors have enacted guidelines on measures that heir members should take to secure the processing of personal data. The EFPIA is drafting a Code of Conduct for the Pharmaceutical Industry on the Processing of Personal Data in Research and Development that will provide for secure processing of sensitive data in the pharmaceutical industry.

10.10. Notification

766. The controller of filing systems for employment administration, visitors, direct marketing, clinical trials etc. must verify whether the applicable data protection legislation imposes an obligation to notify the Data Protection Commission.

767. National laws may exempt notification. This may occur where the controller of the filing system has appointed a personal data protection official who is responsible for (i) independently ensuring compliance with the national provisions implementing the Directive and (ii) keeping a register of processing operations

10.11. Transfer of Data

768. Cross border flows of health data in the pharmaceutical industry take place on different occasions. Data is transferred e.g. if (side) effects of internationally used medicinal products[597] or infectious diseases have to be reported or if one is participating in international epidemiological studies or international multi-center trials[598]. Even the transfer of body material for research purposes requires a transfer of data[599]. Pharmaceutical and medical device companies do sometimes provide personal data from clinical trials conducted in the European Union to regulators in the USA for regulation and supervision purposes.

769. Once the personal data has been transferred to a third country, the law or principles of this third country will apply. In this way, the Directive states that a transfer of personal data to a country outside the EU is only allowed if the third country in question ensures an adequate level of protection[600].

---

[597] Council Directive of 24 June 1993 in respect of medicinal products, *O.J.*, L 214/22, 24 August 1993; Council Regulation of 22 July 1993, *O.J.*, L 214/1, 24 August 1993.

[598] See KUITENBROUWER, F., "Privacy en internationale uitwisseling van persoonsgegevens – een landmozaïek", *Gezondheidsrecht in perspectief*, Hubben, J.H. & Roscam Abbing, H.D.C. (eds.), Utrecht, De Tijdstroom, 1993, p. 124-125; CALLENS, S., *Goed geregeld? Het gebruik van medische gegevens voor onderzoek*, Antwerpen, Maklu, 1995, p. 147-148 & p. 198-199.

[599] PLOEM, M.C., *De EG en de rechtspositie van de patiënt*, Amsterdam, Instituut voor Sociale Geneekunde – Universiteit van Amsterdam, 1994, p. 66; ROSCAM ABBING, H.D.C., *Patiënt en gezondheidszorg in het recht van de Europese Gemeenschap*, Utrecht, Vereniging van Gezondheidsrecht, 1993, p. 61.

[600] Article 25, 1 Privacy Directive

770. The Directive does not give however a definition of what is understood by an "adequate level of protection". It only states that the adequacy of the protection will be assessed in the light of all the circumstances surrounding a data transfer operation or set of data transfer operations; particular consideration must be given to the nature of the data, the purpose and duration of the proposed processing operation or operations, the country of origin and country of final destination, the rules of law, both general and sectoral, in force in the third country in question and the professional rules and security measures which are complied with in that country[601].

771. Following Article 25, 6 of the Privacy Directive, the Commission may find that a third country ensures an adequate level of protection, by reason of the domestic law or the international commitments it has entered into, particularly upon conclusion of the negotiations for the protection of the private lives, basic freedoms and rights of individuals. In the course of this procedure the Committee for the protection of individuals with regard to the processing of personal data has to give its opinion to the Commission.

772. Following this procedure the European Commission analysed a proposal of decision concerning a project of convention with the USA. While the United States and the European Union share the goal of enhancing privacy protection for their citizens, the United States take, for example, a different approach to privacy from that taken by the European Community[602]. The United States uses a sectoral approach that relies on a mix of legislation regulation and self regulation. Given those differences, many US organisations have expressed uncertainty about the impact of the EU-required "adequacy standard" on personal data transfers from the European Community to the United States. To diminish this uncertainty and provide a more predictable framework for such data transfers, the American Department of Commerce issued a document called the "Safe Harbour Privacy Principles" to foster, promote and develop international commerce.

773. These safe harbour privacy principles contain principles on the information obligation of the organisation towards the individual, on the choice the organisation must offer individuals on the disclosure and use of their personal information, on the disclosure of personal information to third parties, on the security measures the organisations must take, on data integrity, on the access to personal information by the individuals and on the enforcement of the privacy principles by the organisation.

774. The draft convention between the European Community and the USA stipulates that each American company, which expressly declares to respect the safe harbour privacy principles is considered to be offering an adequate level of protection. Decisions by organisations to qualify for the safe harbour are entirely voluntary and organisations may qualify for the safe harbour in different ways. Organisations that decide to adhere to the principles must comply with the principles in order to obtain and retain the benefits of the safe harbour and

---

[601] Article 25, 2 Privacy Directive
[602] Safe Harbor Privacy Principles issued by the U.S. Department of Commerce on 28 April 2000.

publicly declare that they do so. Organisations may also qualify by developing their own self regulatory privacy policies provided that they conform with the principles.

775. Organisations may wish for practical or other reasons to apply the principles to all their data processing operations, but they are only obligated to apply them to data transferred after they entered the safe harbour.

776. A transfer or a set of transfers of personal data to a third country which does not ensure adequate level of protection may take place if[603]:

- the data subject has given his unambiguous consent to the proposed transfer;
- the transfer is necessary for performing a contract between the data subject and the controller;
- the transfer is necessary for concluding or performing a contract between the controller and a third party in the interests of the data subject;
- the transfer is necessary or legally required on important public interest grounds, or for establishing, exercising or defending a legal claim; or
- the transfer is necessary to protect vital interests of the data subject; or
- the transfer is made from a register that according to laws or regulations is intended to provide information to the public.

777. A Member State may authorise a transfer or a set of transfers of personal data to a third country that does not ensure adequate protection where the controller ensures adequate safeguards to protect the privacy. These safeguards may result from appropriate contractual clauses. That contract must determine how the responsibility for data protection compliance is split between the transferor and the recipient of data. According to the European Council of Europe and the Working Party on the protection of individuals with regard to the personal data, such a contract must provide that the basic data protection principles apply to the processing of data transferred to the third country, i.e.

- *the purpose limitation principle;*
- *the data quality and proportionality principle;*
- *the transparency principle;*
- *the security principle;*
- *the rights of access, rectification and opposition;*
- *the restriction on onward transfer to non-parties to the contract.*

---

[603]   Article 26, 1 Privacy Directive.

11. LEGAL ISSUES OF THE EXERCISE OF PHARMACISTS

778. The Pharmacy has to comply with rules if it wants to sell medicinal products to the public. These rules are often – but not always – European rules. This Chapter analyses the certificate of the pharmacist (see under 11.1.), the specialisations (see under 11.2.), the monopoly of the pharmacist (see under 11.3.), the rules governing the establishment of a pharmacy (see under 11.4.), the substitution of medicinal products (see under 11.5.) and finally the price reductions for the public (see under 11.6.). The legal issues are analysed from the Belgian viewpoint but this chapter can be used as a guidance for analysing the law on the exercise of pharmacy in other Member States.

11.1. Certificate of Pharmacist

779. The first condition in order to exercise the profession as a pharmacist is the possession of the certificate of pharmacist. The schooling in pharmacy is in an uniform manner regulated in the European Community. Directive 85/432/EEC of 16 September 1985 regarding the co-ordination of the legal and administrative rules of certain activities in the pharmaceutical field fixes the minimum duration of the courses at 5 years, whereof at least 4 years consisting of theoretical study and at least a 6 months during practice in a public pharmacy or a hospital pharmacy. The Directive also imposes a minimum number of compulsory courses.

780. The structure of the study is, in Belgium, regulated by a Decree of the Communities. To obtain a title as a pharmacist, first, a certificate of candidate in the pharmaceutical studies is needed (2 years). The title as pharmacist itself takes 3 years. The academic board decides over the program for each academic study. The program is not fixed in the Decree, but is left to the freedom of the academic board.

781. Directive 85/433/EEC provides for a reciprocal recognition of the certificates. A citizen of a Member State can exercise his profession in every other member state, without the obligation to fulfil additional requirements regarding courses or certificates.

782. Articles 44sexies and 44septies of the Belgian Royal Decree No 78 of 10 November 1967 implement this Directive. Citizens of other Member States, who wish to enjoy the benefits of these measures in Belgium, receive within 3 months after filing their application a document of the Minister of Public Health that indicates that they can operate under the same conditions as a Belgian licensee. Belgian citizens, who wish to exercise their profession in another Member State, have the same facilities.

783. The pharmacist may only take charge of a pharmacy or act as a substitute when his certificate is visa'd by the Medical Commission of his province and when he has obtained his registration on the list of the Council of Pharmacists.

784. The visa is a procedure, that gives the public authority the possibility to prohibit persons, who are no longer, physically or psychically, capable to exercise their profession. A certificate cannot be withdrawn because the academic authorities deliver it. The registration on the list of the Council of Pharmacists can be suspended for deontological reasons.

11.2. Specialisations in Pharmacy

785. After obtaining the certificate as pharmacist, the licensee can specialise in following fields:

- industry-pharmacist;
- hospital-pharmacist;
- pharmacist-specialist in the bioclinical analyses.

The industry-pharmacist and the hospital-pharmacist are also visa'd according the Directive 85/432/EEC. A pharmacist who has finished an education of 5 years does not have to comply with additional requirements. An additional job experience, however, can be asked. The bioclinical analyses do not fall within the scope of the Directive, so an additional certificate can be asked for.

11.2.1. The Industry Pharmacist

786. To be allowed to exercise this profession in Belgium, it is required to be registered on a list, kept at the Belgian Ministry of Public Health. Every person who can prove that he has a certificate as a pharmacist or a certificate from another Member State of the European Community can be registered on this list. He must visa his certificate with the competent Medical Commission and must have practical experience in an enterprise, located in a member state of the European Community, which has a license to market drugs.

787. This practical experience must enclose at least one year. If the person concerned already has a certificate as an industry-pharmacist, the duration is reduced to 6 months. These measures, mentioned in Articles 11 and 12 of the Belgian Royal Decree of 6 June 1960 regarding the manufacturing, the distribution in wholesale and the delivery of medicinal products are not against the Directive because the certificate of industry-pharmacist is facultative. Someone who only practices in an enterprise can begin after one year. A person who wants to get his certificate must spend 18 months: 12 months at university and 6 months doing practice.

788. The presence of an industry-pharmacist is obliged in every enterprise that manufactures medicinal products. If that enterprise imports medicinal products in full package, without performing any activities in Belgium, the enterprise must order an industry-pharmacist or a recognised lab to perform quality controls.

11.2.2. The Hospital Pharmacist

789. The Royal Decree of 7 July 1986 stipulates that person, connected to a hospital pharmacy as title-holders or adjunct-pharmacists, must be holders of the certificate of hospital pharmacist, delivered by a Belgian university. The Royal Decree of 4 March 1991 regarding the requirements for hospital pharmacies to be recognised has repeated this obligation. Favourable terms were provided for pharmacists, already working in hospital pharmacies. But, because of infringement of the previously mentioned Directive (no additional certificates), the European Court of Justice has condemned Belgium.

790. Therefore, Article 18 of the Royal Decree of 4 March 1991 has been replaced by a new article: hospital pharmacists and all pharmacists, connected to a hospital pharmacy must practice at least 500 hours during a period of 12 months. With this rule, the Belgian regulation is no longer against the Directive.

791. The additional academic education as a hospital-pharmacist provides for a practical course of 500 hours, but one can also choose to do 500 hours in a hospital pharmacy without passing university exams.

792. From the point of view of finance, a certain part of the lay-day charges shall be diminished with 10%, if the hospital invokes the help of a non-registered pharmacist. To obtain such a registration, the title of hospital pharmacist is needed. If a hospital engages someone without title (what is legally allowed), the hospital will be penalised through the lay-day charges.

793. A hospital-pharmacist is obliged in every hospital, and the number is a function of the number of hospital beds.

11.2.3. The Pharmacist-Specialist in Bioclinical Analyses

794. Clinical biology is a branch of medicine. Its purpose is the tracking and diagnosis of illnesses in human beings. According to Article 2, 1 of the Royal Decree No 78, the exercise of clinical biology is reserved to persons who are holders of a title in medicine. Article 5, 2 of the same Decree, however, stipulates that the holders of a legal degree in pharmacy or chemical sciences are assigned to perform analyses of clinical biology, according to the rules, laid down by Royal Decree.

795. Since 1984, the duration of education is equal for pharmacists and physicians. The duration is at least 5 years, with 2 years basic education and 3 years higher education. The basic education includes theoretical and practical knowledge. Every branch, namely medical chemistry, haematology and microbiology, consists of 6 months. For the higher education, the choice exists between 3 years of one of the 3 branches or 3 years of combination of two or three branches.

796. The practical course is only possible at the level of trainee teachers and trainee services recognised by the Ministry of Public Health. Before commencing the practical course, the candidate-trainee sends his trainee scheme to the Recognition Commission of the Ministry of Public Health. This trainee scheme embraces the start and end dates of the practical course, the details of the studies, the name of the trainee teachers and trainee services where the education will be followed In an annual report, the commission must be informed about the progress of the course, the changes in the scheme and the eventual interruptions.

797. At the end of the 5-year during education, an application for recognition is filed at the Ministry of Public Health, which will inform the federal institute for sickness and disability insurance in order to ensure refund for his performances. A clinical laboratorium can be under the direction of a physician-biologist or a pharmacist-biologist.

11.3. The Monopoly of the Pharmacist and Exceptions

11.3.1. Monopoly

798. Monopoly is in fact a badly chosen term. It means that a certain person has the sole right to sell something. But the pharmacist does not sell merely. He delivers and at the same moment takes full responsibility for what he delivers. This sole right of preparing and delivering of medicinal products has its legal basis in Article 4, 1 of the Royal Decree No 78. To be able to exercise in pharmaceutics, a title as pharmacist is needed.

799. The following is considered as unlawful exercise by pharmacies: the habitual exercise by a non-pharmacist of all activities, with as purpose: the preparation, the sale, the retail and the delivery, even for free, of medicinal products[604].

800. It has to be noted that for the delivery of medicinal products only the retail is meant. Wholesale falls not within the scope of exercising pharmacy. Regarding the composition of medicinal products only those preparations done in the pharmacy are meant, not those in the industrial business.

11.3.2. The Exceptions on the Monopoly

801. Article 4, §2 of the Royal Decree No 78 enumerates cases where non-pharmacists may deliver medicinal products:

- branch managing physicians if they have, according to the law of 12 April 1958, an authorisation. But no new authorisations are given anymore;
- branch managing veterinary surgeons. They must, according to the law of 22 August 1991, inform the Medical Commission of their wish to have a branch. After simple request, this authorisation is given;

---

[604] *Habitual* means that for an infringement, the habit must be proven. According to the jurisprudence, there is only a habit when a certain act is performed at least three times. Article 38, §2 of the Royal Decree No 78 considers that a habit is not needed for persons who are already condemned for unlawful exercise of pharmaceutics, for persons who have used publicity to perform such acts and those persons who have used striking measures or used a title to convince others that he is legally competent.

- physicians (without branch) and dentists may deliver medicinal products under certain circumstances;
- the delivery of certain objects with a prophylactic purpose against contagious diseases.

802. Furthermore, there are two exceptions, enumerated in the Royal Decree of 6 June 1960 regarding the manufacturing, the wholesale and the delivery of medicinal products, i.e.:

- the Minister can make a list of medicinal products, which can be sold outside the pharmacy;
- the State has the right to prepare medicinal products and to deliver.

Nevertheless, all exceptions are limited; only a limited delivery is possible and the origin of medicinal products is strictly regulated.

11.3.2.1. A Limited Delivery

- The branch-managing physician may only deliver medicinal products to patients, who are treated by him.
- The branch managing veterinary surgeon may only deliver for treated animals and only for the duration of that treatment, without having a public pharmacy. A royal decree can formulate a list of ex-tempore preparations, but until this moment, no such royal decree has been promulgated.
- The physician (without branch) and the dentist may only delivery necessary and urgent samples.
- Only certain centres may deliver the prophylactically aimed objects.
- The Minister can only put those medicinal products on the list that are, because of their nature or qualities not fit for normal pharmaceutical distribution, such as radioisotopes or certain vaccines.
- The State must restrict itself to prophylactic campaigns against contagious diseases (e.g. poliomyelitis) or other exceptional circumstances (e.g. disasters).

11.3.2.2. The Origin of Medicinal Products

- The branch-managing physician must get his medicinal products from a public pharmacy of the province where the branch is located.
- The branch managing veterinary surgeon must also get his products from a pharmacist.
- Regarding urgent medicinal products, there is no purchase. The delivery may not cause profits or fees. The normal provisioning is through the Pharmacy.
- Regarding the samples, they may only be delivered by the persons responsible for the marketing to the persons, who are authorised to prescribe such medicinal products. In hospitals, the distribution happens through the hospital pharmacy. No samples containing psychotrophic or narcotic substances may be distributed. The total amount of samples for the same prescriptor is restricted to 600 per year and only delivered in the smallest form.

11.4. The Rules on the Opening of New Pharmacies

803. The delivery of medicinal products can only be regulated in a sufficient manner if patients can obtain the products in their neighbourhood. For this reason, some member states have a compulsory spreading of pharmacies. No specific European directive exists so it is left to the competency of Member States.

804. In Belgium, Article 4, §3 Royal Decree No 78 gives a legal ground for the promulgation of, at first, Royal Decree of 9 February 1970, later the Royal Decree of 27 October 1972[605]. After their nullification, the law of 17 December 1973, amended by a law of 13 May 1999, gave a legal ground. This law only embraces public pharmacies, not hospital pharmacies. The reasons for a spreading of public pharmacies are:

- a concentration too strong in cities and large centres can cause severe concurrence and the disproportionate use of commercial techniques can lead to automedication, misuse of medication, unlawful delivery in order to gain clients…;
- to avoid a lack of public pharmacies in the country side;
- the numerous functions of a pharmacist and the need of expensive material: the grouping of existing pharmacies becomes necessary;
- in other member states the same measures exist.

805. A ministerial authorisation is needed for the opening, the transfer and the fusion of pharmacies. Such an authorisation is personal and is granted to one natural or one legal person. At the earliest, the authorisation is transferable 5 years after the opening of a pharmacy. The licensee is not, per definition, the owner of the building where the pharmacy is located. In the event of the take-over of a pharmacy, the valour of it is legally fixed. Pharmacies, which are redundant, can be closed permanently if they are offered for a take-over. A special fund can be created for payment in case of compulsory closing or help for marginal pharmacies, necessary for an efficient supply of medicinal products. The maximum number of pharmacies can be regulated by royal decree. Measures are possible in the light of a temporary or definitive closing of a pharmacy for force majeure or on the initiative of the licensee. The minister of public health can, for reasons of public health, suspend the license. There is a compulsory registration procedure for all public pharmacies and must be followed also in case of a take-over.

806. The following criteria applies for the opening of a new pharmacy:

- in communities with more than 30.000 habitants: 3.000 habitants for one pharmacy;

---

[605] Against both royal decrees, a request for annulment was formulated at the *Conseil d'Etat* for excess of competencies. This Council has annulled both decrees because they did not only contain measures for the protection of the public health, but also economic reasons, namely the protection of the existing pharmacies.

- in communities between 7.500 and 30.000 habitants: 2.500 habitants per pharmacy;
- in communities with less than 7.500 habitants: 2.000 habitants per pharmacy.

It is, however, important to mention that in the three cases, the number of population must be diminished with 5.000 habitants for every pharmacy with two or more full-time pharmacists if this situation existed already at the moment of filing for an authorisation.

807. In a community with less than 7.500 habitants, at least two pharmacies must be open and in communities with more than 9.000 habitants at least three pharmacies.

808. The applicant, who did not get his authorisation, can renew his request one time only during three years from the date of introduction.

809. The investigation procedure consists of a consultation of the governor, the Medical Commission, the Pharmaceutical inspector and the most representative organisations. After the final report of the inspector-general, the file will be transferred to one of both Commissions for the Spreading of Pharmacies (French or Dutch), which will bring advice. This advice is transferred to the applicant and the above mentioned instances. Within a month after delivery, appeal is possible at the Commission of Appeal. In case the decision is positive, the minister still can refuse the opening. If the decision is negative, the minister can grant the authorisation in a motivated way. If within two years of notification of the authorisation, no new pharmacy is opened, the authorisation is withdrawn. A moratorium is installed regarding the maximum number of pharmacies in 1995 for a duration of 5 year. A new moratorium is installed in 2000 for a duration of 10 years.

810. Also, for the transfer, an authorisation is needed. The formalities are the same as for the opening of a new pharmacy, with exception of the criteria for a transfer in the neighbour. Further, the opinions of the different instances must not be asked for if the transfer is within the immediate neighbour (e.g. with a radius of 100 mm), thus facilitating and shortening the procedure.

811. The fusion of two or more pharmacies may be allowed if they are located in the same community or in neighbouring community and the number of pharmacies in each community is not more than the one mentioned in par. 806.

11.5. Substitution of Medicinal Products

812. The pharmacist must deliver the medicinal products mentioned on the prescription. Normally, he may not replace a certain, prescribed medicinal product for another, even with the permission of the patient. This prohibition is the result of Article 2, §1 Royal Decree No 78 that considers the performance of a treatment, such as the prescription of medicinal products as medicinal acts. A pharmacist who interferes with this act would unlawfully perform medicine. Furthermore Article 11 of the mentioned royal decree indicates that no restrictions may be placed on the therapeutical freedom of a physician. A pharmacist who unaided would substitute a medicinal product would restrict this therapeutical freedom of the physician.

813. Article 11 is complemented by Article 34 of the law of 6 August 1993. According to Article 34 the King may, through a Royal Decree, discussed in the council of ministers, take measures and execute decrees according to which a pharmacist may substitute a pharmaceutical speciality by another, on the condition that the active substances are the same, the prescriptor does not object and the price for the patient is cheaper. This Royal Decree has for the moment not yet been promulgated, so this system is not yet in force. In the near future, the pharmacist will have the possibility to substitute, except when the prescription mention an explicit prohibition. It is not necessary that the physician always indicates whether the substitution is allowed. The medicinal product must be cheaper. It is clear the legislator wants to encourage the use of generic medicinal products. According to the existing regulations, they must be up to 16% cheaper than the reference product. In most cases at the registration of that product, the Commission of Medicinal Products asks for a bio equivalence study to be sure that the generic product is therapeutically equivalent to the referenced product.

814. At the moment, there are also medicinal products registered according to the provisions of Article 2, 8°, a), 2° of the Royal Decree of 3 July 1969, which are also 16% cheaper. They are only registered with published scientific literature and not with clinical studies (regarding the toxicological – pharmacological part). These products also have most of the time not the statute of a generic product, and thus no bio equivalence study is asked for. In the case of a substitution, the patient will not have the certainty that that product is therapeutically equivalent to the reference product. This can cause problems for the Ministry of Public Health. In the case of products with a small therapeutical index (the difference between the therapeutic doses and the toxic doses), a substitution between two products can be even more dangerous when there is no bio-equivalence study.

815. In product substitution, only the active substances must be equal. The other substances may differ, even if a certain substance causes an allergy. The question is: who will be responsible for the undesired effect after substitution: the pharmacist or the physician? It will be difficult to find out if the undesired effects are the result of the active substance or the other substances.

816. It will take a while before the Royal Decree will be promulgated, because of resistance from the physicians. They consider the Decree as an attempt to restrict their therapeutical freedom, an intrusion of the relationship with their patients and an endangering of the therapy faith. The pharmaceutical industry also is opposed to the measure, stating that it is competition-tampered by enhancing the sale of generic products, thus giving it a preference treatment. Substitution leads the pharmaceutical industry to a considerable financial loss, endangers the possibility of financing research, and the development of high technological products necessary for certain diseases. Even if the State would benefit from a lower price, it is not in proportion with the damages for research. Substitution is also in contradiction with the actions by the government concerning the prescription behaviour of physicians. Physicians can no longer take responsibility if the pharmacist alters their prescriptions. For the government, it is doubtful if substitution will lead to much economisation. It is possible that the more expensive pharmaceutical speciality mentioned on the prescription will be charged to the insurance, and that the cheaper generic product is delivered to the patient.

817. The Council of Pharmacists is at the moment more indulgent and allows substitution under certain circumstances. The pharmacist must always have the agreement of the physician; the pharmacist must respect the physician's will and not substitute without his knowledge. Thus, he will not damage the psychosomatic value of the relationship between patient and physician and that is partially retraceable in the prescribed medicine. The pharmacist decides how he must obtain the agreement of the physician: by personal interference, through a specific indication on the prescription or as a result of specific settlements with the health institution. The substitution may in no way cause doubts with the patient. The pharmacist must give all necessary information to assure that he will stay faithful to therapy. Profits as a result of the substitution are not forbidden nor may third parties impose substitution. The pharmacist bears full responsibility for his choice of medicinal product and for his equivalence. Substitution is always possible in urgent situations, or in the case of guard duty, when the commencing of a treatment is crucial. The range of this deontological rule is limited to the substitution of a medicinal product for a product with the same active substance, the same dosage, and the same pharmaceutical form, with an equal bio availability.

11.6. Price Reductions for the Public

11.6.1. The Price Regulation

818. Price Regulation is a national matter. Before, the law of 14 February 1961 regulated reductions, with maximum prices, maximum profit margins and maximum reductions. Also, a Royal Decree of 17 April 1964 was promulgated, that indicated a reduction of maximum 10% on the public price. The reduction was not immediately deductible; the pharmacist must give a ticket with the reduction and could only pay after four months after closing the year. The law of 9 July 1975 has replaced the law of 14 February 1961. Since the first of January 1983, the non-repayable medicinal products falls under the scope of the law of 22 January 1945 and the repayable medicinal products, since the first of January 1990, under the law of 22 December 1989. Neither regulation any longer contains legal basis for reductions. The royal decree of 17 April 1964 was implicitly lifted. But, because not everybody came to the same logical conclusion, the royal decree of 27 February 1995 explicitly lifted that former royal decree. Therefor, no regulation for reduction any longer exists.

11.6.2. Article 10 of the Law of 25 March 1964 on Medicinal Products

819. This Article forbids direct bonuses or benefits at the delivery of medicinal products. It only covers deliveries from pharmaceutical companies to pharmacists, but not the exercise of medicine, as laid down in the Royal Decree No 78. Reductions to the public can therefore not be considered as bonuses or benefits in the sense of Article 10, and they are not forbidden by the law on the exercise of pharmacy. The logical conclusion is that reductions are permitted, that the percentage is not regulated and that they are immediately deductible from the sum paid in the pharmacy.

11.6.3. The View of the Council of Pharmacists

820.   According to the first, deontological rule of the Council of Pharmacists, the pharmacist on duty may not misuse his guard duty to lure patients to his own pharmacy, which would be the case if he could promise reductions. The second deontological rule stipulates that personal publicity is forbidden. Reductions could be seen as a form of personal publicity. The third deontological rule states that it is forbidden to promise price reductions and bonuses. The mentioning of lower prices is not deontological.

821.   The Announcement No 13 of the Council of Pharmacists reminds us that the Provincial Committees are competent to restrict certain practices, such as ristornos, when they are attended with activities contrary to the honour, the dignity and the modesty of the profession.

822.   One could consider being a pharmacist as an independent profession, deciding for himself to give or not to give price reductions, but in an advice of 20 October 1993, the Council of State has stated that deontological rules, specific for the profession, can restrict this freedom of pharmacists. The Council of Pharmacists has no legal basis to forbid ristornos, but is however competent to restrict deontologically all misuses and can pronounce sanctions, such as a warning, a reprimand, or, eventually, a suspension.

INDEX